Environmentalism and Economic Justice

Society, Environment, and Place

SERIES EDITORS

Andrew Kirby and Janice Monk

Laura Pulido

Environmentalism and Economic Justice

Two Chicano Struggles in the Southwest

The University of Arizona Press   Tucson

The University of Arizona Press
© 1996
The Arizona Board of Regents
All rights reserved.

Manufactured in the United States of America

01 00 99 98 97 96   6 5 4 3 2 1

Library of Congress Cataloging-in-Publication Data
Pulido, Laura.
   Environmentalism and economic justice : two Chicano struggles in
the Southwest / Laura Pulido.
      p. cm. — (Society, environment, and place series)
   Includes bibliographical references and index.
   ISBN 0-8165-1424-0. — ISBN 0-8165-1605-7 (pbk.)
      1. Environmentalism — Southwestern States. 2. Mexican Americans —
Social conditions — Southwestern States — Case studies. 3. Social
ecology — Southwestern States. 4. Sustainable development —
Southwestern States. 5. Social justice. I. Title. II. Series.
GE198.S86P85   1996
363.7′0089′6872073 — dc20   95-32449
                                                              CIP

British Cataloguing-in-Publication Data
A catalogue record for this book is available from the British Library.

Contents

List of Figures   vii

List of Tables   ix

List of Abbreviations   xi

Preface   xiii

1   Subaltern Environmental Struggles   3

2   Poverty, "Race," and Identity in the Creation of
Subalternity   31

3   The Pesticide Campaign of the UFW Organizing
Committee, 1965–71   57

4   Ganados del Valle: Resource Management as Contested
Terrain   125

5   Politics, Identity, and the Future of Environmentalism   191

Notes   213

Bibliography   229

Index   271

Figures

3.1 California political map, southern San Joaquin Valley 61

3.2 Occupational disease attributed to pesticides and other agricultural chemicals, 1967 80

3.3 *El Malcriado* cover, February 1969 92

3.4 Pesticide warning prepared by the UFWOC 106

3.5 *El Malcriado* cover, October 1969 110

3.6 Ad for Zapata buttons 111

4.1 Map of the Chama Valley, New Mexico 126

4.2 Los Ojos, Chama Valley 131

4.3 Population growth in Rio Arriba County 134

4.4 Income from tourism in Rio Arriba County, 1981–90 140

4.5 State park visits in Rio Arriba County, 1982–86 141

4.6 Signs at the Bill Humphries Wildlife Area 159

4.7 Pastores Feed and General Store in Los Ojos 166

4.8 Ganados newsletter 176

4.9 Antonio Manzanares conducting a news conference 178

Tables

1.1   National environmental lobbying organizations   21

3.1   Occupational disease in California attributed to pesticides
and other agricultural chemicals, 1954–67   78

3.2   Occupational disease in California attributed to pesticides
and other agricultural chemicals, 1967   79

3.3   Administrative actions and lawsuits regarding pesticides   98

4.1   Gross receipts and employment in Rio Arriba County,
1986   136

4.2   Employment in Rio Arriba County, 1981–89   138

4.3   Grazing schedule for the Rio Chama, Humphries, and
Sargent Wildlife Areas   172

Abbreviations

AFL	American Federation of Labor
AFL-CIO	American Federation of Labor and Congress of Industrial Organizations
AUM	Animal Unit Month
AWOC	Agricultural Workers Organizing Committee
BLM	Bureau of Land Management
CAL-EPA	California Environmental Protection Agency
CAWIU	Cannery and Agricultural Workers Industrialized Union
CDFA	California Department of Food and Agriculture
CRLA	California Rural Legal Assistance
CSO	Community Service Organization
DJ	Dingell-Johnson Act
EDF	Environmental Defense Fund
FIFRA	Federal Insecticide Fungicide Rodenticide Act
GDV	Ganados del Valle
HEW	Health, Education and Welfare (Department of)
IPM	Integrated Pest Management (Systems)
INS	Immigration and Naturalization Service
LULAC	League of United Latin American Citizens

NAACP	National Association for the Advancement of Colored People
NFWA	National Farm Workers Association
NWF	National Wildlife Federation
NMCF	New Mexico Community Foundation
NMDGF	New Mexico Department of Game and Fish
NMSU	New Mexico State University
NSM	New Social Movement
PLAN	Public Lands Action Network
PR	Pittman-Robertson Act
SHRIC	Southwest Research and Information Center
SIPI	Scientific Institute for Public Information
SWOP	Southwest Organizing Project
SWP	State Water Project
UFWOC	United Farm Workers Organizing Committee
USDA	United States Department of Agriculture
USFS	United States Forest Service
USFWS	United States Fish and Wildlife Service
WIN	Water Information Network
WMA	Wildlife Management Area

The environmental struggles of the poor—from Chipko to antitoxic battles—are becoming increasingly widespread and altering the very nature of environmentalism. The fact that they have captured so much attention has caused them to be presented, and sometimes reified, as class, livelihood, gender, and national liberation struggles. While all environmental action is rooted in some ideology, it is only recently that unprecedented numbers of activists are explicitly linking their vision of environmental quality to specific agendas for social change. The subaltern—those who are socially and economically marginalized—are now speaking out on environmental issues. Because they occupy a position different from that of traditional environmentalists, they are expressing a new articulation of the problem. For example, indigenous populations in Latin America argue that the protection of a particular habitat is contingent upon their political autonomy. In the United States, low-income minority communities point to environmental racism in which racial minorities are disproportionately exposed to environmental hazards and systematically excluded from environmental decision making. Both sets of activists are as interested in changing the prevailing power relations as they are in reducing pollution or preserving biodiversity.

Despite widespread publicity, it is still not clear what these struggles are about. How do we understand them? Are they a basis for transformative change? Are they examples of the fragmented political landscape of postmodernism? This book attempts to clarify our understanding of the environmental/livelihood struggles of marginalized communities within the context of political economy, social movements, and identity politics.

This book explores two specific social and environmental struggles that have much in common with other struggles around the world. The first case is the 1965–71 pesticide campaign of the United Farm Workers Organizing Committee (UFWOC) and the second is a grazing conflict involving Ganados del Valle (Livestock Growers of the Valley), a community development group in northern New Mexico. Both instances of collective action embody elements of material struggles, identity politics, and environmental concerns. To shed light on the dynamics and forces that gave rise to and shaped these struggles, my analysis focuses on the economic structures and role of racism in creating conditions of subalternity. It also examines how an ethnic and cultural identity was constructed and used in attempting to overcome the forces of marginalization. Looking closely at what constituted these struggles and what they were really about illustrates how grassroots activists are contributing to an environmentalism concerned with much more than nonmaterial quality of life issues.

Much attention has been paid to subaltern activists' assertion that, for them, the environment and environmental problems are different from those typically associated with the mainstream movement. They argue that their definition of the environment includes poverty, poor housing, and the Third World debt. According to one activist, "To black folks the environment is not just forests and wetlands; the environment is where you live, so the housing crisis should also be considered an environmental issue" (Stephenson in Ruffins 1989, 6). There is little doubt that environmentalism is being redefined and that the concerns of environmental justice activists vary from the dominant environmental agenda. But I am less interested in how definitions of environmental issues vary than in how people intersect with them in the context of larger social and political relations, and how they go about organizing around them.

Instead of simply recognizing such environmental concerns as different, I argue that the rise of subaltern environmental struggles poses an-

other set of issues. In effect, they force us to explicitly locate environmental concerns within the context of inequality and attempts to alter
dominant power arrangements. This challenges the common understanding of environmentalism as a new social movement (NSM) concerned with questions of identity and nonmaterial quality-of-life issues.
Rather, subaltern environmentalism is embedded in material and power
struggles, as well as questions of identity and quality of life. Dominated
communities engaged in environmental struggles do not disaggregate
their various identities and needs. Although they may engage in strategic essentialism, the practice of reifying aspects of one's identity for
political purposes, they recognize their multiple-identities and the various lines of domination and power that need to be resisted and challenged. They build complex movements which simultaneously address
issues of identity as well as a wide range of economic issues (production,
distribution, and uneven development), thereby defying the various
models and paradigms social scientists have created to impose meaning
on collective action, in particular, environmentalism.

From the perspective of marginalized communities, environmental
problems reflect, and may intensify, larger existing inequalities and
uneven power relations. This relationship of environmental quality,
political economy, and inequality manifests itself in several ways. First,
in much of the Third World, capitalist development causes major social
and ecological dislocation, as growth becomes the mantra of newly
industrializing countries. It is clear that both lack of development and
persistent poverty in the Third World also contribute their own set of
environmental problems that include insufficient capital to provide for
pollution control or regulatory oversight. From a different perspective
we know that the poor may actively contribute to resource degradation
through the cultivation of marginal lands or the overexploitation of
natural resources, both of which are frequently linked to skewed land
tenure and disarticulated agrarian economies. Yet, it is also the poor
and marginalized of the world who often bear the brunt of pollution
and resource degradation—whether a toxic dump, a lack of arable
land, or global climate change—simply because they are more vulnerable and lack alternatives. The privileged can reduce their vulnerability by insulating themselves from environmental problems through

assorted mechanisms including consumption (such as the purchase of bottled water or sunscreens) or exportation (such as the deforestation of other countries).

Recognizing the severity and complexity of these problems, dominant political and environmental actors have proposed the concept of sustainable development (World Commission on Environment and Development 1987). While originally an innovative solution that sought to address the conditions of both environmental degradation and human suffering, it has since mutated into a fairly meaningless concept best described as "controlled capitalism" (Lewis 1992). This corruption signifies that sustainable development can no longer claim — if, indeed, it ever could — to include the needs of the marginalized. This is seen in the continued self-serving actions of corporations and development institutions that operate under the mantle of sustainable development. Although controlled capitalism may appear to be the only reasonable path to pursue, we delude ourselves by thinking that it bears the seeds of lasting environmental and social change, especially given capitalism's dependence on continued growth and consumption and the inequality it spreads in its wake. Those desiring a more socially and ecologically just world may be frustrated by the fact that at this moment there is no readily identifiable alternative to capitalism. At the same time, this is a period of exploration that is allowing us to venture beyond the confines of a narrowly conceived left or right. Consequently, one development which has garnered wide attention is the recent outpouring of grassroots action. While it may be true, as geographer Lakshman Yapa (1993a) has pointed out, that these social movements cannot eradicate poverty because they are primarily from within the region of poverty and the causes of poverty are far more structural and international in nature, it is also true that grassroots action will form an important component of any new social order or counter-hegemonic effort.

Postmodern scholarship has made several important contributions that help us understand the political landscape of the late twentieth century. By turning our attention to the local and particular, it has shown us the diversity of resistance as well as how hegemonic power is reproduced. Most importantly, it has offered us greater political space

in which to maneuver. Yet it offers only limited hope of creating fundamental social change and argues for the futility of such a project. The
most that postmodern identity politics hopes for is that by being open
to identifying and joining with other marginalized and oppressed others we can move toward "empowering a multiplicity of resistances
rather than searches for that ... singular transformation to precede and
guide all others" (Soja and Hooper 1993, 187). While appreciating the
strides this intellectual trajectory has made — and not longing for the
old days of single identities, meta-narratives, and universal projects
from which, as a Chicana from a working-class background, I was
routinely excluded — I do see the need to reinsert political economy into
identity politics and social movements. Michael Watts has suggested
that "mapping the spectrum of cultural forms, onto spatial, class and
social identities in the context of global interconnectedness might constitute an important frontier for geographic inspection" (1991, 10),
and, I would add, political action.

These cases offer, I believe, a positive example of how postmodern
identity politics can be linked to concrete material struggle. (The lack of
such a link has led to frequent criticism of adherents of postmodernism
and cultural studies.) These conflicts go beyond the false duality offered
by an old and new social movements construct and defy efforts to reduce them to class struggles. In each of these struggles, identity politics
is neither incidental nor an afterthought. Instead, it is germane to the
structuring of the problem and the struggle itself. People consistently
drew upon their identities and oppression as sources of empowerment
and tools in the course of action. I will illustrate the complexity of these
struggles and demonstrate that, for the actors themselves, the questions
and frameworks posed by scholars (such as, "Is class or racism responsible for my oppression?") miss the mark. Participants experienced a
far more complex reality that required resistance and change on multiple fronts.

This book has several purposes. First, on an empirical level, I show
that subaltern environmental struggles fit the mold of neither old nor
new social movements. Instead, they combine elements of economic
struggles, identity politics, and quality of life issues. Second, I make
clear that the environmental struggles of the marginalized are very much

about power. Only through gaining more power to change their conditions can oppressed people live in dignity and work toward social equality. This necessarily implies conflict through challenging dominant orders and practices since power is never given, but rather taken. Third, I demonstrate that, for subordinated communities, environmental issues also are economic. Mainstream environmentalists at times categorize subaltern struggles as economic or civil rights issues without seeing them as environmental ones. This position overlooks the fact that, because of their economic and social marginalization, subaltern environmental concerns are encountered within the context of inequality.

Although this book focuses on a single ethnic group — the Chicano/ Mexicano population of the southwestern United States[1] — aspects of its politics and analysis are applicable to other marginalized groups (whether colonized people, occupied nations, or racial minorities), even though the precise conditions of subalternity vary from case to case. The point is to gain an understanding of how multiple forces interact in creating inequality and oppression, and how complex struggles form to overcome it.

Since most of the scholarship on oppositional environmentalism in the United States focuses on the anti-toxics movement (Szasz 1994; Bullard 1990; Freudenberg 1984), often located in urban areas, I chose my two case studies carefully, to add a new dimension to the literature that would emphasize inequality rather than the particular issue per se. Accordingly, both are rural and neither is about waste. While there are plenty of contaminated rural communities, neither of these cases deal directly with incinerators or dumps. The first case examines an environmental and occupational hazard — pesticides — that has been closely associated with the environmental justice movement. The early pesticide campaign of the United Farm Workers is a clear example of how a highly marginalized and powerless group organized to gain greater control over their lives, including their environment. Many people have since questioned the UFW's motives, suggesting that they used the issue to gain greater support. This may or may not be true, but it's not the concern of my study. The point I wish to emphasize is that the fight against pesticides was part of a larger struggle to improve farm workers' lives, including better wages and more respect for workers. It was one of the most influential events in the development of a Chicano identity. There is no denying that pesticides were (and are) a serious problem, and one of the few ways to improve the situation was to garner more power for the workers and their union. (Thus the fight against pesticides cannot be divorced from the struggle for union recognition and a strong contract.) Not only would it have made no sense for individual workers to go after pesticides by themselves, it would have done nothing to address the workers' extreme poverty and lack of power. Poor peoples' environments can rarely be improved without acquiring more power. In this case, it was necessary to address uneven power relations within a racialized division of labor.

The second case focuses on inequality within the context of natural resource policy. Little attention has focused on natural resource use in this country and its relationship to poverty, uneven development, racism, and cultural identity. But for Ganados del Valle, a community development cooperative, these structural forces are at work, circumscribing people's lives. Because of history, racism, uneven development, and the division of labor, the Hispano communities of northern New Mexico are in economic and social decline. They have sought to alter the situation by creating a community-development corporation that not only empowers individuals and provides a renewed cultural and ethnic identity, but also seeks to improve their economic well-being in an environmentally sustainable fashion by building a series of integrated businesses based on sheep. The fact that mainstream environmentalists oppose Ganados' controlled use of elk-grazing habitat underscores their inability to accept the reality that people transform nature in order to reproduce themselves, and that hegemonic methods of resource management may be counter to the cultural and economic needs of marginalized populations. The case again highlights the fact that oppressed people must challenge dominant power relations in order to change their circumstances. Like the UFW, Ganados is not just about the environment; instead, they have a comprehensive plan to restore economic and cultural vitality to northern New Mexican communities that includes a careful use of the local environment, the fostering of an affirmative identity, and a concern for quality of life issues.

In both of these situations, people are fighting for a more dignified and sustainable livelihood, but "dignified livelihood" is more than just attaining material well-being and learning to tread lightly on the land.

For oppressed communities, a dignified life means being able to live free of cultural oppression and racial and ethnic inequality. Hence, while culture and racism are critical to understanding oppression, they are also essential to illuminating the process of mobilization. At times, various forces may rise to the surface and become the dominant projection of the struggle — such as, for example, a cultural identity. This happens either because activists interpret their actions within such a context or know it is a strategy that will increase their support. Heavily biased interpretations may also come about from outsiders, or the larger public, who choose to see particular factors as the framing issues. The task is to see beyond the surface representation, clarify the politics engendering such representations, appreciate the distinct forces shaping struggles, and investigate how they interact.

Structure of the Book

The first chapter lays out the theoretical argument of the book and introduces the idea of subaltern by sketching out two such environmental movements: resistance struggles in the Third World and the environmental justice movement in the United States. I then discuss mainstream environmentalism within the context of NSMs, identifying how subaltern environmental movements are both similar to and different from the mainstream movement and its political agendas.

The second chapter lays out what I consider to be the key analytical categories in understanding these specific subaltern environmental struggles: economic relations, 'race', and ethnic and cultural identity. The interplay of these elements within these communities not only oppressed people but were crucial to understanding how people tried to change their circumstances in meaningful ways. They were also critical to differentiating between mainstream and environmental justice (or subaltern) movements since poverty, racism, and cultural inequality — defining features of oppressed people's lives — are often only secondary considerations for more privileged people.

The third and fourth chapters are devoted to the case studies themselves — the United Farm Workers' Organizing Committee (UFWOC) and Ganados, respectively. Each chapter lays out the historical and geographical context of the struggle and tells the stories of each group, paying special attention to the various players and their positions. The last chapter offers a detailed discussion of the struggles, assessing their contributions and shortcomings in the larger struggle for social justice and suggesting some of the political implications and lessons of each.

A Word on Methodology

Most of the research for this book was conducted in 1990 and 1991, as part of my dissertation. Given the time lag between completion of the field research and publication date, I have made only a limited effort to bring the historical accounts into the present. Instead, I have chosen to present them as two discrete events which offer insights into larger struggles. Both the UFW and Ganados continue to exist and evolve and face new challenges and opportunities. I present historical snapshots of each.

Although the two cases are separated by almost thirty years, they both required that I reconstruct a series of historical events and give them meaning within the context of subaltern environmentalism. I examined documents pertaining to the UFWOC at the following places: the Walter Reuther Archives of Urban and Labor Affairs, Wayne State University, Detroit, Michigan; the Bancroft Library, University of California, Berkeley; the Chicano Studies Library, University of California, Berkeley; the Kern County Library, Bakersfield; and numerous courthouses throughout California. Besides archival work, I interviewed many people involved in the early UFWOC, now scattered across California, many of whom are still involved in social justice activities.

Several sources provided access to documents and materials necessary to an investigation of the Ganados case: Ganados del Valle, Los Ojos; New Mexico Department of Game and Fish, Santa Fe; New Mexico State Library, Santa Fe; United States Fish and Wildlife Service, Albuquerque; and the Coronado Room, University of New Mexico, Albuquerque. Many individuals opened their personal files to me, and I interviewed extensively people involved in the Ganados grazing conflict, including not only the members of Ganados themselves, but members of the New Mexico Department of Game and Fish, the United

States Fish and Wildlife Service, state officials, and New Mexican environmentalists.

This project is important for several reasons. For one, I believe that inequality and environmental degradation are two of the more serious problems facing our world today. These problems call out for intervention, and growing numbers of communities are becoming involved. Although fraught with their own problems and contradictions, subaltern environmental struggles are reshaping local geographies and challenging our theories of environmentalism, social movements, identity politics and class struggle. As such, they force us not only to rethink our ideas of environmentalism but also our theories on collective action and organizing, particularly in a time of rapid social change.

An undertaking such as this book is of necessity a collective project, both in terms of the people who shared part of their lives with me, and the people in my life who supported and assisted me in various ways.

I gratefully acknowledge the financial support of the Woodrow Wilson Rural Policy Dissertation Fellowship Program, the Southwest Regional Studies Center of the University of New Mexico, and the Inter-American Cultures and Chicano Studies Program of UCLA.

Figures 3.1 and 3.3 were drawn by Caroline Holsted and Carol Kalt of the geography department of California State University, Fullerton. Tom Do of California State University, Long Beach, sketched figure 4.1, which is based on a map provided by Duane Griffin. All other graphics are credited to the work of Angel M. Alcala, who also solved a number of computer and other technical problems.

In addition to financial assistance, many individuals contributed to this book in ways too numerous to mention. It is impossible to thank them all. The following alphabetical list names some of those who helped make this book: Angel M. Alcala, Sara and Angel R. Alcala, Shirl Buss, Ernie Chavez, Lisa Duran, Leo Estrada, Monica Fisher, Margaret FitzSimmons, Lisa Garcia, Bob Gottlieb, Duane Griffin, Allen Heskin, John Horton, the Labor/Community Strategy Center, Joel and Victoria Ledesma, Chris Mayda, Donna Mukai, Devon Pena, Stephanie Pincetl, Ann and Richard Pulido, Craig Pulido, Ken Pulido, Louis and Bertha Pulido, Ron Pulido, Maria Samora, the Serrano family, Velia Silva, Valentina Valdez Martinez, Abel Valenzuela, Maria

Varela, Clyde Woods, Angus Wright, and the extremely supportive geography department at the University of Southern California.

To all who were interviewed and gave their time, I express my deep thanks. Although not everyone will agree with my interpretation of the events, I have done my best to portray accurately various viewpoints, and I take responsibility for all interpretations offered.

Environmentalism and Economic Justice

Subaltern Environmental Struggles

Mainstream environmentalists have welcomed the adoption of environmental concerns and activism by decidedly nonelitist groups such as peasants, those who dwell in slums, farmworkers, and racially oppressed groups, among others. This blossoming of environmentalism among the subaltern diversifies the mainstream's ranks, broadens the interests of the movement, and allows its spokespersons to speak with greater authority. For many, this burgeoning environmental concern is a testament to the diffusion of environmental consciousness, emanating, of course, from the core.[1] Indeed, some take direct credit for it. "Concern for the resource base is now shared worldwide, and the U.S. movement deserves much of the credit" (Brown Welsh 1988, 291).

Despite such self-congratulatory rhetoric, it is true that the mainstream environmental movement of the core countries has played no small role in making environmentalism an issue and in providing a dominant frame so to speak, in which to locate nature-society relations. But a direct transfer of U.S. mainstream environmentalism does not adequately explain the rise of subaltern environmental struggles. This apparent upsurge is due to several developments. These include changing perceptions and meanings of environmental problems and actions on the part of both observers and actors, as well as subordinated groups' responses to continued economic and political marginalization, struggles over identity, and concerns for quality of life, and the continued degradation of the physical environment. Any analysis of environmental resistance struggles should not underestimate the role of interpretation in understanding them. Oppressed groups frequently have long histories of resisting the forces that seek to undermine them, and they have always intersected with resource use and environmental concerns — the difference is that an environmental template is now placed over them.

There are instances when subaltern actors consciously articulate a clear environmental meaning not only because it reflects their struggle but because they realize the political leverage it offers. Increased environmental activism, however, cannot be attributed simply to language or signification. There has been a real increase in activism and social movements in general (Ekins 1992; Escobar and Alvarez 1992; Dalton and Kuechler 1990; Scott 1990; Slater 1985) and environmentalism in particular (Johnston 1994; Friedmann and Rangan 1993a; Gedicks 1993; Taylor, Hadsell, Lorentzen, and Scarce 1993). In the Third World, segments of the population are rejecting the modern concept of development that has left vast social and ecological destruction in its wake (Escobar 1992b; Shiva 1989; Slater 1985). In the First World marginalized communities are resisting threats to their physical well-being as well as to their continued subordination in a highly racialized, capitalist economy (Bullard 1993a, 1990). Given these multiple meanings it is necessary to flesh out environmental resistance struggles in order to understand what they are about, if and how they may differ from more established forms of environmentalism, and what are their political consequences.

This new form of environmentalism goes by a variety of headings: grassroots, popular, livelihood, resistance, environmental justice, and resource struggles. What they all share is a counterhegemonic, or subaltern, location — they exist in opposition to prevailing powers. Ranajit Guha defines subaltern consciousness as different from a working-class consciousness in that it is not confined to class relationship but encompasses other forms of domination and subordination, such as colonialism, caste structures, and, I would add, racism — defining features of many societies.

The key here is a relationship of structured and institutionalized inequality. "[S]ubordination cannot be understood except as one of the constitutive terms in a binary relationship of which the other is dominance, for subaltern groups are always subject to the activity of ruling groups, even when they rebel and rise up" (Guha 1988a, 35). Such a conceptualization of domination and resistance offers insights into the environmental struggles of the subordinated. Even though their struggles may be categorized as class conflict, racism, or patriarchal resistance, what is usually at stake are multiple forms of domination, exploitation, and resistance, that narrow applications of class may prevent us from appreciating.

The concept of subaltern allows us to see the entrenched and all-encompassing ways in which power relations are constituted and experienced. "Subalternity was materialized by the structure of property, institutionalized by law, sanctified by religion and made tolerable and even desirable — by tradition" (Guha 1988b, 45). Here Guha describes a severely unequal set of power relations that have existed and do exist in colonized countries. While we typically associate such inequality with less industrialized countries, we must recognize the extent to which they have also occurred in advanced industrial societies like the United States (Kaplan and Pease 1993).

Given this oppositional location, one theme which resonates throughout subaltern environmental struggles is the notion that they exist distinct from traditional, or mainstream, environmentalism, which is largely thought to be concerned with narrowly defined quality-of-life issues. Writing from the perspective of environmental justice activists in the United States, Bryant and Mohai note that

> environmentalists have long been remiss for not observing the urban environment as one that needs attention. As a consequence they are viewed by suspicion by people of color. . . . To champion old growth forests or the protection of the snail darter or the habitat of spotted owls without championing clean safe urban environments or improved habitats of the homeless, does not bode well for future relations between environmentalists and people of color, and with the poor. (Bryant and Mohai 1992, 6)

Ramachandra Guha, in referring to Indian environmental struggles, makes a similar observation: "Two features distinguish these environmental movements from their Western counterparts. First, for the sections of society most critically affected by environmental degradation — poor and landless peasants, women, and tribals — it is a question of sheer survival, not of enhancing the quality of life. Second, and as a consequence, the environmental solutions they articulate deeply involve questions of equity as well as economic and political redistribution" (Guha 1989, 81).

Both of these passages reflect a preoccupation with survival, economic and social inequality, and social justice — themes that have not been closely associated with mainstream environmentalism.

Although many have noted this increase in environmental activism among the "others," there has not been a serious attempt to conceptualize it in a coherent way. Instead, the problems and solutions of the First World have largely remained distinct from those of the Third World, despite the fact that grassroots activists are in the process of forging connections (see Pulido 1994b). One of the few to see the similarities is Ben Goldman. "The calls for environmental justice that have emerged from communities throughout the United States are echoed by parallel community concerns throughout the world" (Goldman 1994, 27). Unfortunately, this observation has not been widely recognized or acted upon.

One factor that intensifies this distance is that activists may use language and frameworks with which other marginalized groups do not readily identify. For example, while U.S. activists emphasize racism in understanding their subordination, this may not be the same lens by which Filipino communities see their situation. Moreover, the racism Filipinos do experience is not the same as that of racially dominated groups in the United States; it is constituted in a different political and economic context.

These seemingly disparate struggles, however, do have something in common, and subalternity provides one possible framework to understand them in a more systematic fashion. This is not meant to imply that the struggles of Third World subsistence producers are the same as those facing inner-city residents opposed to an uncontrolled hazardous waste site, but common threads run through them that can strengthen our understanding of oppositional environmental movements. By choosing case studies located in the United States, it will become apparent that they have similarities with the struggles of the less-industrialized world. Despite the fact that nonwhites in the United States often refer to themselves as "Third World" people, U.S. environmentalism is frequently perceived as all rich, white, and powerful. In reality, the struggles of marginalized communities in the First World may be just as much about livelihood and economic issues as in the Third World, where these issues are more clearly recognized as legitimate.[2] Before proceeding to examine subaltern environmental struggles in more detail, I will briefly review current debates in social movement theory in order to better contextualize mainstream and subaltern environmental action.

Environmental Action and Social Movements

Alan Scott has defined a social movement as "a collective actor constituted by individuals who understand themselves to have common interests and, for at least some significant part of their social existence, a common identity. Social movements are distinguished from other collective actors, such as political parties or pressure groups, in that they have mass mobilization, or the threat of mobilization, as their prime source of social sanction, and hence, of power" (1990, 6).

Social movements have long attracted scholarly attention, and numerous frameworks and paradigms have been developed in order to provide meaning to these events. I will focus primarily on New Social Movements (NSMs) and identity politics because both are closely linked to environmentalism.[3] Because environmentalism is considered an NSM, I will consider its applicability to subaltern struggles while also looking at the general concept in a more critical light. For NSM researchers, identity has emerged as a key area of focus. For this group of scholars, understanding how individuals coalesce and fashion new collective identities is the crucial question in understanding the emergence of social movements.

The concept of NSMs was developed to explain the type of movements that rose in the advanced industrialized countries beginning in the 1960s (Dalton, Kuechler, and Bürklin 1990) during what was the beginning of the transition from a Fordist to a post-Fordist economy (Buttel 1992).[4] These post-Marxist movements (Boggs 1986) are considered new for several reasons. First and foremost, NSMs are seen as distinct from class-based movements such as labor or agrarian struggles (thought to be on the decline anyway during this period). Accordingly, NSMs are not closely associated with economic issues per se, but are

more aligned with the expansion of rights and quality-of-life issues —
what Inglehart (1990) has called postmaterialist values. Hence, this
period has witnessed the ascendance of quality-of-life movements (environment and peace) and identity politics (feminism and gay rights)
that are contingent upon people fashioning new collective identities
that allow them to work together.

A second distinguishing feature is that NSMs are not perceived to be
struggling for a grand or universal transformation. Instead, they are
considered to be local efforts seeking to change small portions of the
social totality over a limited geographic area. Further distancing NSMs
from previous forms of collective action is the lack of unity between the
agent and the social conflict, such as that between workers and class
struggle (Laclau 1985). This is a central point in understanding the idea
of NSMs. Instead of people mobilizing on the basis of some objective
reality, NSMs develop around themes, and it has been argued, reflect the
politicization of domains previously considered apolitical, or strictly
personal (Melucci 1988; Slater 1985). One group of writers described
the set of differences in the following way:

> Research on "old" social movements (labor, agrarian, racial) often stresses
> the class basis of these conflicts. These movements derived from a combina-
> tion of economic interests and distinct social networks. In other words, they
> arose to represent the particular interests of a clearly defined social aggre-
> gate, and the movement depended on an organizational social aggregate
> that integrated members of the class collective. Social movements were a
> vehicle for groups that lacked access to political power through other politi-
> cal channels. . . . A distinguishing feature of new social movements is that
> they lack the narrow special interest appeal to any one social grouping. *New
> social movements are not drawn from the socioeconomically disadvantaged
> or from repressed minorities.* (Dalton, Kuechler, and Bürklin 1990, 12,
> emphasis added)

Typically, NSMs, including mainstream environmentalism, are seeking changes that often cannot be contained within an industrial economy. These movements transcend the confines of both conventional
Marxism and liberal democracy (Boggs 1986). NSMs reflect the fact
that people are yearning for more than a steady paycheck. There is a
deep desire for greater meaning, participation, quality of life, and acceptance of difference by the larger society. Thus, people have mobi-

lized around a wide range of issues: sexism, racism, environmental degradation, alienation, ability, and sexual orientation.

A third feature of NSMs is that these mobilizations feature a distinct mode of operation. Previous (or old) movements were thought to be closely identified with either the state apparatus or highly entrenched institutions, such as established labor unions, that were relatively hierarchical and undemocratic. In contrast, the actions and actors of NSMs are rooted in civil society, are more dispersed, and emphasize democracy and process within their structures and activities.

While identity formation is emphasized within the context of NSMs, there also exist identity politics that have emerged as a subcategory of NSMs. Generally, identity politics refer to the unprecedented level of activism seeking to affirm various forms of otherness, the expansion of rights, and the addressing of social difference (Young 1990). Penrose and Jackson have argued that "rather than assuming that identities are fixed and singular . . . [they are] dynamic and plural. Such a plurality immediately gives rise to a *politics* of identity as groups and individuals become aware of their differences, attach significance to certain dimensions, and contest the relevance of other designations" (1994, 207, emphasis in original). Such a description reveals the extent to which identity politics are associated with postmodern scholarship and politics.

For one, the description reflects a renewed emphasis on the individual rather than on macrostructures. "The individual subject has become more important, while our models of 'the subject' have altered. We can no longer conceive of 'the individual' in terms of a whole and completed ego or autonomous 'self'. The 'self' is experienced as more fragmented and incomplete, composed of multiple 'selves' or identities in relations to the different social worlds we inhabit" (Hall 1991, 58–59).

Stuart Hall's quote also alludes to the second connection between postmodernism and identity politics: the destabilization of the center, in this case, "the subject." This simply refers to the recent recognition of the fact that we all have multiple identities and positions. Individuals may simultaneously identify as consumers, citizens, feminists, workers, and human-rights activists, differing markedly from the previous construct that conceived of the individual either as a worker, a black, or a woman. While this development more clearly reflects reality, it does present us with a whole new set of political questions and challenges. In fact, the challenges are so great that some have categorized NSMs as obstacles to creating real social change by the way they have relativized all forms of oppression and domination, and displaced what were once central struggles for social justice — usually 'race' and class (Handler 1992; Harvey 1993 and 1991). "The new social movements can be considered the archetypical form of postmodern politics — grassroots, protest from below, solidarity, collective identity, affective processes — all in the struggle against the established order outside the 'normal' channels. . . . On the other hand, there is no grandiose plan for a better society" (Handler 1992, 719).

Not all critics of NSMs and postmodernism entirely reject these new trends, but they do see the proliferation of identities as a political challenge. "The task of incorporating such aspects of social organization as race, gender, sexual orientation, religion, and ethnicity within the overall frame of historical materialist analysis . . . and class politics . . . is one of the most profound challenges to socialist thinking at the present time" (Harvey 1991, 75).

Of course, the mere fact that social science paradigms have changed does not necessarily mean that people's identities and behavior have actually been modified. Anthropologist June Nash has summarized well how social scientists' expectations and interpretations may be only tenuously linked to reality. "The Modern age's drive for a unified dominant theory seems to have blinded us to the fact that most people who are not part of the scientific community are not discomfited by the diversity of claims to truth that sprout in any social movement. Third World people were living in a postmodern world long before it was discovered by theorists" (Nash 1992, 292).

Despite what may appear to be a decisive qualitative shift in the types of movements occurring throughout the world, several scholars have forcefully challenged this assumption. Alan Scott, in his influential book *Ideology and the New Social Movements* (1990), argues that NSMs are not new at all. The primary reason observers think so is that they are fetishizing mobilization itself, instead of paying adequate attention to the goals of movements. If we were to do so, Scott argues, we would see that most movements eventually become incorporated into society as their objectives become adopted and mainstreamed. Thus, it is only because we have chosen to focus on the struggle that we misread the nature of the movement. David Plotke (1990), in contrast, acknowledges that there is something new about NSMs but argues that the claims have been greatly exaggerated primarily because the concept of NSMs was developed in response to Marxism. Accordingly, in an effort to create significant distance between Marxism and NSMs, we now act as though workers' struggles were not cultural and social struggles.

> Proponents of new social movement discourse are right to insist that contemporary collective action really is about culture, not merely about the cultural expression of class elements. But this is not very new. In the United States class conflict has always existed alongside cultural, ethnic, and racial struggle, never as a pure form for other movements to express.
>
> . . . There are significant novel elements in both the context and the substance of the cultural emphases of new forces. First, explicitly cultural elements have more weight in new movements than was the case in most prior periods of U.S. history, even if cultural efforts have always been present. Second, these cultural concerns are increasingly framed in terms not only of general social values and norms, but also of the definition and maintenance of identities for individuals. The notion of a conflict over culture necessarily entails a conflict over identity, as norms have to be lived. (Plotke 1990, 89)

Nowhere is the murkiness surrounding the distinction between new and old social movements more pronounced than in the area of 'race'. On the one hand, some writers see movements for racial equality as an expansion of rights and fundamentally different from class struggle, therefore considering it to be a NSM (Harvey 1991). On the other hand, analysts such as Dalton, Kuechler, and Bürklin (1990) place racial struggles in the category of old movements. Both Plotke (1990) and Aronowitz (1994) have touched on this contradiction. Plotke suggests that the struggle for black liberation historically and in the present has always had strong elements of both. "New social movement discourse is right to insist on the importance of cultural themes within that movement, and wildly wrong to treat it (then or now) as mainly a cultural movement uninterested in legal and distributive issues. The coexistence of legal, distributive, and cultural elements in the themes of the Black movement is evident" (Plotke 1990, 91). This differs somewhat from

Aronowitz's conclusion in which he categorizes some efforts on the part of nonwhites (such as those pertaining to redistribution) as old and other forms of activism (including Black Nationalism) as an NSM (Aronowitz 1994, 16–17). Thus it is possible for an antiracist struggle to contain elements of both.

Building on the insights of Plotke (1990) and Scott (1990), I believe some movements and their claims, including environmentalism, are new, but many are not. To assume that NSMs have become the norm simply does not bear out under close scrutiny. While mainstream environmentalism embodies many of the tendencies of NSMs, it represents only one kind of activism. Other forms of environmentalism and collective action are not NSMs. The concept of NSMs has become problematic precisely because it has been so widely applied. In reality, its true value is in helping us see what is unique about a limited number of movements.

Because of the turbulence coursing through social movement theory, there is a great debate over how to conceptualize social movements — which approach to take, what questions to ask, and most importantly, how to understand them. The difficulty of these questions is most striking in reference to the mobilizations of poor and subaltern groups, largely because the most prominent theories are formulated in reference to the middle classes of the First World. Yet, the unparalleled rise in social movements in Latin America (Escobar and Alvarez 1992; Slater 1985) and elsewhere (Moghadam 1994) insists that we directly confront these issues. We must ask ourselves how applicable First World theories are to the struggles of often impoverished, marginal populations existing in states which are only nominally democratic.

Despite apparently different contexts, scholars from Latin America accord significant attention to the process of identity formation and social movements.[5] This should not imply, however, that the movements of the First World and Third World are the same. Yapa forcefully disputes the idea that the struggles of the poor can be equated with the identity politics of the First World. "Social movements of the poor differ from politics of identity in a major respect; [the] poor do not wish to affirm their poverty, they wish to negate it by moving out of it" (Yapa 1993a, 5).

This insight is critical to understanding subaltern environmental struggles. As the Latin American literature intimates, identity plays a crucial role in the struggles and movements of the poor, but in no way can those struggles simply be reduced to quality-of-life issues or to identity politics, particularly in light of the fact that people may be resisting murderous regimes, the violence of development, imperialism, and destruction of their resource base. Identity is but one component of these struggles — affirmation of difference is hardly the paramount objective. Instead, subaltern movements are simultaneously about both material concerns and systems of meaning, thereby challenging the notion that identity issues are not of concern to those struggling to survive. The reality of many contemporary movements and struggles is that they are not simply about a search for identity or improved quality of life — needs upon which those who are financially and physically secure can focus. Nor are they only about brute class struggle centered on production and its larger vision of uniting the workers of the world. Arturo Escobar (1992a,b), writing about social movements in Latin America, has observed:

> It is essential to recognize the importance of economic factors and their structural determinants. But just as crucial as the reconstruction of economies — and indelibly linked to it — is the reconstitution of meanings at all levels, from everyday life to national development. Social movements must be seen equally and inseparably as struggles over meanings as well as material conditions, that is, as cultural struggles. . . . Contemporary social movements in Latin America have a multiple character, as economic, social, political and cultural struggles. (Escobar 1992b, 69 and 82)

I would argue that the same could be said for the environmental struggles of the subaltern, regardless of their location. While most Latin American movements and struggles are situated within the context of development, First World subaltern struggles are situated in terms of racism. This is not an attempt to reduce these movements to one specific form of oppression or another but rather to identify the frameworks within which activists themselves have placed their struggles. Certainly this is the case for environmental justice activists in the United States who have gone to great lengths to articulate an intensely racialized identity and experience (Pulido 1994a).

Drawing on the insights of writers such as Plotke and Escobar allows

us to move beyond the old and new social movement binary by suggesting the richness and complexity of oppositional forms of collective
action. Let us now turn directly to subaltern environmental struggles to
see how these issues are played out in both theory and practice.

Subaltern Environmentalism

Disciplines such as geography and anthropology have long focused on
Third World resource and environmental problems. This has included
work on natural hazards, "traditional" forms of agricultural production, and resource use. The neo-Marxism of the 1970s, however, had a
profound impact on the whole field of nature-society relations (Harvey
1974) that culminated in political ecology, which approaches environmental issues from a political economy perspective (see Emel and
Peet 1989 for a complete review). Instead of seeing rural peasants
and workers as backward groups in need of modernization (see Zimmerer 1993), greater consideration was given to structural forces that
produce conditions of environmental degradation (see, for example,
Wright 1992; Watts 1983).

Continuing on this intellectual path (and responding to an upward
surge in mobilizations), many researchers became increasingly interested in questions of agency, which in terms of nature-society relations,
were manifest in resource struggles and resistance. Because rural communities were the focal point of most investigations, it soon became
evident that such struggles were inseparable from issues of livelihood
and environment (Wisner 1995; Friedmann and Rangan 1993a; Redclift 1987) and thus presented a far different paradigm than that of traditional environmentalism. An emphasis on agency and the local also
led to a critical reexamination of development as a modern project. Not
only were conventional development projects blamed for much environmental degradation, but the targets of modernization themselves
resisted these schemes and began the search for alternatives (Shiva
1989). Although many sectors (including most states) still embrace a
modern development agenda, many others have come to reject it on
several grounds, including its limited efficacy. Yapa makes the case for
this failure by bringing to our attention the fact that "industrial production has grown fifty-fold in this century, four-fifths of that growth com-

ing since 1950. If economic growth of such massive proportions in the past did not eradicate poverty, I fail to see . . . that a new round of accelerated growth will eliminate poverty" (Yapa 1993a, 30). Moreover, because of the debt crisis, the decade of the eighties witnessed a reverse flow of capital from the periphery to the core, accompanied by a dramatic rise in human misery and want. In addition to this aggression, development and the forces of the global economy have played no small role in contributing to ecological degradation through a host of mechanisms that include the eradication of common resources, the usurpation of subsistence production, the displacement of local people and knowledge, and the imposition of capital-intensive production practices typically geared towards increasing export revenues and not toward meeting local needs. (For an overview of development and environment, see Peet and Watts [1993]. For a different viewpoint, see Lewis [1992].)

For all these reasons, Third World movements are closely associated with livelihood issues, which can be defined loosely as a community's struggle "to gain access to and control over the natural resources upon which their lives and livelihoods depend" (Friedmann and Rangan 1993b, 4). The precise political economic system and social relations under which appropriation, domination, and resistance occur will vary, but it is clear from the literature that the prevailing forces of an international capitalist economy, including the project of development, structure the unequal relations which give rise to subaltern environmental struggles.

These movements and struggles have been studied through various lenses, but most have sought to uncover the structural origins of the movements and to clarify how they differ from more elitist forms of environmentalism. Much less attention has been paid to identity politics, nor has there been an attempt to apply some of the insights of cultural studies (Jackson 1989) to these problems. For example, researchers have attributed Third World environmental degradation and resistance to capitalism (Guha 1990), patriarchal maldevelopment (Shiva 1989), colonialism (Broad and Cavanagh 1993), corporate power (Gedicks 1993), and the State (Peluso 1992). In contrast, fewer studies addressed simultaneously questions of meaning and political economy. For example, Bebbington (1993) and Bebbington et al. (1993) detail how

Ecuadorian Indians have striven to create a suitable ethnic identity based on the selective appropriation of old and new cultural elements. By carefully cultivating those fragments that support their development objectives and their vision of appropriate resource use, they are able to fashion a meaningful ethnic identity.

While most writers are sympathetic with the subordinated in subaltern environmental struggles, a number of analysts have offered important insights that prevent us from developing simple or unitarian interpretations of them. Both Rangan (1993) and Pulido (1996) have examined the romanticization of resource struggles and outlined some of the political pitfalls of this strategy. Going a step further, Pezzoli (1993) has demonstrated that communities engaged in what appear to be environmentally related struggles at times may not be committed to an environmental agenda. Even when they are, idealized visions of resource use may be impossible to implement due to social divisions (Someshwar 1993). Nor should we think that the success stories we hear, such as that of the Brazilian rubber-tappers, are simply won by subaltern resistance. Melone (1993) points out that their achievements are partly due to working with mainstream environmentalists of the First World.

Despite these observations, it is difficult to deny that the environmental concerns of marginalized social groups are removed from their livelihood. "[T]o those close to . . . the ground . . . reality is a seamless mesh of social and environmental constraints which it makes little sense to atomize into mutually exclusive categories" (Cleary in Friedmann and Rangan 1993a, 4). Because of the interconnected nature of this reality, these movements extend beyond environmental and economic concerns to include issues of gender, ethnicity, cultural production, and political autonomy.

Environmental Justice in the First World

An analogous but different set of movements is occurring in the First World particularly among racially stigmatized minority groups in the United States. In this instance, marginalized communities are organizing themselves against a variety of environmental hazards and threats, as well as the exclusionary practices of the mainstream environmental movement in environmental decision making. While Third World struggles are rooted in livelihood, First World activists have voiced a distinctly racial interpretation of their environmental concerns. Due to the highly racialized nature of U.S. society, this is entirely appropriate. Environmental quality is no different from other social issues in that racially dominated groups encounter them within the context of subordination.

The discovery of environmental racism—defined as racial minorities' disproportionate exposure to environmental hazards—has unleashed a fury of activism and action on both the grassroots and policy levels. It should be pointed out that the environmental justice movement—a movement fighting environmental racism and hazards in local communities—is a *multiracial* struggle and includes Anglo individuals, communities, and organizations (Szasz 1994; Hofrichter 1993). However, increasingly, a distinct but prominent submovement is being formed that is limited to people of color (Pulido 1994a), which is, in fact, becoming a movement in its own right and will be the primary focus of my discussion.

People of color in the environmental justice movement have articulated a broad but problematic conceptualization of racism that has allowed racism to subsume and become a metaphor for all forms of inequality impacting nonwhite groups. Activists are acutely aware that racism is manifest in every corner of society and that racist attitudes are deeply entrenched and institutionalized, but they have not developed a textured understanding of how racism interacts with various economic forces and hegemonic forms of cultural life. Instead, they have emphasized overt forms of discrimination, as evidenced in a growing literature which seeks to affirm or refute the existence of racist pollution and hazardous land use patterns (Anderton et al. 1994; United Church of Christ 1987; and Bullard 1990; see also Goldman 1994 and Cutter 1995). Within this framework, racism exists if 'race' is shown to be a statistically significant variable in pollution and siting patterns. If not statistically significant, then racism does not exist even though class might be a factor. In this scenario, racism and class structure are almost autonomous. Efforts to deny the existence of environmental racism, as well as the larger history of racism and civil rights in the United States, have placed antiracist activists and scholars in a defensive position, which partially explains this problematic framework.

It could be argued that for racially oppressed groups, racism is the primary axis of domination. All encounters of the oppressed — whether in the job market, at school, at home, or as a consumer — are experienced through racial subordination. Conversely, the racialized structure of the United States results in a benefit to whites. White privilege is so hegemonic that few whites are even cognizant of it. What appears to be natural and fair to whites may be reinforcing the inequality and subordinated status of nonwhites. This level of racism often escapes notice and articulation in favor of more discrete and visible patterns of discrimination. Yet understanding that white privilege exists, which may be more in the arena of ideology, is crucial to understanding and challenging racism.

One scholar of environmental racism has offered us a clue as to why meaning is overlooked in favor of quantitative analysis. "[T]he stigma of being branded a racist organization is so odious that the accusation demands proof" (Greenberg 1993, 236).[6] Implicit in this statement is the belief that only conscious actions driven by biological prejudice constitute racism. Few of those participating in the discourse of environmental justice, however, have sought to uncover these assumptions and place the debate in terms of ideology. By focusing on the inequitable siting of hazardous facilities and disproportionate exposure to pollution, we ultimately fetishize skin color or phenotype (as seen in the title of one article, "Black, Brown, Poor and Poisoned" [Austin and Schill 1991]) instead of developing a broader and deeper understanding of how inequality is reproduced. Likewise, few have critically studied the environmental justice movement itself, preferring either to document inequalities or to present examples of environmental resistance on the part of people of color (Bullard 1993a; Alston 1990), thereby contributing to a unified image of resistance. A number of popular writers and scholars (Cole 1992; Austin and Schill 1991; Kerr and Lee 1993; Alston 1990; Russell 1990) have presented overviews of the rise and contours of the movement, most of which affirm the distinction between environmental justice and mainstream environmentalism.

More theoretical insights have been garnered from studies directed at the entire environmental justice movement, not just nonwhites. Most of this scholarship seeks to uncover the strategies, resource utilization patterns, and group dynamics of the movement and its participants. Particular emphasis has focused on movement formation (Capek 1993; Cable and Benson 1993), as well as comparisons between the mainstream and environmental justice movements (Taylor 1992). The most influential work by far has been done by sociologist-activist Robert Bullard, whose work has shown that African Americans were not overly concerned about environmental issues until they were seen in light of civil rights and inequality. "The key to . . . inclusion rests on linking environmental issues with the social justice concerns of minority communities, whose problems to date have not been sufficiently addressed" (Bullard 1993a, xiii).

This is critical to understanding the dominant discourse of subaltern environmental struggles in the United States. Racism and the struggle for equality are the entry point for marginalized groups in the United States; livelihood is the entry point for Third World communities. This does not mean, however, that all struggles by nonwhites in advanced industrial societies qualify as subaltern. Racialized domination may be an important component of a subaltern status; however, if those dominated are economically integrated into the larger society and share the same culture as the dominant society, they are not subaltern but victims of racism. In the 1940s almost all African Americans were subaltern because their subordination was complete — it was economic, social, political, cultural, and institutionalized by law and custom. In the 1990s many but not all African Americans are subaltern. Take, for example, the telling label "underclass." It refers to people who are economically and culturally subordinate as well as socially and spatially segregated. Their very existence is seen as problematic and offensive to the dominant society.

Subalternity, as stated earlier however, is much more than economic status. Contemporary farmworkers, who are routinely held up as victims of environmental racism (Moses 1993; Perfecto 1992), provide an opportunity to examine more closely the nature of subalternity. In the 1990s farmworkers throughout much of the United States are drawn from Mexico and, increasingly, from non-Spanish-speaking indigenous groups (Nagengast and Kearney 1990). These workers occupy a very

low position within the international division of labor, and their exploitation by growers sets the stage for their more general subordination. Aside from their extreme poverty, these individuals frequently
lack legal status, do not speak the dominant language (English), suffer
abuse from labor contractors, and lack public support, being seen by
the general public as an eyesore, and a threat to their way of life. The
fact that farmworkers suffer pesticide exposure is only one of the many
indignities they endure. Any organic strategy to address pesticide exposure that emanates from this subaltern group will need to come to
terms with the economic, racial, and cultural domination they face.
Latino farmworkers, nonunionized immigrant workers, and inner city
youths are all examples of subaltern populations in the First World.

One of the goals of this book is to suggest a broader definition of
environmental racism, one that includes livelihood as well as forms
of cultural domination. By juxtaposing the livelihood struggles of the
Third World with the environmental justice movement of the First
World, we see parallels that are captured by the term *subaltern*. There
are, of course, many differences in these struggles, but there are also
similarities that may indicate larger patterns of domination and resistance in resource use and pollution exposure, and that may clarify counterhegemonic environmentalism. In order to comprehend subaltern environmental struggles, it is necessary to understand what they
are existing in opposition to, in terms of both the dominant society and
mainstream environmentalism. I will next discuss environmentalism
within the context of social movements, looking at how it might differ
from subaltern struggles.

Mainstream Environmentalism

It is difficult to speak of such a disparate movement as environmentalism in monolithic terms (Dunlap and Mertig 1992). Environmentalists
cross the ideological spectrum and have undertaken an assortment of
political projects (Ingram and Mann 1989, 142–44) ranging from bioregionalism (Alexander 1990), to deep ecology (Devall and Sessions
1985; Manes 1990), green capitalism (Anderson and Leal 1991; Lewis
1992), and ecofeminism (Seager 1993; Warren 1990; Zimmerman
1987; Diamond and Orenstein 1990). Even the term "radical environ-

Table 1.1. National Environmental Lobbying Organizations

Name	Year Founded	Member-ship*	Budget (millions)*
Sierra Club	1892	560,000	$35.2
Audubon Society	1905	600,000	35.0
National Parks and Conservation Assoc.	1919	100,000	3.4
Izaak Walton League	1922	50,000	1.4
National Wildlife Federation	1936	975,000	87.2
Defenders of Wildlife	1947	80,000	4.6
Environmental Defense Fund	1967	150,000	12.9
Friends of the Earth	1969	30,000	3.1
Natural Resources Defense Council	1970	168,000	16.0
Environmental Action	1970	20,000	1.2

Source: Adapted from Mitchell et al. 1992, 13.
*Figures based on 1990 membership and budget.

mentalism" denotes an array of beliefs, values, and actions (Merchant 1992). Nevertheless, there is a hegemonic or dominant sector of the movement, known as "mainstream" or traditional environmentalism, described by Gottlieb and Ingram (1988). "The largest of these groups, either in membership size, access to funding sources, or both, have become most recognized by policy-makers on the national and state-wide levels as representatives of the environmental point of view, and are solicited by media outlets, elected officials and their aides, and members of the bureaucracy for their opinions and positions" (p. 374).

Mitchell, Mertig, and Dunlap (1992), while recognizing the importance of large budgets and staff, see lobbying as one of the central features defining the most influential national-level organizations. Table 1.1 lists the names, membership, and budget of the most prominent organizations.

> They have several million dues-paying adherents, command multimillion-dollar budgets; employ corps of full-time lobbyists, lawyers, and scientists; and enjoy widespread support. . . . Although these twelve organizations

engage in other activities, such as education campaigns, research, and litigation, they are distinguished from other national environmental organizations by the fact that they openly lobby for the development and implementation of environmental legislation. (Mitchell et al. 1992, 12)

Designation and status as mainstream are also derived from the high
degree of institutionalization within society, which is partially achieved
by claiming the historical legacies of such figures as John Muir, Gifford
Pinchot, and Rachel Carson. History is an essential tool of legitima-
tion, and the vast majority of historical accounts all substantiate and
reinforce the role of mainstream environmentalism as *the* environmentalism, while other forms of environmentalism are considered more peripheral (Sale 1993; Shabecoff 1993; Scheffer 1991; Hays 1987 and
1959; Cohen 1988; Fox 1981; see also Gottlieb 1993; Darnovsky
1992).

Conventional histories of environmentalism trace its roots to the
earlier movements of romanticism, transcendentalism, and conservation, concerned with the wise and efficient use of natural resources.[7]
This utilitarian perspective differs from the values associated with environmentalism, which is oriented towards producing a collective post-
material good (environmental quality). Although various authors offer
different analyses of environmentalism, they all attest to the mainstream movement's preoccupation with quality of life versus subsistence, or production, issues. As early as 1957, David Brower, then of
the Sierra Club, recognized that the environmental agenda allowed
little room for non-nature considerations. "Whether justifiably or not,
those who work for conservation of natural scenery and wildlife have
come to be known as conservationists, a term which excludes people
who have a role in managing a resource for profit, even though they
may conserve it in doing so" (quoted in M. Cohen 1988, 219). This bias
obviously precludes the participation and traditions of people directly
involved in transforming nature either for profit or livelihood. They are
excluded from the construct known as environmentalism regardless of
how they may care for the land.

While there have been a few notable attempts within the histories of
both conservation (Koppes 1987, 1983; Wilmsen 1994) and environmentalism (Smith 1974b) to address issues of equity and social justice,

they stand as exceptions. A survey of environmental organizations conducted in the 1970s revealed a consistent desire to separate environmental concerns from other social issues and to maintain its quality of life orientation. Survey respondents reported opposition to the environmental movement "concerning itself with the conservation problems of such special groups as the urban poor and ethnic minorities." Even the socially conscious did not see environmental organizations as the vehicle to carry out such work. "When I want wilderness preservation, I join a wilderness group. When I want civil rights, I support the NAACP" (Smith 1974a, 6–7).

Environmentalism grew dramatically during the 1970s and 1980s, as large numbers of Americans supported improved environmental quality (Dunlap and Mertig 1992). Starting in 1960, with the Clean Water Act, environmentalists were active in developing, securing the passage of, and implementing a watershed of environmental legislation affecting air, land, wildlife, pollution, waste, and wilderness. This led to what FitzSimmons and Gottlieb (1988) have called the professionalization of the movement, as it evolved from a loosely knit coalition of groups to an highly organized, technocratic, and powerful lobby based in Washington, D.C. Previously informal groups became institutions, complete with lawyers, scientists, and lobbyists ready to sue, study, and advise.

It was within this context that the "Group of Ten" emerged, a self-designated title reflecting their influential status as leading environmental organizations. The group included the Audubon Society, Defenders of Wildlife, Environmental Defense Fund, Environmental Policy Institute, Izaak Walton League, National Wildlife Federation, Natural Resources Defense Council, National Parks Association, the Sierra Club, and Wilderness Society (note the overlap between the Group of Ten and the names in Table 1.1). Ironically, at the point when the Group was seeking to establish a tentative national agenda (Cahn 1986), they found themselves increasingly out of touch with large segments of the population, including the burgeoning grassroots movement that was springing up in response to toxic hazards (Freudenberg 1984).

The people in important mainstream organizations are very largely white and very largely well-off, the more so as you move from membership to board of directors, and they're very largely male as well. Whether charges of "racism" and "elitism" against them are quite fair . . . it is true that their concerns have tended to mirror those of the white suburban well-to-do constituencies and that the kinds of people who have been attracted to the staffs have tended to be college graduates, often professionals, and of the same general milieu as the people they deal with in legislatures and board-rooms. (Sale 1993, 98)

Mainstream versus Subaltern Environmentalism

Given this sketch of mainstream environmentalism, we can now identify several key points on which it differs from subaltern environmentalism. One of the first is the ideological and political orientation of each form of environmental action. Paehlke (1989) makes the case that environmentalism is a new ideology that is neither left nor right (see also Bramwell 1989). Instead, it draws upon elements of both and may find expression anywhere along the ideological continuum. To a large degree, Paehlke is correct, as evidenced by the adoption of environmental concerns by free-market advocates (Anderson and Leal 1991), and the conciliatory posture many mainstream groups have assumed in their relations with industrial polluters (Krupp 1986).

At the same time, however, numerous environmental groups, particularly from the grassroots, are intent on holding corporations responsible for their pollution and demanding greater democracy in production matters (Mann 1991). Paehlke's argument falls short when we look at the relationship between these ideologically opposed strands of environmentalism. The fact is they have neither united nor placed their environmental concerns before their ideological commitments. To what extent can we speak of an environmental ideology when some groups identify more with corporate America and others with efforts to unionize marginal workers? Subaltern struggles are explicitly oppositional; they are seeking to change the distribution of power and resources to benefit the less powerful. Their politics may not necessarily be called "left" (given Paehlke's rather dated definition which equates left with industrial socialism), but they clearly seek greater social justice.

Secondly, another comparison between the two takes into account the different types of communities involved in each form of environmental action. Mainstream environmentalism typifies an NSM in that it attracts people concerned with an issue who have only a limited personal connection to it. NSMs are vehicles for individuals to organize and seek change for an issue for which a political channel does not exist (Dalton, Kuechler, and Bürklin 1990, 12). In contrast, subaltern environmental struggles draw people who already exist as a social or spatial entity in some way—perhaps as workers, a village, or a racialized class.

Finally, it is widely believed that mainstream environmentalists address issues that are not of concern to subaltern communities. Many grassroots activists have attacked the mainstream for focusing on what are perceived to be elitist or racist concerns, such as endangered species and wilderness preservation. This perception has been substantiated by historical analyses, such as Hays' (1987) authoritative history of mainstream U.S. environmentalism in which he argues that societies, as they become wealthy and industrialized, have the time and energy to devote to such luxury issues as environmentalism.[8] Such analyses have reinforced the role of issue saliency. "The narrowness of the mainstream movement, which appears to be more interested in endangered animals (nonhuman) species and pristine undeveloped land than at-risk humans, makes poor minority people *think* that their concerns are not 'environmental'" (Austin and Schill 1991, 72).

It is true that environmentalism has at times been exceptionally racist (see Jordan and Snow 1992), and this inevitably informs the process of issue identification, but we must be wary of seeing this as the sole difference between subaltern and mainstream environmentalism. The reality is far more complex and contradictory.

I argue that the issue of positionality is most important in distinguishing mainstream and subaltern environmentalism. Activists of all sorts may be involved in the same environmental issue and even have the same political line, but mainstream and subaltern actors hold different positions within the socioeconomic structure that, in turn, frame their struggles differently. It is important to realize that positionality does not refer to a specific person or group per se but is rather a position that can be filled by any individual (Fuss 1989, 32). Take, for instance, a debt-for-nature swap or a pesticide exposure issue. In both cases, mainstream activists are involved in negotiating policy. They may stand in solidarity with the affected community, but for subaltern actors it is *their* land and *their* bodies that are at risk. This is not a minor matter in seeking to understand various forms of environmental action. This question of positionality has been lost amid charges of racism and elitism, especially by those emphasizing issue relevancy.

Because of their importance, it is worth looking more closely at positionality, participation, and political economy in terms of environmentalism. Despite clear evidence of broad-based support for mainstream environmentalism (Dunlap, Gallup, and Gallup 1993; Fortmann and Kusel 1990; Mohai 1990; Lowe, Pinhey, and Grimes 1980; Mitchell 1979), *participation* has been drawn largely from the ranks of the middle class (Mohai 1985). In an effort to better understand this pattern, several researchers have delved into the relationship between socioeconomic position and environmental action.

Not only has participation been found to be the province of the middle class, but more specifically, it has been associated with employment in the service sector — versus either the primary or manufacturing sectors (Cotgrove and Duff 1980). Likewise, the rise of environmentalism is strongest within postindustrial societies (Pierce et al. 1989; Dominick 1988). Thus, both the individuals actively involved and the sites of elaboration are distinctly not subaltern. Scheffer (1991) captures (rather crudely) the perceived relationship between the poor and mainstream environmentalism. "The underprivileged and dispossessed among us will always complain, I suppose, that undue attention is being given to environmental issues, while others — mostly the better off — will counter that earth keeping is a perennial and fundamental responsibility" (p. 19). What these indicators all confirm is that mainstream environmentalism has *not* attracted those who are economically insecure (Paehlke 1989, 8) or who have engaged in traditional production activities. This supports Inglehart's observation (1990) that NSMs reflect a shift "from an emphasis on economic and physical security above all, toward greater emphasis on belonging, self-expression, and the quality of life" (p. 11).

A large number of environmental groups in the 1990s (both mainstream and otherwise) are dealing with issues of interest to various subaltern populations, but most identify with those in power — such as corporations, business leaders, the state, and international development institutions and organizations (Stavins 1989; Carpenter and Dixon 1985). Within mainstream environmentalism this is evident in the Environmental Defense Fund's "Third Wave." In this latest phase of environmentalism, organizations seek to cooperate with corporations through, for example, market-driven strategies (Krupp 1986). Because of their position and politics, organizations have not challenged the distribution of profits and other benefits of development. Essentially, equity and social justice considerations are raised only within the framework of traditional economic and power relationships, and under the current arrangement, it is only through general economic growth that poor people can attain economic well being. "Capitalist states depend on the expansion of their national economies to ensure that the poor receive enough of the national income to survive. Indeed, economic growth is a major instrument for social policy. By sustaining hope for improvement, it relieves the pressure for policies aimed at more equitable distribution of wealth" (Rees 1990, 12). Reduced consumption, ecological sustainability, and basic needs are not seriously considered. In short, environmentalists of all stripes are deeply involved in political and economic issues, but most take a status-quo perspective (Clifford 1994).

Nevertheless, a number of environmental groups seek to work with subaltern populations. This often leads to conflict because the needs and objectives of subaltern communities are fundamentally different from those of groups who prioritize the environment. In the case of Chipko ardent environmentalists were successful in securing restrictions on forestry that have greatly harmed local communities in need of economic development. "Local leaders found their demands for local industrial development and employment being submerged by the environmental rhetoric that demanded the preservation of the Himalayas in its own right" (Rangan 1993, 170).

In a previously mentioned study, Bebbington (1993) reveals how the actual needs and desires of indigenous populations represent an amalgam of interests and do not conform to the agenda of environmentalists, religious communities, development projects, or anyone else. The same conflicts occur in the United States. Both of the case studies in this book represent contentious relationships between mainstream environmentalists and subaltern communities. In the case of Ganados, most environmentalists would not allow local Hispanos to use land set aside for elk in a project they otherwise considered sustainable. In the case of the UFWOC, environmentalists were not only hesitant to support a cause they saw as a civil rights or social justice issue, but when they subsequently did address pesticides, they worked to reduce pesticide residues while ignoring the larger problem of worker exposure. These conflicts are ultimately attributable to positionality.

Contrary to mainstream efforts are the actions of subaltern environmental movements who, because of their position, are not in control of the economy and, in general, do not benefit from a continuation of the status quo. For these individuals, environmental issues are important in that they affect their livelihood or impact their health and physical well-being. Consequently, not only are they more physically and socially vulnerable, but they may require a change in the prevailing social relations to reach a satisfactory solution. Hence, on a very fundamental level, participants in subaltern struggles encounter environmental concerns not only from a different perspective, but also from a different structural position that may entail entirely different solutions and courses of action.

Having made some effort to differentiate subaltern and mainstream environmental struggles on the basis of positionality, it is important to review their commonalities. If we take the concept of the NSM, we can see some overlap between subaltern and mainstream environmental movements. While mainstream environmentalism has been dubbed "the master NSM issue" (Buttel 1992, 14), this does not mean that subaltern struggles do not share some similarities, including attention to identity and quality-of-life concerns. For example, one reason for the success of Ganados del Valle's economic development initiative was its richness as symbolism that drew upon and affirmed Hispanos' identity as pastoralists. It was not accidental that Ganados' project is predicated on land, grazing, sheep, wool, and weaving — all elements of a past and an identity that continues to mean a great deal to local people. Their struggle was as much to salvage that past and transform it into a viable identity as it was to increase their household income. Indeed, the struggle for identity was part and parcel of their mobilization. I believe that, as human beings, the poor and dominated are as concerned with questions of identity as anyone else. Thus, it is not surprising that their livelihood or environmental struggles resonate with these questions, particularly in terms of oppressed ethnic groups where one's body and cultural practices and identity are important signifiers in everyday life that may circumscribe one's opportunities.

Subaltern environmental struggles are also about quality of life, but not as routinely associated with more privileged groups. For subaltern groups, quality-of-life issues are expressed *within* their economic projects. "People fight not only for more but for the possibility of defining a way of life expressive of deeply held values" (Plotke 1990, 93).

Subaltern environmental struggles also diverge from the NSM model in important ways. Many are local; some are not. Even though the UFWOC case study is based largely in California, the UFWOC itself became international and, at one point, their vision of farmworker unionization sought to include workers in both the United States and Mexico. Thus, subaltern environmental movements cannot categorically be considered local. Although it is generally held that old social movements were striving for universal transformations, I believe that remains an open question, particularly in terms of the subaltern. It appears to be true, as Escobar (1992b) has pointed out, that social actors are searching for identities and autonomy (as opposed to grand structural transformations) within the context of domination. "Reflection on daily life has to be located at the inter-section of micro-processes of meaning production, on the one hand, and macro-processes of domination, on the other. Inquiry into social movements from this perspective seeks to restore the centrality of popular practices, without reducing the movements to something else: the logic of domination or capital accumulation, the struggle of the working class or the labor of parties" (p. 30).

Undoubtedly, however, the most important differences lay in the areas of economic relations, domination, and positionality. Given the conditions in which marginalized communities find themselves, their point of entry into environmental concerns is usually framed by inequality and often related to access, production, and distribution issues in intimate ways. Due to their position, the subaltern are not able to distance themselves from the political and economic consequences of either the problem or the proposed solutions. Because they encounter environmental problems through inequality, their resolutions may be contingent upon an alteration of local power relations, cultural practices, systems of meanings, and economic structures.

A deeper understanding of subaltern environmental struggles, particularly in relation to the mainstream movement, allows us to break the theoretical and political impasse that has been posed by the idea of NSMs, particularly the belief that NSMs are not about economic issues. For the poor, environmental issues are very much about material and political struggle. At the same time, the insights of postmodern scholarship allow us to cultivate a richer understanding of subaltern struggles, which combine to give rise to an environmentalism of everyday life. In previous times, we might have tried to make these struggles conform to our narrow definition of class struggle, ignoring the critical roles of identity formation and quality-of-life issues that social agents care enough to mobilize around and that are, in fact, critical to any form of collective action. By the same token, however, we must strive to connect identity politics to a larger materialist analysis instead of focusing on the actions of what appear to be autonomous individuals.

Poverty, "Race," and Identity in the Creation of Subalternity

In order to understand the origins and meanings of subaltern environmental struggles I have chosen to focus on three specific analytical categories — poverty, 'race', and identity. I am not only interested in uncovering the structural origins of oppositional environmental movements and struggles, but I am also concerned with revealing how the subjects themselves perceive such struggles as well as what they mean to the communities in question. This entailed seeing the actors as complex subjects capable of making decisions as to how they interpret and represent their stories. One could approach these issues using such tools as a survey of community perceptions. I felt, however, that detailed fieldwork, in-depth interviews, and archival work, followed by a rigorous deconstruction of the resulting story, would be the best method.

Listening to what people said, observing their actions, and placing them within the larger historical and geographical context convinced me that these struggles were first and foremost about livelihood, or the material well-being of the communities in question.

Even though I privilege economics, I recognize how economic relations are mutually constituted by racism and issues of identity. A materialist analysis is crucial in identifying the structures and forces leading to the formation of subaltern environmental struggles. Were these populations more economically secure, they would not, by definition, create an oppositional struggle centered on livelihood and their ability to reproduce themselves. The task is to identify the ways in which racism, cultural oppression and identity interact with economic forces to create unique forms of domination and exploitation. John Rutherford (1990, 20) has suggested the challenge is to conduct a materialist analysis in a nonreductionist way. He notes that economics "is felt in the first instance, setting the conditions of articulation, but in no way determining their outcome."

Indeed, the mutually constitutive nature of these forces is evident in the way that social actors often choose to emphasize specific facets or representations of their struggle. This in itself offers us a window into the multiple ways in which people choose to identify and interpret the world around them and often choose to identify a particular representation for specific political ends. Consequently, Ganados frequently portrayed their struggle as a cultural conflict; the UFWOC emphasized the racism to which farmworkers were subjected and the role of the farmworkers' struggle in the formation of the larger Chicano identity and movement of the 1960s.

We can briefly demonstrate, using the case of the UFWOC, how these forces interact. Let's begin with racism. Clearly, racist ideologies have been effectively developed and deployed for the purpose of economic exploitation or gain, as seen in the quest for cheap labor, land usurpation, colonization, and so forth. In no way, however, can racism be *reduced* to material objectives. Racism also operates independent of economic processes. Racism may become such a deeply rooted and naturalized system of meaning that it sometimes exists contrary to anyone's rational interest. Racism is a very real form of domination that must be challenged in the economic as well as in the social and cultural spheres — not that these spheres can ever be fully divorced since work and production as economic activities are also *social*. Thus racism was critical to the creation and maintenance of a highly exploited nonwhite work force.

Consequently, while the UFWOC's movement is a class conflict, it was also an antiracist struggle. It was antiracist in its efforts to counter the racialized division of labor, a racist class structure, as well as the larger racist ideology which rendered rural Chicanos as a despised population. Chicano marginalization (political and social) not only contributed to a very real economic oppression and exploitation, but it fueled the forging of both identity and struggle. Part of any resistance and struggle for empowerment is a real effort to salvage and re-create one's cultural identity in an affirming way. The process by which people organize and collectively seek to restore and re-create their identities is ethnicity. Once an ethnic identity has been established (and even during the process), it can serve to facilitate a larger movement to achieve economic or political objectives. Conversely, the mobilization of a community on a material and political issue may inspire the development of an ethnic identity.

When poverty, racism, and culture come together to oppress people, they also interact to create unique forms of oppression that become the basis of resistance. Each of these forces must be countered individually and collectively, and one of the first steps in attempting to do so is the creation of an affirming, collective identity. In turn, this can lead to a politics of identity, as identity itself may become contested.

One important axis of domination and resistance that I have not included is gender. Within both of the case studies, as well as throughout most of the world, gender largely defines one's role and status within the community, but gender oppression and identity was not an articulated community or group objective in these struggles. I could have made gender a subject of inquiry because whether it is articulated or not, it is central both to the constitution of a community and to the nature of struggle itself. Emphasizing this line of inquiry, however, would have taken the analysis in a different direction, emphasizing *unspoken* forms of consciousness and interaction. Historical and contemporary analyses indicate the gendered structures of the UFWOC (Rose 1988) and of Ganados (Varela 1991a), and there is ample evidence of how both resource use (Merchant 1989; Shiva 1989) and mobilization (Pardo 1990), in general, are gendered. Nevertheless, the fact remains that gender was not strategically used by the organizations in either understanding their oppression or mobilizing against it. For this reason I did not make it a separate category. Instead, it is interwoven throughout the discussion and reflects not only individual gender consciousness, but its intersection with other dynamics that create fully textured lives.

That the group identity and demands were framed by the participants in terms of ethnicity, and not gender, is hardly surprising, as research has shown that in the course of politicization Chicanas, like other nonwhite and ethnic women in the United States, tend to adopt an ethnic consciousness and identity first. Rose's (1988) study of Chicanas in the UFW found that they did not develop an overt feminist consciousness; however, the groundwork was laid for a possible challenge to a rigidly gendered and patriarchal culture. Through subsequent involvement in political struggle, many women do develop a feminist consciousness and demand changes in the patriarchal order of both the ethnic group and the larger society. Recent literature and political praxis suggest that women of color are increasingly resisting a single identity — either race or gender (Hill Collins 1991) — and are calling for a recognition of the many feminine identities that exist, rather than being limited to any universal construct of "woman" whose hidden subtext is "white" (Hill Collins 1991; Anzaldua 1990; see also Pardo 1990).

In the following sections I explore more fully the meanings and practices associated with poverty, 'race', and identity.

Poverty

As noted in the previous chapter, a crucial part of subalternity's definition is economic marginality. While subalternity denotes a general relationship of structured inequality resulting in a relationship of domination and subordination, the specific economic circumstances and relations may vary. I want to expand more on the specific economic relationships that frame my case studies.

Typically, when discussing economic status the term *class* is used to refer to a variety of phenomena when in reality it is a very specific relationship between workers and owners. To focus strictly on the Marxian definition of class would exclude numerous other economic relationships, forces that actively shape people's lives and the landscape. In short, there are many ways to be poor and economically marginal which are beyond the bounds of class. Understanding the specific conditions and relationships which give rise to poverty and inequality is essential in order to analyze them and to ascertain the motivating forces of struggles. Now that economic meta-theories are less privileged, we have the space to explore other theories that may be less comprehensive, but better capture the complexity and diversity of the economic forces that shape places and people. These case studies illustrate the various economic relationships and processes that have created relatively powerless subaltern Chicano populations.

Questions of scale are crucial in identifying the various economic conditions that shape the physical environment, struggles, and identities. In this period of growing internationalization, we are all increasingly vulnerable to the aftershocks of decisions and events made in distant places (Massey 1994). People and locales become displaced or thrown into poverty for reasons far beyond their individual control, such as investment patterns, political events, and decisions on the part of global financing. Uneven development refers to the spatial expression of capital's patterns of investment and disinvestment which produce international, regional, and local sociospatial inequality. The results of disinvestment, or capital flight, include the loss of industry and jobs, increased levels of underemployment and unemployment, and growing poverty. Disinvestment may occur for a variety of reasons, such as militant unions, the existence of cheaper labor elsewhere, or a climate not considered sufficiently conducive to capital accumulation.

At other times, places are simply bypassed by the forces of development, leaving them to continue on in precapitalist forms of production and social relations, often creating regions of deep poverty. Because they have been relatively exempt from the homogenizing forces of modernity, such communities often carry the illusion of a traditional lifestyle, one that is considered quaint by outsiders. This is the case in northern New Mexico, where Hispano poverty is historically entrenched and due to uneven development (coupled with some maldevelopment) and racialized local economic activity.

It is imperative to understand the role of capital in the creation of places. While other factors, such as resistance, also contribute to the production of place, the power of capital should not be underestimated (Massey 1984). Intense capital investment can dramatically transform a region leading to an entirely new geography. Consider the radical changes occurring on Mexico's northern border, or the newly industrializing Asian states, the so-called Tiger-economies. Both of these regions are confronting a host of new environmental problems, rapidly expanding infrastructure needs, and new sets of social relations.

Conversely, the withdrawal of capital from the upper Midwest reconfigured a once strong working-class region into the "rust belt."

Development and disinvestment patterns are so powerful that they have created sociospatial categories which are ingrained in our image of the world and institutionalized in terms (such as North and South, Core and Periphery) and in particular places (such as Appalachia, the rural South, and northern New Mexico). Moreover, specific forms of uneven development are associated with particular social relations (such as those found in colonialism) in which one place directly benefits from the resources of another, often leading to stunted or disarticulated economies. Colonialism and contemporary uneven development help account for the immigration of Mexican workers to California. Mexican workers have been leaving a place of limited economic opportunity for a site of rich capital investment for decades.

Uneven development is not an aracial economic process; instead it can be an expression of racism, illustrative of how racism and economic processes may intersect. One of the most vivid examples of racist development patterns is the deindustrialization of South Central Los Angeles. Once a thriving industrial region providing upward mobility for African Americans, a hemorrhaging of industry occurred after the Watts uprising of 1965 as capital followed whites out to the suburbs (Hamilton 1989). Thirty years later, the locale suffers still from limited employment opportunities as few manufacturers have ventured back into the area. Thus, place is as important as one's skills and economic position in determining if and how one's basic needs are met, and the degree of social and political power accompanying one's economic status.

The division of labor is a different but equally important economic category. It refers to one's role within a production process or in the provision of a service (Sayer 1992). Division of labor commonly intersects and overlaps with other defining categories, such as gender, 'race' and ethnicity, and immigration status. Consequently, certain groups are associated with particular jobs, such as Mexicans with California farmworkers or females with secretaries.

One's place within the division of labor translates into a particular lifestyle based on income, education, status, authority, and power. Division of labor is an important but slighted analytical category, found in all advanced economies whether capitalist, socialist, industrial, or rural (Sayer and Walker 1992). While most of us fall into the category of workers, there is a world of difference in terms of power, lifestyle, and income between the lawyer who works in a downtown high-rise, the support staff who answers the phone, and the janitor who cleans the building. These differences, however, are a function of the division of labor, not class.

There may at times be racial/ethnic contradictions in the division of labor, or there may be an almost perfect fit, leading to a racialized division of labor. Nowhere is this seen more clearly than among California farmworkers. During the period under investigation, growers were overwhelmingly Anglo, while field hands and labor contractors were nonwhite, the majority being Mexicano. There were other farm personnel (workers) who were largely Anglo and more privileged than field hands. This so-called "middle class" did not identify with Mexicano farmworkers because of racism and the division of labor. Here, racism worked to fragment the work force and that worked to the benefit of capital. Understanding these structures and divisions helps account for the obstacles the UFWOC faced, the tactics they used, and the goals they established for themselves. Regardless as to whether or not a region is prosperous or impoverished, there will always be inequality based on the division of labor. Moreover, this division will often be structured along natural lines of difference, such as gender and 'race' that serve to justify inequalities as inevitable and appropriate (Kobayashi and Peake 1994). The division of labor shows, once again, how sexism and racism both contribute to economic oppression, are intensified by it, but cannot be reduced to it. Sexism and racism must be challenged within the division of labor as well as outside of it.

The final relationship to be considered in this discussion of poverty and inequality is class. Class refers to one's position in relation to the means of production, but suffers from a somewhat problematic usage. On the one hand, the term and concept of class are casually used to cover a range of economic and power relationships while glossing over very real structural differences. On the other hand, traditional social science has confined class analysis to studying white men in factory settings (Vanneman and Cannon 1987), which does not begin to address the many ways and places in which people are exploited. In Marxist terms, class is a relational category defining workers in opposition to capital. I want to emphasize the *relational* aspect of class, that is, a group existing in relationship to another group.

Recent innovations in class theory have sought to make the concept better reflect reality, such as Gibson and Graham's (1992) recognition that any one individual can simultaneously occupy a number of class positions. This important insight captures the reality of a post-Fordist economy in which a large percentage of the population cannot subsist solely on a single wage-paying job. By stressing the role of appropriation and the distribution of surplus value as defining class, they acknowledge that an individual may concurrently be a worker, self-employed, and an exploited homemaker (p. 119). By emphasizing class as a process rather than as a social grouping, they not only allow more activities and relations to fall under class relations, but they also expand the spheres where appropriation and distribution occur to encompass not only the shop floor and the fields but also the household. They do this by defining class as "the social process of producing and appropriating surplus labor . . . and the associated process of surplus labor distribution" (Gibson and Graham 1992, 113).

This conceptual development is extremely relevant to the case of Ganados because these rural individuals and households are involved in diverse economic pursuits defying easy classification. How do we conceptualize someone engaged in petty commodity production, who is also a member of the rural proletariat, but derives part of their livelihood from subsistence activities? This is an important intervention in allowing us to focus on material inequality without limiting our analysis to a factory setting and the relationship between capitalists and workers — a construct that excluded many other real forms of exploitation, such as the household, the informal economy, and relationships with the state.

As a complement to this, Sacks (1989) suggests that working class membership need not be based on individual status. Within "a community that is dependent on waged labor, but that is unable to subsist or reproduce by such labor alone, . . . class emerges as a relation to the means of production that is collective, rather than individual" (pp. 543, 546). Her definition encompasses the activities of women who are not employed in wage labor, as well as poor people who are not continuously employed. At the same time, it includes struggles that are not rooted on the shop floor but instead are more community-based, though still related to questions of production. Sack's observations are useful in that traditional formulations of class that consider only the individual have proven problematic. For example, a factory worker is a member of the working class. But what about his or her family? Their respective communities? This amplification helps us conceptualize what we might call community-based class struggles. These communities, although differentially constituted, are engaged in production struggles that exist in opposition to another class. Clearly, conventional class analysis does not adequately depict their complex realities.

Space and community enhance our understanding of class, and are also essential to the formation of collective identities that, as the NSM literature suggests, play a large role in mobilizations. Not only is place important to identity formation, but both Ganados and the UFWOC's struggles were about who would control the production of a particular place. Would the UFWOC's vision of California agriculture prevail or would agribusiness? Would Ganados' plans for "visitor tourism" be implemented, or would the region become just another tourist place employing the local residents as maids rather than as active subjects building a sustainable and dignified economy?

Of course, neither poor people nor workers automatically constitute a class. Only when people unite to struggle on issues related to production, the appropriation of surplus value, and domination — only when they exist in opposition — do they then become a class. This inevitably brings up the question of domination and power. Inherent in class relations is domination, but class is much more than domination. Richard Walker (1985) has observed that "class in the Marxist sense requires an object of power, and an end other than domination itself" (p. 169) — which is the appropriation of surplus value.

Domination in class struggle occurs, for example, when farmworkers resist the conditions under which they work. Many elements of their pesticide campaign were efforts aimed at resisting domination by acquiring more power for workers. Controlling pesticide use would reduce group vulnerability and exposure to hazardous conditions. Domination has become a large part of what we see today as class struggle. What Miliband (1988) describes as efforts to "modify or improve the conditions in which subordination is experienced" (p. 334) is also known as "thin opposition" (hooks and West 1991). Until recently, domination was sometimes regarded as a poor substitute for the supposedly "real" struggle of workers to gain control over the means of production. Fortunately, domination is being given greater consideration not only in its own right (see James Scott 1990), but also because it creates other types of oppression that, in turn, can reinforce exploitation. For instance, cultural denigration, which is closely related to racism, contributes to an ideology which allows differential treatment of certain groups, in this way potentially reinforcing their exploitation.

In summary, both of these case studies can be seen as forms of class conflict by drawing upon the insights of Sacks (1989), and Gibson and Graham (1992). Both grassroots groups discovered they had more power to change their economic situation as a collective than as individuals. The UFWOC struggled for greater control over the means of production; Ganados continues to struggle for access to the means of production. Class alone was not enough to explain either groups' economic marginality or the various forms of domination they experienced. The role of both uneven development and the division of labor must also be considered to understand the assorted economic forces and structures shaping their lives. Both were opposed by the state and other interested parties. These were power struggles in which poor people attempted to gain greater control over their lives in the form of money, dignity, power, and security. They confronted and addressed environmental issues as part of their struggle. Neither group focused solely on an environmental problem; the environmental problem was embedded within a larger set of unequal economic and social relations. Because of their relatively powerless position, these groups could not significantly change either their economic or environmental conditions without engaging in conflict and struggle. As racialized minorities, however, their struggles were very much about fighting racism, and were interpreted as racial struggles by many.

Racism

Racism looms large not only in the UFWOC's and Ganados' environmental struggles, but also in almost every conflict involving nonwhite groups in the United States. Racist ideology plays a crucial role in creating subaltern conditions because as a system of meaning its purpose is the exclusion of different groups. Though few will deny the role of racism in the creation of a subaltern group, or even in the production of environmental racism, there is debate in both scholarly and popular circles as to the precise role of racism in the evolution of inequality. Witness the "race or class" debate enshrouding social policy (Boston 1987; Wilson 1980) and environmental racism (Mohai and Bryant 1992), to name just two arenas. Let me outline how 'race' and racism participate in creating a subaltern status.

In order to understand racism, we must first be clear on what is commonly meant by the term 'race'. Critical reflection on the idea of 'race' reveals a highly contradictory concept. Essentially, race is a social construct — an ideology developed within the context of uneven power relationships — that has little to do with biology (Jackson and Penrose 1994; Goldberg 1993; Muir 1993; Miles 1989; Jackson 1987). Writing on the British experience, geographer Peter Jackson (1987) defines racism as "a set of interrelated ideologies and practices that have grave material effects, severely affecting black people's life chances and threatening their present and future well-being" (p. 3).[1] This is a useful definition that can be applied to the U.S. experience as long as we redefine black to refer to all racialized minorities.

In the United States, the idea of skin color, or phenotype, and ancestry are at the heart of the system of racial signification.[2] Though this is considered common sense, it is a social artifact, not a truth or an inevitability. In reality, there are any number of ways to categorize 'racial' groups, all of which would be problematic. Indeed, the idea of ancestry itself is fraught with contradictions. For example, how do we categorize people of mixed parentage? Until very recently, anyone with a drop of "black" blood was considered black. More recently, those of mixed background are consciously choosing to adopt one or both ethnic identities. That they do so is evidence not only of the ideological nature of 'race', but also of the system of domination and subordination that racism creates.

Why would we legally and socially consider someone black if they can "pass" for white? The answer is found both in ideology and in political economic systems. By developing the idea of an inferior black race, whites could reap the benefits of white privilege. This privilege could only be maintained as long as some "racial," or color, line was continuously defined and enforced. Additional insights can be drawn from the practice of choosing a racial and ethnic identity. How can you "choose" what supposed biological category you belong to? Selecting to adopt a black identity is, for many, an affirmation of resistance and struggle against centuries of racist oppression. Furthermore, it demonstrates that racial categories are contestable, and can be appropriated or subverted by the dominated (Gregory 1993).

A quick glance at systems of racial stratification illustrates the various racial schema societies have devised (Rodriguez 1992; Rodriguez and Cordero-Guzman 1992; Webster 1992). These schema differ not only over space but over time, and they testify to the contingent nature of race. Consider for a moment that both Jews and Irish were once considered racial groups, or the fact that the racial category "white" had to be consciously constructed (Allen 1994). Likewise, while Mexicans were once labeled a "mongrel race," the U.S. government has more recently declared that "Hispanics" are not a 'race', although they remain a racialized minority. Although most Mexicanos are *indio* or *mestizo* in appearance, there is tremendous variation, with darker Latinos experiencing more discrimination than fair-skinned ones (Rodriguez 1991; Telles and Murguia 1990; see also Bohara and Davila 1992). These examples show that 'race' is not fixed but varies with larger political projects and systems of domination.

It should be patently clear that though we are all racialized, some of us are subordinate (nonwhites) and some of us are dominant (whites). Whites in fact are hegemonic, as they are equated with "normal" while the rest of us deviate in some way (health, ability, culture, level of development, etc.). The case of Mexicanos (a nationality) embodies the many contradictions inherent in the concept of 'race' and exemplifies how its exercise is related to power.

Throughout the history of the United States, the Mexican origin population has been treated as a racialized other and has been incorporated, in a subordinated status. From Tejas to California, Mexicanos' land and identity were appropriated in the imperialist expansion of the United States through the Mexican-American War (see Peet 1985 for a discussion of imperialism and racism). Conceptualizing Mexicans as a racially inferior people not only justified these actions, but had many convinced this would lead to the uplifting of the Mexicano. Mexicans have continued to enter the United States during episodes of civil unrest and poverty. As the "workhorses" of the U.S. Southwest who built the railroads, picked the crops, worked the mines, and tended white children (Barrera 1979) — Mexicanos continued to suffer from imposed segregation and legal discrimination.

Despite being subject to racism, Mexicans, as a national group, are a troublesome 'race' since mestizos defy the very idea of race. This contradiction is illustrated in Martha Menchaca's (1993) study of the legal treatment of Mexicanos in early U.S. history that found ambiguous legal experience. In certain times and places, Mexicanos were treated similar to African Americans (such as in the Jim Crow practices of Texas); at other times, like American Indians; and at still other times, like Anglos. Though their legal treatment was uneven, economic marginalization and social exclusion all served to cast Mexicanos as a subaltern group.

Having established the socially constructed nature of 'race', we can now move on to a discussion of racism. As an ideology, race shifts with the political and economic winds. For this reason, racism (Giroux 1993; Omi 1992; Baron 1985), racial orders (Montejano 1987), racist ideologies (Blaut 1992), and racial formations (Omi and Winant 1987) are not stable. Furthermore, not all nonwhites experience the same kind of racism since racism is refracted through gender, social status, culture, and I would add, phenotype.[3] This is an important point to which I will return.

In discussing racism, on which there is markedly little consensus, we must acknowledge that the most fundamental but least recognized form of racism is the existence of a racist ideology that allows for the creation of racial groups. In order to be effective, a racist ideology must become so pervasive and natural that it becomes hegemonic, and therefore, rarely questioned. An example of the hegemonic nature of racist ideology can be seen in the process of nation building, where the formation of an imagined community is defined in opposition to others (Smith 1994; Gilroy 1991). The lack of recognition of racist ideology is, by far, one of the most critical factors missing from the contemporary public discourse on 'race'. This slighting of ideology helps explain

the extremely convoluted public discourse on racism and the degree of
contestation surrounding the question, What is racism?

The concept of a racial project can help shed light on why there is
such disagreement over what racism is and, at the same time, can illustrate how racism works. Howard Winant (1994) defines a racial project
as "simultaneously an interpretation, representation, or explanation of
racial dynamics and an effort to organize and distribute resources along
particular racial lines" (p. 24). At present, there are numerous and competing racial projects, not just between whites and nonwhites. One of
the more ominous racial projects underway is centered on protecting
Anglo-American culture and identity (Giroux 1993; Omi 1992). Henry
Giroux (1993) notes that the new racism "has shifted the emphasis
from a notion of difference equated with deviance and cultural depriva-
tion to a position that acknowledges racial diversity only to proclaim
that racial formations, ethnicities and cultures pose a threat to national
unity" (p. 2).

The idea of 'race' and culture intersects in numerous ways and represents one of the strongest points of contention as to what constitutes
racism. In tracing the evolution of racist ideologies, Blaut (1992) notes
that previous ideologies were based on perceived biological criteria (see
van den Berghe 1967), while today's are based on culture. In attempting to understand the new racism, as well as the racial projects of nonwhites, we must pause and consider the "object" of prejudice within a
racist ideology. Although much of our racial discourse centers on the
words "color" and "skin" — and although many people continue to be
racist based solely on the idea of phenotype — skin color has essentially
become a signifier for behavior considered objectionable by the dominant group.

At work is a merging of racial groups and cultural characteristics that
Yehudi Webster (1992) calls an "alignment of race and culture." It is not
possible for 'race' to be connected to any culture since it is not a biological category; it is conceivable for a racist ideology to be linked to cultural
traits. For example, in the state of California there is an ongoing and
spreading hostility toward the Spanish language. This has surfaced in
opposition to bilingual education, a curtailing of public translation services, and the passage of English-only legislation. Are these anti-Spanish
actions racist? To many, no. The reason many do not see it as such is due

to the lack of understanding of racism as an ideology. The Spanish language has become, however, *racialized* in California, that is, it has been imbued with a racial meaning through its association with Latinos.

A different interpretation of racism, and a different racial project, is illustrated by the scholarship surrounding environmental racism. By stressing racist outcomes, or discrimination, almost to the exclusion of ideology, environmental-justice activists have created a situation where statistics are being used to confirm or deny the existence of racism. The research framework, however, is predicated on finding racial patterns in which racial minority groups, defined by the U.S. census, are impacted to a statistically significant degree by various forms of pollution. According to this conceptualization, should statistical tests not indicate significant disproportionate exposure, racism does not exist.

This approach has led at least one group of researchers (Lester, Allen, and Milburn-Lauer 1994) to compare the situation of African Americans and Hispanics to that of various white ethnics, including British and Eastern European groups. Moreover, it has prompted numerous scholars to fall into the race-versus-class trap (see Mohai and Bryant 1992). By successfully identifying racist patterns, researchers garner support for their cause and provide another window into the racist nature of America.

There is no denying the important policy implications of such findings, but it is equally important to uncover the underlying motives or racial projects to which such research contributes. Clearly, there are those who seek to debunk the racist hypothesis because they do not want to see nonwhites make any additional moral or material claims upon either the state or white society. In fact, pollution exposure itself may not even be the central concern, but its role in substantiating racist claims is what is problematic to some.

Those who insist on the existence of environmental racism are also partaking in a racial project. By confirming environmental racism, scholars and activists hope to pressure the state into solving the pollution problem, provide more employment opportunities for nonwhites, redirect policy to enhance nonwhite communities, and provide funds to nonwhite environmental initiatives. Clearly, they are trying to funnel more resources and power to subordinate racial groups.

But by cutting racism off from its ideological roots and insisting on the primacy of racism over class, we fail to acknowledge the different types of racism that exist. Consequently, it is assumed that the racism that a Chicano executive encounters is the same racism that an undocumented worker selling fruit on the street corner experiences. They are not. Racism combined with marginal economic status creates subalternity. David Harvey (1993) provides a useful insight into comprehending the efforts of environmental-justice activists to reify 'race'. He notes that an oppressive identity (such as racism) may sometimes be instrumental to a victim's "sense of livelihood. Perpetuation of that sense of self and identity may depend on perpetuation of the processes which gave rise to it" (p. 64).

This conceptualization of racism, anchored in documenting racist outcomes, and its concomitant racial project is based on what Iris Young (1990) has called a material distribution strategy that emphasizes a redistribution of resources rather than countering oppression. Challenging racist ideology (an undoubtedly difficult task) would focus on the social and cultural practices that render some as the other, and on the system of racist ideology as a whole. Instead, the predominant racial project of nonwhites seems to both essentialize and concretize racial identities and differences. Regardless of which racial project is in question, both have material consequences and are struggles over the nature and power of various identities.

Identity

Having traced the way subaltern communities encounter environmental issues within a context of inequality and a concern for survival, we now turn to the role of identity. As NSM literature demonstrates, the formation of a collective identity is a necessary first step in building a movement. People, regardless of how oppressed they might be, do not inevitably have a common identity. A shared identity must be cultivated and refined through interaction and struggle with other groups. The development of a collective identity allows people to forge an emotional attachment to each other, but it is more than that. Subaltern people, like anyone else (and perhaps more so), have a need to create an affirmative identity since their identities have been maligned, distorted, or subject to attempted erasure by the dominant society.

It is, of course, impossible *not* to have an identity, but for those who daily receive the message that they are despised and worth nothing, the internalization of these perceptions can lead to a negative identity contributing to oppression and self-destruction.[4] Resistance, let alone a movement, will never occur if the oppressed lack either a collective or an affirmative identity. But while an affirmative identity will not necessarily lead to mobilization, it is, at the least, crucial to retaining one's dignity in the face of oppression.

Although the NSM literature, and identity politics as a whole, recognizes the upswing in articulations of and mobilization around assorted identities, it has perhaps overemphasized the newness of this phenomenon while incorrectly conceiving of identity politics as separate and divorced from economic struggles. Any attempt to merge a materialist analysis and identity must be handled carefully. Yapa's observation (1993a) that the poor do not want to affirm their identity as poverty-stricken people is well taken, but the fact in class struggle, as in any other form of collective action, is that there is a clear need to form an identity, and in the case of marginalized groups this means the negative identity must be appropriated and reconstructed. Obviously, the creation of an affirmative identity can never be fully distinguished from resistance because the action and consciousness required to build such an identity, even if it simply allows one to live with a shred of dignity, is an act of resistance and an exercise of power itself. It is the power of self that is the crucial first step in imagining the possibility of resistance or another reality.[5] In my study of subaltern Chicano environmental struggles, ethnicity was the primary form of identification, and culture provided much of the raw material for that identity.

Ethnicity

Ethnicity, like the idea of race, is a social construct. It is an identity developed in conditions of difference and often in conditions of inequality and subordination. The following is a useful definition of ethnicity that emphasizes domination. "Ethnicity is the identity which members of the group place upon themselves, race is a label foisted on to them by non-members. . . . While racial identity may be a crippling disability, ethnicity acts as a positive force for the protection and promotion of group interests" (Aldrich, Cater, Jones, and McEvoy in Cater and Jones 1987, 191). Given this definition, we can conceptualize ethnicity as a response to racism, economic exploitation, and racialized economic marginalization (although ethnicity also arises in instances of difference that lack dramatic inequality).

This definition also allows for the changing and fluid nature of ethnicity. Since it is socially constructed, ethnic identification and mobilization change in response to political-economic conditions in both international and local arenas (Nagel and Snipe 1993; Hanson 1989; Nagel 1986; Nagel and Olzak 1982), as well as to agency. "How people define themselves and are defined by others is a dynamic process. Cultural identity is not a fixed and static entity; rather it ebbs and flows as history itself unfolds" (Gutierrez 1986, 80).

Moreover, at any particular moment, people may choose to emphasize or deemphasize an ethnic identification in a process Padilla (1985) calls "situational ethnicity," to change the boundaries that define who does not belong to an ethnic group. Nagengast and Kearney (1990), Roosens (1989), and Nagel (1982) have all shown how different groups have either created or changed an ethnic identity in response to political conditions. The important point is that ethnicity is neither primordial (Eller and Coughlan 1993) nor fixed. Instead, it is deliberately and consciously developed by groups as a way of coping, or as a useful political tool. "In a world where power, wealth, and dignity are unevenly and illegitimately distributed within and among nations, ethnicity is a resource in political, economic, and cultural struggle" (Nash 1989, 127).[6]

Despite the fact that the U.S. government categorizes all Spanish-speaking persons as belonging to a single ethnicity, this is somewhat fallacious (see also Tienda and Ortiz 1986). While the all-encompassing ethnic-category strategy of Hispanic may work for bureaucratic purposes, it epitomizes the political nature of ethnicity, because it includes all persons belonging to any national-origin group that has Spanish as the dominant language. This includes those of Cuban, Mexican, Dominican Republic, Puerto Rican, and Argentinian origin, to name but a few. Aside from some connection to the Spanish language, they have little in common and only a weak collective identity — moreover, one that is continuously changing.

Take the case of the Mexican American population, which is by far the largest of all Hispanic groups, constituting 62 percent of all Latinos in the United States (United States Bureau of Census 1990d) (a percentage even higher in the Southwest). Because of the social and spatial heterogeneity of Mexican Americans, there was not, until the 1960s and 1970s, a strong ethnic identification across the Southwest where their history and numbers are the greatest. What is commonly called the Chicano Movement, or *el movimiento*, was an attempt to create a Southwestern Chicano identity (Munoz 1989). This does not mean that more localized, or even regional, ethnic identities did not previously exist, but there was not a coherent one that stretched across the Southwest.

Because of this sociospatial variation, there are significant differences in Mexican-American culture that led to assorted identities. There is considerable variation, for example, between, Tejano, East L.A. Chicano, northern New Mexican Hispano, and Mexican immigrant cultures. Most share a common language, religion, identity as mestizo, and have some connection to Mexico, but differences arise from the incorporation experience, geography, urban versus rural status, 'race', and class position.

Regardless of these differences, there were attempts to form a more collective identity starting in the 1940s and 1950s with such groups as the League of United Latin American Citizens (LULAC) and the G.I. Forum (Gomez Quinones 1990). In contrast to subsequent mobilization efforts, these organizations sought to promote assimilationist goals in order to be accepted by the dominant Anglo society (for important exceptions, see Rosenbaum 1986).[7] Instead of affirming a Chicano identity, they strove to portray themselves as worthy Americans, as defined by Anglo America. According to Carlos Munoz (1989), the 1960s Chicano youth movement was the first real attempt to create an anti-assimilationist identity that resonated with "brown pride" and drew upon Chicanos' Indian roots.

Examining the Chicano movement a bit closer not only illustrates the situational nature of ethnicity but provides a useful framework in which to place both the UFWOC's and Ganados' struggles, because they are both connected to the Chicano movement and its politics. The Chicano movement can best be described as a series of tenuously linked struggles representing the common yet distinct aspirations of various

Chicano communities. Each state of the Southwest was the site of numerous struggles, for example, the farmworkers in California, Reies Lopez Tijerina and La Alianza in northern New Mexico, Corky Gonzalez and the Crusade for Justice in Denver, and José Angel Gutierrez and La Raza Unida party in Texas. Moreover, these distinct struggles were overlaid by student and youth activism across the region.[8]

They all shared a powerful cultural component, including great pride in an indio heritage, and took a strong stand against racism and discrimination while seeking greater political power. Together, these struggles, plus hundreds of others, comprised the Chicano movement. An important part of the struggle for a meaningful identity included the search for a homeland or the mythical Aztlan, thought to be situated somewhere in what is now the southwestern United States.[9] A geographic identity and homeland were central to the newly emerging Chicano identity of the 1960s and 1970s (J. Chavez 1989) that was based on a conceptualization of Chicanos as victims of Anglos, particularly in terms of the loss of historic lands (Saragoza 1990).

As the more militant segments of the movement sputtered out by the mid-1970s, it became apparent that its results were mixed.

> In stressing self-determination, pride, and even violence, the leadership of the Chicano movement during the period between 1960 and 1970 was moderately successful in making the larger Anglo society acknowledge the discrepancy between the democracy it professed and the reality in the barrios. This leadership undertook the strong action needed to enable the more moderate elements to enter institutions. In reviewing the accomplishments of the sixties, what was achieved were token reforms, representation, and limited mobility. Chicano self-determination was not even attempted, let alone accomplished. The problems confronting the movement were universal almost without fail: the lack of explicit class constituency; the lack of a radical program to which a constituency was deeply committed; a lack of resources; the lack of structured disciplined organizations; the lack of stable, competent, committed leadership; and the lack of a common critical ideology. (Gomez Quinones 1990, 144)

The movement lapsed, or was transformed, as the result of changes in the larger political climate, changes that gave a new generation of youth far more advantages, and of changes in the class composition of the Chicano population — successes of the movement itself. Indeed, one of the most important legacies of *el movimiento,* the War on Poverty, and most importantly, the black civil rights struggle was the creation of an African American and Chicano middle class (see Cruse 1987) that along with the changes mentioned above had profound implications for Chicano ethnic identity.

Chicanos encountered and underwent dramatic changes in the 1980s which forced a further change in ethnic identification. These changes have presented new opportunities as well as new conflicts and tensions. Paralleling the larger society, Chicanos experienced increased class fragmentation and income polarization (L. Chavez 1991; Harrison and Bluestone 1988). Acuna (1989) argues that the rise of a Chicano middle class has created "power brokers" (a phenomenon that occurs in civil rights, environmental justice, and other movements) who position themselves to speak for the Latino population. Because of their solid middle-class credentials and their "brown skin," government and corporate America listen to them (Ortiz 1991). Only recently, as political and economic fragmentation has increased, have alternative Latino voices emerged. In a recent book, conservative writer Linda Chavez (1991) offers a scathing attack on the Hispanic civil rights establishment for portraying Latinos as disadvantaged and oppressed. The fact that such a voice has emerged (a power broker) attests to the social and economic diversity of Latinos.

Furthermore, because of massive immigration from other parts of Latin America, the term Chicano is no longer inclusive. The Chicano subject has been decentered.

Although Mexicans and Mexican Americans are still the single largest Latino group, one cannot ignore the growing Central American, South American, and Caribbean presence, all of whom are Latino. These two developments, increased economic fragmentation and tremendous immigration, have shattered any pretense of a coherent Chicano identity. In reality, there are a number of nuanced identities, such as Chicano, Hispano, Latino, Salvadoreno, Guatemalteco, Mexicano, Hispanic, and Mexican American (see Heskin 1991), whose significance may be lost on outsiders, especially those who simply see a racialized homogeneous group. The splintering of old and emergence of new identities (Nagengast and Kearney 1990) demonstrates the precarious nature of ethnicity, in this case resulting from much larger political-economic dynamics, and the changing structure of inequality. Although I have argued for the complex and variegated nature of this population, there are present efforts underway to build a more united Latino ethnic identity (Padilla 1985), a process known as "panethnicity" (Lopez and Espiritu 1990). On the one hand, there is increasing pressure to identify as one group for the ease of government handling as well as for the strength to be derived from large numbers. On the other hand, the diverse experiences of inequality make it increasingly difficult to fashion a shared meaningful identity. It is true the Chicano middle class is marginalized in very real ways due to racism, but they are not subaltern in the way that undocumented immigrants, farm workers, or the rural poor are — an important obstacle in trying to create a collective identity.

It is still unclear how these structural forces will shape Chicano/Mexicano/Latino ethnic identity. Only one thing is certain: it *will*. By focusing on a particular set of cultural forms — praxis, artifacts, values and beliefs (Bauman 1973) — we can better highlight the way or ways in which culture is used in the forging of a collective identity and its role in contributing to the larger success of a movement.[10]

As suggested in the previous section, subalternity by definition includes the denigration of one's identity. In conditions of subordination, the very symbols, things, beliefs, and the way of life that help define an individual may be outlawed (see, for example, Trevor-Roper 1983), subject to punishment, or ridiculed. During the 1940s and 1950s, for example, it was commonplace for Chicano children to be physically punished by teachers for speaking Spanish on the playground. Because such practices become the focal point of domination, they may also become the catalyst and embodiment of resistance. The reappropriation of these cultural forms provides insights into the process of identity formation as they constitute a crude map of where mobilization develops.

Despite the significance of culture, Donald and Rattansi (1992) caution why those interested in antiracist and, I would add, subaltern politics must be wary of culture and cultural arguments, particularly in light of both the way antiracist efforts have degenerated into meaningless talk of a multiculturalism (devoid of any reference to power and domination) and of the way the political right has so skillfully appropriated and controlled the discourse on culture (Giroux 1993; Omi

1992). To ignore culture is to ignore a vast terrain of human consciousness and action, an act that would be simply unacceptable. The task is to find a level and method of analysis still connected to political economy that does not lose sight of domination and subordination (see Roseberry 1989).

The first set of cultural concepts to consider is Bauman's concepts of differential and hierarchical culture. This construct recognizes that all societies have cultures that provide meaning but that these differ. This concept of differential culture has not always existed. It arose partly in response to the need to explain contrasting levels of economic development (Bauman 1973, 36).[11] Differential culture, in conjunction with racism and economic inequality, can give rise to hierarchical culture, which maintains that some cultures are better than others. This is the traditional relationship of dominance that has characterized Anglo-Mexicano relations. However, the idea of hierarchical culture can also be turned on its head by subaltern movements.

In both case studies Chicanos became aware of how their culture not only differed from, but was also maligned by, mainstream Anglo America. They chose to use this difference as a form of resistance. Knowing their culture had been denigrated by prejudice and racism, they sought to use their culture not only to organize people, but also to show the world who they were. Once shameful cultural icons were appropriated and turned into symbols of resistance. In some instances, they turned the tables by implying that their culture was superior (hierarchical) to the dominant Anglo one. This happened to a limited extent in Ganados' grazing conflict where Hispanos drew upon their pastoral history and heritage to enhance their ecological legitimacy by portraying their nature-society relations as morally and environmentally superior to those of Anglos.

This brings us to the second cultural concept, that of values and beliefs and material culture. Subaltern populations are acutely conscious of the fact that they are different from the dominant group. They know the ways in which they differ and the outward symbols and expressions of those differences, because they are often the subject of disdain. These cultural forms, onto which a subaltern identity is grafted, may include food, religion, language, clothing, family size, and family structure. They are actions, beliefs, and objects that, taken together and separately in the context of unequal power relations, signify subaltern. For example, a focal point of Chicano and Mexicano Catholicism is the Virgin Mary (La Virgen de Guadalupe), which is considered highly problematic by the dominant society. In the course of building a movement, farmworkers and activists publicly turned to this belief — openly displaying statues and posters, and praying (displays of material artifacts and performative acts) — not only as a source of solace and inspiration but also (and far more consciously at times) as an expression of resistance and tool of mobilization. By openly engaging in ritual prayer, they asserted their identity to the larger society.

An entirely different use of material culture can be seen in Ganados' economic development project, which is based on producing high-quality woven goods. The woolen products — such as *rebozos* (shawls), pillows, and throws — are material objects that are symbolic of the region, the people, and their emotional and historical attachment to the land. By initiating a project that combined elements of grazing, sheep, craft production, and localized forms of production and management, material culture was both affirming and enabling as a powerful tool of resistance. The heavy use of symbolism was instrumental both in attracting participants and in affirming locals' sense of history and identity. It offered them a different interpretation of the present: instead of being impoverished rural Hispanos whose culture was "dying" (see Carlson 1990), they became skilled artisans creating a link to their "rich" history. They were trying to preserve or re-create a treasured culture that was endangered.

The third cultural concept I consider is praxis. Praxis is action. It is the social relations that actually create a culture. It is the stuff of which culture (and life) is made. Praxis usually refers to practices of which people are not overtly conscious but which appear to be the natural way of doing things. An illustration of praxis is how people organize their family life. Praxis is critical to understanding domination, mobilization, and resistance. Culture as praxis deals with how resistance is carried out, down to the smallest detail. For example, what forms of defiance does a community choose to engage in? What is the division of labor? How is mobilization orchestrated? How is it gendered? What role does gender play? How do indigenous leaders go about organizing and consolidating a community? These questions all pertain to praxis.

In order for a movement to be successful, it must begin where people are. It must begin with the familiar and everyday. One reason that both of these case studies were successful was the emphasis on praxis, which allowed people to feel comfortable in new experiences and situations.

Theorists too often ignore culture, insisting that people will do what is economically rational, perhaps even violating cultural structures. Experience has shown that such forms of planning and development fail. Organizing, planning, and movement building must be done within an appropriate cultural context. What's more, seeing the efficacy and strength of one's own culture can help reinforce a strong ethnic identity. This happened in the case of the UFWOC struggle when entire families were sent out on the boycott circuit. The UFWOC decided to pursue this strategy because families were found to be far more effective organizing units than individuals, who often became homesick and were subject to conflicting pressures (Rose 1988). Although Mexican families (especially large ones) are often construed as problematic by the Anglo majority—responsible for problems ranging from deviance, psychosocial maladjustment, self-inflicted poverty (see Temple-Trujillo 1974), and environmental degradation—the success of families serving as the basic boycott unit demonstrated all that was good and empowering about Mexicano families.

The three usages, or concepts, of culture presented have shown that culture, in all its many forms, is important to oppressed communities in several ways. First, culture is crucial in the production and exercise of subalternity. By the same token, however, it plays a key role in mobilization efforts both by providing familiar and meaningful guideposts and by facilitating the fashioning of a collective identity. The use of symbols, praxis, and hierarchical conceptions remind people of who they are, of their shared traditions and past (however romanticized), and of what they can achieve by uniting and acting collectively. Although ethnicity may be a response to racism and other forms of inequality, the materials from which it is carved are cultural.

By appreciating the individual yet interlocking roles of poverty, racism, and identity, we can better grasp how subaltern communities are created and how they begin the long process of resistance and movement building. Creating an oppositional movement is such a daunting task, it is fairly remarkable when the oppressed and subaltern of the

world successfully unite and engage in collective action against hegemonic forms of domination. Although the creation of an identity is a
necessary first step, much more — such as appropriate tactics, strategies, and agency — is required. Equally important are factors beyond
the control of the subaltern, such as the potentially far more powerful
forces arrayed against them. Whether they are racists, the state, multi-
national corporations, or religious zealots, it is the powerful, who have
the upper hand, that set the terms of the debate and the engagement. It's
largely by finding chinks in the wall, exploiting changes in the political
climate, and refusing to cooperate (Piven and Cloward 1978) that subaltern communities may change their circumstances.

3

The Pesticide Campaign of the
UFW Organizing Committee, 1965–71

Some people that I know still eat contaminated grapes
Gente que conozco comen uvas contaminadas
Covered with pesticides that poison farmworker children
Cubiertas con pesticidas que envenenan los chiquillos
El Picket Sign, El Picket Sign,
No Compran Uvas
El Picket Sign, El Picket Sign,
Support the United Farmworkers
El Picket Sign, El Picket Sign,
For safe jobs, safe food
El Picket Sign, El Picket Sign,
Stop Environmental Racism
From the fields of California Cesar Chavez has been saying
De los files de California Cesar Chavez anda deciendo
That the Struggle is for everyone, but some are acting dumb
Este lucha es para todos, pero unos se hacen pendejos

El Picket Sign[1]

Pesticides have been recognized as an important environmental issue
since the dawn of the contemporary environmental movement in the
early 1960s. Large mainstream environmental organizations, such
as the Sierra Club and the Natural Resources Defense Council, have

routinely addressed pesticides, but did so far differently than the United Farm Workers' Organizing Committee did in the period from 1965 to 1971. While the UFW boycott of the 1980s is relatively well known in environmental and social justice circles, the union's earlier campaign is more obscure.

As part of the UFWOC's[2] attempt to build a union and secure contracts, they waged a multifaceted campaign against pesticide abuse, illustrating how the subaltern encounter environmental issues within the context of material and political inequality. Throughout the struggle, the UFWOC's demands for union recognition and its associated benefits cannot be separated from their pesticide concerns and strategy. Although in the 1980s the UFW was accused of exploiting pesticide concerns in order to attract support, this should not detract from the danger of pesticides, particularly among unorganized field-workers.

Related to such accusations, some have suggested that the farmworkers' pesticide struggle is not an environmental issue but an economic struggle with an environmental component. These interpretations force us to delve more deeply into the movement in order to better understand the nature of oppositional resource struggles. If we place the UFWOC and other subaltern group struggles within the context of NSMs, with their preoccupation with identity and quality of life, then the UFWOC struggle might seem oddly out of place. By fully appreciating the conditions structuring the lives of the subaltern and their precarious economic circumstances, however, it becomes apparent how NSM and subaltern environmental concerns differ dramatically, resulting in the need for a new understanding of environmentalism.

The UFWOC campaign diverged from other pesticide strategies because it did not approach pesticides from a narrow perspective. For example, mainstream environmental groups working at the same time sought to intervene in the spraying of pesticides in national parks or in their use in mosquito control. More contemporary strategies seek to link pesticides to food residues and children's consumption patterns. Both sets of action, however, focus on quality-of-life issues in which the social actors are fairly removed from the actual threat. The UFWOC, in contrast, sought to organize a subaltern group in order to enable them to gain more control and power over their lives. It was a class struggle that became a social movement onto itself, and it was an integral part of the larger Chicano movement of the time. The UFWOC's objective was to improve the lives of farmworkers in terms of wages, job security, and community and workplace conditions, including greater control over and reduction of pesticide use. Because farmworkers experienced pesticide exposure through their subordinated status and relative powerlessness, the only way they could reduce their vulnerability was by engaging in a major power struggle to alter the conditions of their powerlessness.

An examination of this subaltern environmental movement allows us to better grasp how a marginalized group intersects with environmental issues, provides insights into the centrality of economics and racism in producing subalternity, and sheds light on how the oppressed respond to domination. The story of Cesar Chavez and the UFWOC has been the subject of numerous books and studies precisely because it is the ultimate David and Goliath story (Jenkins 1985; Majka and Majka 1982; Kushner 1975; Levy 1975; Day 1971; Matthiessen 1969). A highly subaltern population managed to build an effective, charismatic, and broad-based movement to challenge the power of agribusiness and the state. This movement was successful not only because of its size and strength, but also because of the political period in which it appeared. The 1960s were, of course, a time of great unrest and mobilization, as the political space existed to push the boundaries defining marginal groups (Jenkins 1985). The UFWOC's struggle was an important part of this larger political picture, particularly in California, and its prominent role is alluded to by the way in which it is sometimes equated with a Chicano civil-rights struggle. While it is true that both the UFWOC and the larger Chicano struggle were very much about identity and rights, the former was indisputably a class struggle that became a social movement.

Farmworkers received pitiable wages and were subjected to deplorable working conditions because of their marginality, which in turn was due to their class location, their position within the international division of labor (the Mexican origin population provides most of California's farmworkers), and racism. The UFWOC won agricultural workers the right to unionize, improved working conditions in the field, and regulated pesticide use. A sophisticated campaign against pesticides was waged on a number of fronts — through the courts, boycotts, contracts, and the legislature — with only minimal assistance from established environmental organizations. This multipronged approach indicates the various strategies needed when confronting hegemonic power in the form of both growers and the state. Because of the farmworkers' position, their environmental concerns were never detached from their political and economic reality. This also presented numerous contradictions in waging a campaign. A detailed look at this struggle illuminates the sources of exploitation and domination, the details of resistance and how it is created, and the various meanings attached to the movement by individuals.

Geographical and Historical Context

The scene of the UFWOC story is the southern San Joaquin Valley (fig. 3.1), known simultaneously for its agricultural productivity and its violent history of agricultural organizing. This is where the UFWOC began.[3] Because of the region's history and agricultural base, the class structure and racial and ethnic lines were drawn fairly sharply, with the Anglos occupying positions of authority as community leaders and growers and the Mexican-origin population serving as a highly marginal, socially stigmatized, impoverished work force.[4]

The Central Valley is a large structural depression which runs the length of most of California, from the Tehachapis to the Cascades, a total of 450 miles (675 km). The San Joaquin is the southern part of the Central Valley, while the northern part is known as the Sacramento. Politically, the southern San Joaquin consists of Fresno, Kings, Tulare, and Kern Counties, which with the exception of Kings County are known as the "Big Three" in reference to their bountiful agricultural production (University of California 1982, 106). The region is characterized by rich, fertile soils and enjoys a Mediterranean climate with long, hot, dry summers and mild, moist winters, allowing for a growing season of 285 days (University of California 1982, 107). Precipitation averages less than six inches annually, making intensive agriculture possible only through groundwater extraction or surface diversions, both of which have played a pivotal role in the production of the physical and social landscape.

Passing through the southern San Joaquin one encounters endless

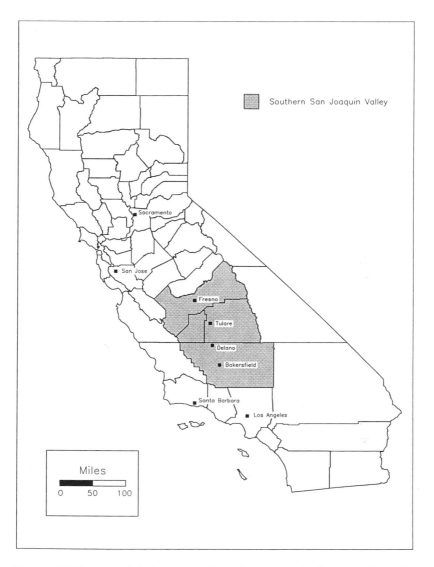

Fig. 3.1. California political map, southern San Joaquin Valley. *Map drawn by Carol Kalt and Caroline Holsted.*

miles of orchards, grapevines, cotton, and other crops such as alfalfa, roses, watermelon, and potatoes. This vista is broken only by a few large cities, dusty towns, and oil rigs. The majority of the population is clustered in cities and towns. In fact, California's premier agricultural counties are, statistically speaking, urban counties because of the Bakersfield and Fresno metropolitan areas. Due to the physical geography and intensive agricultural production, the valley suffers from serious air pollution (Pasternak 1991) and severe groundwater contamination.

The area has not always been characterized by such an urban and industrial nature. Although the Spanish knew of the valley, they did not penetrate it. It was only toward the end of the Mexican Era (1834–46) that the valley was settled through massive land grants made necessary by the extensive nature of arid-land cattle ranching. When California was annexed by the United States, the majority of Californios lost their land through legal fees, even though many holdings were adjudicated in favor of the original owners. A series of government programs were instituted to dispose of the lands that had become part of the public domain. These included the Acts of 1841, 1850, and 1853, and the Morrill Act of 1862. These programs were rampant with corruption and speculation, resulting in extreme land concentration (Liebman 1983, 23). Early crop production was anchored in the Sacramento Valley, but the advent of the railroad and refrigerated boxcar enabled cultivation to spread into the southern San Joaquin Valley. By the 1880s sugarbeet production was widespread and growers faced a labor shortage largely attributable to very low wages and more lucrative opportunities in the gold mines (Daniel 1981).

It was at this time that a racialized class structure developed that included the adoption of a racist ideology and served to produce a subaltern class. Field-workers faced legal discrimination, were extremely poor, were relatively powerless, and were considered social pariahs by the dominant Anglo growers. Growers learned that the key to an adequate work force was to limit a group's upward mobility — a strategy that growers ensured by pressuring the government to maintain legal restrictions against farmworkers. The Chinese were the first to fill this position in large numbers. They had little recourse due to legal discrimination that prevented them, for example, from buying land and limited their mining opportunities. Subsequently, different ethnic groups served this function in what has been called "ethnic succession," a reference to the process by which different ethnic groups sequentially replace each other in the fields (L. Jones 1970). As soon as resistance was expressed, activism was suppressed and a new work force was sought.

California historian Carey McWilliams (1939, 117) has identified and described the various work force characteristics growers sought in the creation of an "ideal" work force, that is, a work force over which they exercised total control. Central Valley growers have historically been interested in recruiting an abundant, cheap, mobile, ethnically diverse, and temporary labor pool. An abundance of workers is desirable not only to suppress wages, but also because of the perishable nature of California crops. Inexpensive labor was critical. Growers had always argued that they could not afford to pay higher wages because they had little control over the prices they received. Worker mobility was essential because year-round employment was not available. Consequently, workers were prohibited from wintering in local communities for fear that they might organize, which certainly goes a long way towards creating a socially marginal population. The final work force criterion was ethnic diversity. Though certain ethnic groups dominated fieldwork at various times, growers always sought some degree of ethnic mixing because such a labor force tends to remain segregated, thus hindering worker cooperation, and making it possible to foster worker competition. After the Chinese resisted these conditions, the same sequence of events took place with Japanese, Armenian, Portuguese, Mexican, and Filipino workers. By the 1920s Mexicans had become the dominant ethnic group in the fields, although other ethnic groups were still present. Nevertheless, Mexicans were considered an ideal labor force because they were powerless and available in ample numbers (Daniel 1981). One reason Mexicans have dominated this sector for so long is simply the number of Mexicanos available. Due to Mexico's proximity to California, its poverty, and its place within the international division of labor, there has almost always been a surplus of workers, thereby allowing growers to exercise inordinate control over the work force.

Racist attitudes towards Mexicans also served to rationalize and legitimize their role as workers. "The Mexican is not politically conscious, has no political ambitions and does not, no matter in what numbers he may live there, aspire to dominate the political affairs of the community in which he lives. . . . The Mexican does not intermarry with Americans except in rare instances and has no ambition to do so. He is not, therefore, a menace to the American bloodstream" (in L. Jones 1970, 35–36).

We can see that from the beginning the marginalization of Chicano (and other) farmworkers was a function of both racism and economic position — all suffered from low wages, harsh working conditions, unsteady employment, and low status, which in turn translated into minimal power. Agribusiness's desire for such a highly exploited work force caused them to look beyond white Americans to nonwhite countries and workers who, because of their marginality, would tolerate conditions inconceivable to native white workers and their communities. This is a clear example of how racist ideology aligned with the economic needs of capital and produced a situation of subalternity.

In the case of Mexicans and Mexican Americans, it was not only a people who were racialized but a nation, showing the intersection of racism and nation building — Mexicans were what Anglo-Americans were not. Because of this racism and the global political economy, Mexicans entered the United States in a socially and economically subordinated status. Racism was manifest not only in limited economic opportunities, but in a whole series of social and political inequalities that served to prevent upward mobility. The continued poverty and marginality of San Joaquin Chicanos acted to justify the racist attitudes of the dominant Anglo society. They were seen as dirty, poor, and lacking in political ambition. In the words of one law-enforcement official, "Mexicans are trash. They have no standards of living. We herd them like pigs" (Taylor and Kerr in Chacon 1980, 47–48). Such attitudes enabled dominant Anglos to see Mexicans as less than fully human and not deserving of better working and living conditions.

Few labor organizers were concerned with California field workers before the Great Depression. Despite the lack of interest on the part of organized labor, there is a history of sporadic strikes before the 1930s, although they were single-issue oriented and poorly planned (Daniel 1981; Kushner 1975). Because there was not a systematic effort to improve the working and wage conditions of field-workers, the strikes were not particularly effective. The decade of the 1930s, one of the most violent eras in California history, ushered in a new level of activism. With the influx of Anglo workers, primarily Dust Bowl refugees, organizers anticipated they would not tolerate such conditions and would eagerly unionize (McWilliams 1939, 212). Unfortunately, while organizers were strong on rhetoric and were able to convince workers to strike, the strikes were not carefully planned in terms of scheduling actions or in providing for strikers and their families. Because of this lack of foresight, when a strike was successfully carried out (such as the Cotton Strike of 1933), organizers were not able to translate their victories into a functioning union (Daniel 1981).

By the 1940s labor organizers had abandoned field-workers because of their powerlessness. They simply lacked the power to extract meaningful concessions from growers, which led organizers to forsake them (see Almaguer 1980). That farmworkers were excluded from even institutionalized labor underscores why they cannot be seen simply as workers, or their struggle seen solely as class conflict; they were subaltern. Mainstream organizations, like the American Federation of Labor (AFL), had begun to see farmworkers as a social problem rather than a labor one (Daniel 1981, 281). This interpretation favors government solutions, such as legislation, that may ameliorate some of the worst problems while not addressing the fundamental issue of powerlessness.

Of course, the failure to successfully organize and unionize must not be seen solely as the fault of workers and their organizations. As Vanneman and Cannon (1987) have pointed out, the power of capital must be considered, which in this instance was truly awesome. The fact that workers could not successfully oppose capital was both a testament to their weakness and to the sheer power of agribusiness, which was able to marshal the resources of the state to achieve financial success and social control. The government assisted in the procurement and development of water, land, technology, and labor supply.

> They could summon congressmen to do their bidding, their politicians passed laws favoring agribusiness and blocked legislation that could benefit farmworkers, farmers routinely called on the courts and law enforcement agencies to protect their interests. When farmers needed a supply of water — to supplement the deep wells that were sucking the underground dry — they asked for and received *billions* of federal and state dollars for dams and canals to import water from great distances.

Subsidized irrigation systems, subsidized transportation networks, subsidized research and development of crops and machines, and subsidized marketing all contributed to the "progress" of the San Joaquin Valley. . . . Agribusiness control was absolute! (Taylor 1975, 75, emphasis in original)

The picture emerges of a group of very powerful growers who not only exercised control over their seasonal work force, but also played an influential role in shaping California's growth. Although the valley has many small family farmers, there are a significant number of large, corporate enterprises, including Tenneco, Getty Oil, Chevron Oil Company, Southern Pacific Railroad, and Castle and Cooke (Liebman 1983; Keppel 1987), and a middle strata of powerful growers who dominate local affairs. Growers were (and are) highly organized. The largest statewide organization was the California Farm Bureau, which was open to all farmers. There also were specialty organizations, such as the Grape and Tree Fruit League, the South Central Farmers Committee, and the Desert Grape League. These organizations distributed publications, lobbied effectively, and in the case of the California Farm Bureau, even controlled local labor markets (Galarza 1964). Jelinek (1976), in his study of farm organizations, and Vogeler (1981), in his examination of national agriculture, both concluded that while there was a large number of participating small family farmers, these structures and institutions ultimately worked to the benefit of the larger enterprises. For a wide variety of both economic and ideological reasons, small growers continue to identify with the agenda and goals of agribusiness despite the fact, as Vogeler argues, that they may have more in common with workers.

Agribusiness has become lucrative and powerful not solely on the basis of growers' business acumen but also through government policies. Originally intended to assist family farmers, such policies have instead benefited large corporations, often to the detriment of smaller operations (Vogeler 1981) and rural communities (Goldschmidt 1947). Because of the way power is structured in both rural areas and national arenas, growers have exerted undue influence on a number of fronts: land tenure, water resources, immigration policy,[5] university research, local law enforcement, and the courts.[6]

When discussing agribusiness, particularly in the late 1960s, one cannot overlook its racial, gender, and class composition. Growers in the southern San Joaquin are overwhelmingly white males. Many are sons of immigrants from Italy or Yugoslavia proud of the life they have made for themselves. During the 1960s there were few female and equally few Chicano growers (Females now comprise approximately 11 percent of California growers; Hispanics 4.2 percent of U.S. growers [United States Census of Agriculture 1987, 21].) Farther north, there are a number of Japanese farmers, but few are found south of Fresno. While not all growers are rich, many have become quite wealthy, and the farms are passed down from father to son(s). Agribusiness in the San Joaquin Valley is a male-oriented enterprise. Undoubtedly, women have played important roles in agribusiness, but aside from their portrayal as farmworkers, that history is yet to be reconstructed.

Given the enormous power of large agricultural enterprises, we can see how any attempt on the part of workers would have to be formidable in order to be effective. For example, growers responded to unionization efforts through the Associated Farmers, a vigilante group pledged to "help each other in times of emergency," striking frequently and brutally at camps, strikes, and in the fields under the banner of "fighting the Red Scare" (McWilliams 1939, 240). Grower repression took numerous forms, including blocking food and supplies destined for strikers, boycotting merchants who extended credit or supplies to them, evicting workers from grower-owned housing, prosecuting activists under charges of criminal syndicalism, physically attacking strikers, and in a few cases, firing into crowds (Daniel 1981; Chacon 1980). It was not uncommon for local sheriffs to deputize large numbers of farmers, empowering them to engage in armed vigilante activity. Local law enforcement felt obliged to cooperate with growers. One undersheriff explained the close alliance. "We protect farmers out here in Kern County. They are our best people. . . . [T]hey put us in here and they can put us out again, so we serve them" (Daniel 1981, 182).

The growers' refusal to negotiate and recognize as legitimate the concerns and demands of workers was not merely a function of racism and their response to competitive market conditions. Instead, growers saw the unrest as the result of *outside* radicals, not as the result of low wages and bad working conditions (Daniel 1981, 152). This rationale was in itself racist and patronizing. Growers didn't believe "their" workers were dissatisfied and capable of resisting.[7] Because the growers' power was so complete and the groups were defined by 'race' and ethnicity, it appeared to be only natural that Anglo growers should control Mexican workers. By disregarding real worker problems, growers backed themselves into a position of inflexibility, thus setting the tone for uncompromising and often violent labor relations.

The hegemonic control of growers can also be seen in the process of acquiring workers. State procurement of labor became institutionalized through the Bracero program that provided Mexican workers through a "national scheme of labor importation administered by the government on behalf of and for profit of private industry" (Galarza 1977, xiii). Officially, the program was intended to provide a supplementary labor force, but in many instances Braceros completely displaced domestic workers as they accepted lower wages and were less likely to resist (Galarza 1964, 156). The Bracero program was a serious obstacle to unionization efforts and, in fact, it was hardly coincidental that the first successful strike took place in 1965, the year that the Bracero program was eliminated (Majka and Majka 1982, 167).

The power of agribusiness was also evident in resource development. As early as the 1930s, the federal government, and later the State of California, became actively involved in providing subsidized water to growers. In 1933 the federally funded Central Valley Project allowed for the development of the eastern and central side of the valley. One problem with the federally funded water projects, however, was the 160-acre limitation that restricted the amount of land a water-beneficiary could own. Although California farmers never complied with this regulation, growers decided a nonfederal water project was necessary to preclude any threat (Worster 1985, 290). Thus the State Water Project (SWP) was born. It was the world's largest water transfer system, and it brought water to the San Joaquin Valley via the California Aqueduct. The SWP was completed in the early 1970s and opened up thousands of acres in the western San Joaquin.

California agriculture has also benefited from a close relationship with the University of California (UC) through both research and extension. The university's agricultural research program is dedicated to making California agriculture more efficient, specialized, and productive. This has been accomplished through mechanization, new hybrids, pesticides, chemicals, fertilizers, and biotechnology. Many have argued, including the UFW, that the research agenda of the UC directly favors large growers and agribusiness to the detriment of small farmers, farmworkers, and rural communities, all of whom are part of the UC mandate. Hightower (1976) has summarized the unequal relationship between research institutions, the state, agribusiness, and workers: "Corporate agribusiness received a machine with the taxpayer's help, but the workers who were replaced were not even entitled to unemployment compensation" (p. 94).

This quote sums up well the way in which the state has been complicit in supporting the development of agribusiness with scarce consideration to the well-being of workers and their communities. It also illustrates the highly skewed power relationship between growers and workers. The attempt to improve any aspect of workers' lives — be it housing, education, or pesticide exposure — required a concerted challenge both to the state and to agribusiness.

When Cesar Chavez and Dolores Huerta began organizing in the early 1960s, they confronted a labor force suffering from very low wages, severe underemployment, and a perpetual oversupply of workers. With wages ranging between $.70 and $.90 an hour, the farm union demanded a $1.25 per hour wage during their first strike in 1965 (Huerta 1985, 131). According to a survey conducted by the Assembly Committee on Agriculture, the average hourly wage had increased to $1.40 per hour by 1965. Despite these increases, farmworkers remained relatively powerless and mired in poverty largely because of the seasonal nature of farm work. In 1965 approximately 45 percent of the work force was employed eighteen weeks or less per year (Mines and Martin 1986, 81, 84).

One key to maintaining the prevailing social arrangement was the persistent oversupply of workers. With so many potential workers, a grower could easily dismiss any worker for resistance. Worse, the Bracero program served to sanction and formalize the oversupply. A related problem to the large labor supply was that, on a certain level, foreign workers did have objective interests different from domestic workers. Since foreign seasonal workers spent only a few months a year in California, they could not take full advantage of union benefits. A union could curtail individual earnings by limiting the amount of time worked through the implementation of a seniority system; foreign workers, in contrast, wanted to maximize their earnings during their time in California (Taylor 1975, 29). Yet, despite these drawbacks, both domestic and foreign seasonal workers would have to pay monthly union dues.

The UFWOC was the first farmworkers' union to gain recognition, secure contracts, and win the right to unionize — a right agricultural workers were denied under the Wagner Act. In 1965 farm interests continued to oppose placing farmworkers under national labor laws (Taylor 1975, 11). The situation was somewhat ironic. If workers were not protected under the law, neither were they subject to its limitations. This situation allowed the UFWOC to conduct the first successful boycott, which was instrumental in bringing growers to the table.

The UFWOC resulted from the merging of two organizations; the largely Filipino, Agricultural Workers Organizing Committee (AWOC), led by Larry Itliong; and Cesar Chavez's National Farm Worker Association (NFWA). In the 1950s Chavez became involved with the Community Service Organization (CSO) in San Jose, California. Because of his organizing ability, he became the national director in 1958. Through the CSO, Chavez took on a number of issues and campaigns but found he could only deal peripherally with farmworkers. Because the CSO would not make farmworkers a priority, Chavez left and decided to organize farmworkers full time in 1962.

Chavez spent from 1962 to 1964 building the NFWA in Delano, California. Chavez chose Delano both because he had family there and because the local grape crop was characterized by a large, permanent work force that was relatively well paid — essential components to building a successful organization. As many others had discovered, a largely migratory work force was almost impossible to organize. Likewise, in order to support a union both socially and financially, workers needed fairly stable jobs and incomes.[8] Moreover, because grapes were not a mechanized crop, growers were more vulnerable to strikes.[9]

NFWA was a personal, homey kind of service organization that Chavez saw as the groundwork for a future union. By 1964 Dolores Huerta had joined Chavez. In 1965 the Filipino AWOC was engaged in their first strike in McFarland when more than one thousand NFWA members voted to lend their support (Taylor 1975, 131). In September 1965 the

NFWA launched their first strike in an effort to unionize grape workers. The picket was promptly declared illegal (Matthiessen 1969), convincing the union of the near impossibility of relying on the strike as a viable tactic. The collusion between growers and law enforcement, and the large supply of unemployed workers, compelled the NFWA to consider the boycott.[10] Soon after, the AWOC and NFWA merged to create the United Farm Workers' Organizing Committee (UFWOC).

Growers interpreted the boycott, when compared to the traditional strike, as a sign of the UFWOC's inability to organize and as a lack of worker support (Razee 1966). The UFWOC chose the boycott, however, because of the severe obstacles to waging a picket. Instead, they hoped the public would pressure the growers into granting union recognition. Nevertheless, the UFWOC did have a problem with worker support (Jenkins 1985). Regardless of harsh conditions, many workers were hesitant to picket, strike, or join a union. This was due to their fear of violence and reprisals, not because of idyllic working conditions. Reinforcing the growers' view that outside agitators were the source of the problem was the fact that the picket lines contained many UFWOC supporters, such as students and other social justice activists. This lent an aura of credibility to the growers' charge that outside troublemakers, and not workers, were on strike (Taylor 1975, 149).

The UFWOC's struggle was significant not only because it sought to unionize heretofore unorganized workers, but also because it posed a direct challenge to institutionalized labor. After World War II, labor became increasingly conservative with their demands focused almost exclusively on wages and security. Organized labor in the form of the AFL-CIO epitomized class struggle without a social conscience (Kushner 1975, xii). Even though farmers opposed unionization, they knew wages were the central demand of unionized industrial workers. This was something that was at least understandable, if not agreeable. But the UFWOC was not making simply wage demands: *they wanted to remedy the great power imbalance between growers and field-workers.* Hence, while the UFWOC's demands included traditional wage and seniority matters, they also infringed on management rights, challenging growers on the most fundamental level. For a fairly powerless group, the UFWOC was making unprecedented demands: union recognition plus participation in management.

The unbalanced power struggle made the organizing attempt more dramatic not only for the workers but also for the larger community. In addition to the hesitancy of migrant farmworkers to embrace a union, there also existed a small Chicano middle class anxious for Anglo acceptance. Often small business people, these individuals did not support any activity that made Mexican Americans appear unruly or willing to "rock the boat" (Day 1971, 31). It was in their interest to appear as solid middle-class citizens in order to preserve their social and financial standing.

It is important to paint neither rural communities nor farmworkers with too broad strokes, thus obscuring the intraethnic dynamics and diversity. While farmworkers in the San Joaquin Valley were impoverished, they were not the poorest. While the vast majority of farmworkers were of Mexican origin, there were also Anglo, Filipino, and African American workers. While farmworkers readily supported the union when the first elections were held (Villarejo 1991a), it took a long time for them to reach that point. In the beginning, workers were not so ready to jump on the bandwagon. Worker consciousness had to be raised, trust built, and issues identified. In that process pesticides emerged as one of the key issues.

Pesticides and Positionality

Agribusiness and Pesticides

As argued in chapter 1, in attempting to understand subaltern environmental movements, it is not so much the issue that decides the nature of the struggle; it is one's position in relation to the problem. Of the many groups involved with pesticides, only one approached the issue from a subaltern position — farmworkers. I would like to review briefly the evolution of pesticides in the United States and how agribusiness, the state, environmentalists, and farmworkers all intersected with the issue.

Pest control has existed since the beginning of agriculture but changed significantly after WWII with the introduction of DDT, "the atomic bomb of insecticides" (Dunlap 1981, 17). Although some have argued that early pesticide producers knew the potential danger of the chemicals (van den Bosch 1978), it is clear the public not only did not, but that they welcomed the technological advancement. In contrast to today's technological wariness, it had to be proven that there were negative consequences associated with pesticides in order for public concern to be raised.

Agribusiness embraced pesticides, precluding the development of alternative forms of pest control such as cultural or biological practices. In some areas, tradition and culture influenced farming practices. In Texas, for instance, farmers resisted the chopping and burning of stalks simply because that traditionally was the tenant's job (Dunlap 1981, 28). Instead, farmers were eager for a quick fix. Faced with such attitudes and behaviors, the task for economic entomologists became "not to find a method of control, but to find a method that did not conflict with the social and economic needs and desires of the community." In particular, the public wanted "convenience, simplicity, and immediate applicability" (Dunlap 1981, 31, 35). A new generation of professional entomologists, plus the tremendous potential for profits, also contributed to the dominance of chemicals.

The rise of pesticides reveals much about our society and culture. They were initially welcomed because of expected increases in food production necessary to feed the population and provide trade surpluses. But our heavy reliance on pesticides also suggests an attitude of conquest and domination towards nature. How a society farms exposes its relationship to the land (Berry 1986), and ours is one that seeks dominion over nature. Not only do we alter the landscape and ecosystem, we try to control it completely, even to the point of futility — illustrated by the attitude "the only good bug is a dead bug," despite the growing immunity of common agricultural pests. The objective becomes control simply for the sake of control.[11]

By the 1960s, pesticides were an entrenched part of agriculture and considered essential to any modern operation. Between 1950 and 1969 farmers' expenditures on pesticides increased 15 percent annually, from $87 million to over $1 billion. Likewise, while farmers spent $.25 an acre on pesticides in 1950, that figure had risen to $3.65 an acre by 1968 (Daniels 1969, 1335). Universities, extension, and chemical companies all worked closely together to develop new chemicals for agriculture.

Agribusiness is a set of institutions, businesses, and practices devoted to producing agricultural commodities in a highly industrialized and scientific fashion. It includes growers; farm equipment manufac-

turers; chemical and oil companies that produce pesticides and fertilizers; professional pesticide applicators; seed producers and distributors
(often the same pesticide companies); public and private organizations
that procure water, adequate labor, food processors and distributors;
and state universities charged with pursuing agricultural research and
working with rural communities. These institutions and individuals
have a distinct culture, political viewpoint, and position in terms of
pesticides.

For them, pesticides are, and were, a lucrative business, and any
aspersions cast upon pesticides have been countered with skillful public
relations and marketing. In World War II America pesticides were not
only a valuable commodity, but there existed the sincere belief on the
part of some that pesticides were highly desirable because of their ability to both improve global food production and eradicate pests and
pestilence (Jukes 1971). The position of agribusiness to pesticides was
not only one of direct material interest but also one of ideology, as an
elaborate framework had been constructed to sanction their production and use. Given this orientation and position, any negative consequences associated with pesticides could be supposedly countered
through careful handling.

Given the importance of pesticides to agribusiness, it is not surprising that the federal government did little to protect workers. When discussing pesticide regulation at the county, state, and national level, it is
important to include both law enforcement and the courts because
both routinely defended agribusiness when called upon. Moreover,
Central Valley judges and lawyers were often involved in agriculture
themselves. In short, there was (and in the mid 1990s still is) a dense set
of interlocking relationships between regulators and agribusiness.[12]

Beginning at the federal level, Victoria Elenes has characterized pesticide policy as a tug-of-war between environmentalists and farmers,
in which farmworkers have been ignored. Farmworker protection remained under administrative control, subject to political pressure and
fluctuation, despite efforts to place it under more stable legislative control (Elenes 1991, 16). Besides this structural problem, there was a clear
conflict of interest in the regulation of pesticides. The United States
Department of Agriculture (USDA) not only served as the farmers' ad-

vocate, but was also charged with defending the public's health (Dunlap 1981, 42).[13]

This lack of concern for workers can be seen in a sampling of pesticide laws and regulations that routinely ignored their needs. For example, in 1910 the Pure Food and Drug Act was passed to protect consumers from poisonous foods. The Federal Insecticide Act was designed to protect growers from misrepresentation involving insecticides and fungicides. The original Federal Insecticide Fungicide Rodenticide Act (FIFRA), passed in 1948, was created to protect growers, once again, from false claims regarding pesticides (Elenes 1991, 36–38). Not until 1969 were hearings first held to consider federal regulation of worker exposure (House of Representatives 1969).

During those federal hearings attention shifted to California because of the state's relatively sophisticated regulations, which were under the jurisdiction of the California Department of Food and Agriculture (CDFA) (Fielder 1970). But similar to the federal scene, California actually did little to protect workers. The CDFA developed pesticide regulations which were enforced by local agricultural commissioners appointed by county supervisors.[14] The California Department of Public Health (DPH) collected data and conducted studies but did not formulate pesticide policy. In 1969 the CDFA first explored the relationship between workers and pesticides through a subcommittee that reviewed worker safeguards (Fielder 1970, 1339). Up to that point, there is little evidence of CDFA acting on behalf of farmworkers in terms of pesticides, although a number of aspects of pesticide use were regulated. California required commercial sprayers to obtain a permit before applying an "injurious material" (thirty-five of which were identified in 1968), to file monthly reports detailing pesticide use with the county agricultural commissioner, and to conduct a sampling program to analyze food for illegal residues. Pesticide regulation extended beyond crop residue to protect birds, mammals, and state waters, as seen respectively in sections 3005 and 5650 of the Fish and Game Code. In short, many aspects of pesticides had been considered and regulated (H. Fisher 1964), except workers.

When the UFWOC first discussed pesticides, all California regulatory bodies, including the DPH, discredited their concerns. Then-DPH director Thomas Milby did not support the cause of worker exposure, although he eventually changed his position in response to a Tulare County study.[15] With the exception of Milby, most evidence suggests that regulators in the 1960s aligned themselves with agribusiness. DPH official Donald Mengle, who was responsible for sharing pesticide injury data with county commissioners, concurred with Kern County Agricultural Commissioner Thomas Morley that "no reasonable danger existed" (*Cohen v. Superior Court* n.d., 11). Mengle also sought to discredit Irma West (*Cohen v. Superior Court* n.d., 12), who coordinated the Injury Control Project for the DPH and was one of California's few health professionals committed to ameliorating worker pesticide exposure (West 1969; A. Medina 1991).

In one hearing, the director of the CDFA testified that workers were protected because warnings were required before and after a field was sprayed. "Before any employee engages in handling or applying injurious materials or restricted materials *or is required to work in areas* where residues of such materials remain in injurious amounts, he shall be informed by his employer of the precautions recommended by the manufacturer and by all appropriate industrial safety orders; and shall be provided with adequate protective devices as specified in such recommendations" (CAC Section 2462, Title 3, in Fielder 1970, 1338, emphasis added). As emphasized, farmworkers were not prohibited from working in contaminated fields, a grower was only required to inform workers of the potential danger.

The second method by which CDFA protected workers was by use of a bilingual booklet that explained how to reduce "human error." According to Senator Scherle from Iowa, these booklets should have been adequate protection for workers, since workers were responsible for their own safety: "[W]e can't legislate against the human error, and I think this is the reason for these books, as mentioned a moment ago, in both Spanish and English, to try to help people realize exactly what they are working with and the careful attention that should be paid as far as the spray itself is concerned" (Scherle 1970, 1345).

Booklets were available at the county agricultural commissioners' and unemployment offices. Not surprisingly, neither of these measures were particularly effective in protecting workers. Because of unequal power relations, workers could not easily resist growers' demands that they work in a contaminated field. To assume that they could overlooks not only the particular problems California farmworkers faced, such as a persistent oversupply of labor, but also the structured inequality between worker and employer in which one person is selling his or her labor to another. That is not a relationship of equals. Scherle's analysis also glosses over the possibility that growers might not provide protective equipment, thereby limiting workers' ability to protect themselves regardless of the booklets.

California pesticide regulation is statewide, but implementation is at the county level. County commissioners enforced laws and collected monthly reports of pesticide usage. Pesticide injuries, however, were under the jurisdiction of the California Department of Public Health (DPH). All injuries were to be reported to local authorities, including the agricultural commissioner, and then submitted to the DPH. Once again, while California did have a reporting system, it had serious shortcomings. Thomas Morley, then Kern County agricultural commissioner, once stated that he had never heard of a pesticide injury in all of Kern County and consequently had never reported one (*Cohen v. Superior Court* n.d., 10–11), this despite the fact that on the average 64 percent of all the cases reported in the state annually between 1954 and 1967 were agriculturally related (Table 3.1).

Regardless of widespread and systematic underreporting, a significant number of injuries were reported to the state. In 1958 the DPH issued "Reports of Occupational Disease Attributed to Pesticides and Agricultural Chemicals" that laid out the scope of the problem based on data provided by the agricultural industry itself. There were 910 reported injuries in 1958, two-thirds of which were in agriculture (California Department of Public Health 1958, 7). Table 3.1 indicates a steady increase in reported pesticide injuries in California. Some of the increase is due to greater pesticide use, but much can be attributed to enhanced reporting due both to the requirement that physicians report all suspected poisonings to the DPH and to increased employee awareness.

Still, there was (and is) a tremendous undercount (Moses 1993, 173–76; West 1964). For one, workers may be afraid of reprisals by either the labor contractor or grower. Workers may also be unfamiliar with the reporting system, health care may be inaccessible, or the

Table 3.1. Reports of Occupational Disease Attributed to Pesticides and Other Agricultural Chemicals in California, 1954–67

Year	All Industries	Agriculture	%	Other
1954	391	248	63.4	143
1955	531	326	61.4	201
1956	789	464	58.8	325
1957	749	434	57.9	315
1958	910	599	65.8	311
1959	1093	782	71.5	311
1960	975	668	68.5	307
1961	911	578	63.4	333
1962	827	545	65.9	282
1963	1013	746	73.6	267
1964	1328	821	61.8	507
1965	1340	836	62.4	504
1966	1347	820	60.9	527
1967	1400	838	59.8	562

Source: California Department of Public Health 1967, 23.

worker may simply accept the problem as part of his or her occupation (E. Medina 1991). Often a worker does not know that his or her illness is pesticide related. Nor do all physicians report pesticide related illness, either because they don't recognize it as such (Mizrahi 1970, 1455) or because they fear reporting too many poisonings, particularly if they are a grower's doctor (Valle 1986).

When pesticide concerns were first raised, some insisted that few injuries were attributable to farming, being mainly household or industrial accidents. John Giumarra, a prominent southern San Joaquin grower, testified in 1969, "I also suggest to you that of the 150 to 200 deaths in the United States that a substantial number of those are children in the urban area who will take ant poison, roach poison, who have spray cans of DDT and other things that are sold to the consumer in the marketplace and it does not specifically relate to the farm worker"

(Giumarra 1970, 3771–72). Growers obviously sought to diminish any dangers associated with pesticides, particularly in terms of occupational use. Table 3.1 shows that over time agriculturally related pesticide injuries have continuously accounted for over 60 percent of all reported injuries. Table 3.2 presents data for agriculturally related diseases reported in 1967.

Table 3.2. Reports of Occupational Disease Attributed to Pesticides and Other Agricultural Chemicals by Industry Group and Clinical Type of Disease, California, 1967

Industry	Total	Systemic Poisoning	Lung Cond.	Skin Cond.	Chem. Burn	Eye Condition
Agriculture	838	179	37	268	108	371
Farms	661	81	36	254	43	185
Pest Control	156	96	—	9	9	19
Others	21	2	1	5	1	10
Manufacturing	223	36	10	63	18	54
Food Products	52	3	1	18	2	16
Agricultural Chemicals	103	28	8	12	10	27
Other Chemicals	19	2	—	6	4	4
Other	49	3	1	27	2	7
Construction	29	1	1	9	13	5
Transportation, Communications, and Utilities	50	5	2	11	4	15
Trade	50	3	3	13	5	20
Structural Pest Control	17	1	—	9	2	5
Government	121	11	8	29	5	42
Unspecified	72	4	8	28	8	16
TOTAL	1400	240	69	430	108	371

Source: California Department of Public Health 1967, 31.

Fig. 3.2. Numbers of occupational diseases attributed to pesticides and other agricultural chemicals as reported by the California Department of Public Health in 1967. *Map drawn by Carol Kalt and Caroline Holsted.*

Within the general term *agricultural* there is a subtle distinction with important policy and political implications. "Pest control" refers to the actual preparation and application of the chemicals, commonly referred to as mixer/loader/applicator activities and usually performed by professionals. The "farms" category, constituting a full 47 percent of all statewide injuries, refers to general farmwork, such as pickers being exposed to residues in still highly contaminated fields. This reflects a significant distinction in terms of the division of labor. Pesticide applicators were considered professionals. They had greater status and recognition, were trained and licensed to work with pesticides, and suffered fewer pesticide injuries. In contrast, general farm laborers were racially and ethnically distinct, were considered disposable, were not trained to work with pesticides, and had the least protection even though they represented, by far, the greatest number of individuals on a farm who had the greatest contact with residues (Pease et al. 1993, 27–30).

Pesticide injuries were concentrated in heavily agricultural counties (fig. 3.2). Los Angeles County, once a rich farming area, had the greatest number of reported injuries in 1967, with a total of 139. The next highest-ranking counties were Fresno (113), Kern (109), and Tulare (81) — the "Big Three." Other considerations besides total pesticide usage also influenced the nature and extent of injuries, such as cropping patterns. Even though the southern San Joaquin produced vast amounts of cotton, to which many gallons of DDT were applied, neither were responsible for many injuries since cotton is a highly mechanized crop. In contrast, fruit crops that are not mechanized, particularly crops like grapes, are responsible for many more injuries simply because workers have extensive contact with dense foliage, and it is the foliage that causes many poisonings (Pease et al. 1993, 23–26; Milby 1970, 1389–90). Other factors such as wind strength and direction can affect pesticide exposure by carrying pesticides to adjoining areas.

Regulators and Pesticides

Regulators who supported agribusiness insisted that growers cared about their workers. Then CDFA Director Fielder boasted that "through the years California farmers have supported legislation and regulations that provide the most comprehensive control over sale and use of pesticides of anywhere in the world. . . . Fortunately, agricultural producers share our concern and are most cooperative in the regulation and control of pesticide uses, and are strong proponents of 'safety first'" (Fielder 1970, 1337, 1340).[16] While it is true that California did have the most comprehensive program, it can hardly be said that growers supported those regulations or that they truly cared. Testimony by an extension entomologist demonstrates his allegiance to agribusiness and suspicion of the UFWOC:

> We have worked with applicators, chemical companies, agricultural commissioners, farming organizations, state and county health departments, individual farmers, highway patrol, California Department of Highways, state and local medical societies, Medic-Alert, and many others. At no time have we even been asked to work with the UFWOC. . . . Pamphlets in English and Spanish on safety have been available in all of our county extension offices and an extended effort has been made to contact the workers in the field. . . . Whenever cases of injury from pesticides are brought to our attention we try to find out the cause and see if we can do something to improve the situation. . . . Our relationship with those agencies who have the responsibility of enforcing laws and regulations pertaining to safety have been very close and we have found that they will act very decisively and quickly when laws pertaining to safety are broken. Also Dr. Bailey has worked with many physicians and has found those in the farming areas to be very much aware of the problems associated with and the diagnosis of pesticide poisoning.
>
> . . . With this effort and desire to improve the safety standards of this state, it causes me to wonder about some of the testimony given at the hearing. For example, all those who testified were from one locality, all were associated with grape harvest and those during the first day admitted that they were members of UFWOC. What is the significance of this? It would seem to me that if such carelessness existed throughout the state, as was implied, and if neither the medical profession nor the enforcement agencies were doing their job, we should have had testimony from other farming areas in the state or if this was only confined to grapes, at least we should have heard from grape field workers from other parts of the San Joaquin Valley or the rest of the state. (Swift 1970, 1546)

The regulator's statement exhibits fairly hostile feelings toward the UFWOC. He seeks to discredit UFWOC testimony, arguing that if pesticide poisoning was widespread, a more diverse set of workers would have testified. This completely ignores the marginality of most farmworkers at the time. It is highly unlikely that a monolingual Spanish-speaking farmworker would arrange to testify as an individual. As a group, however, workers have far more power and strength. Swift also claims close working relationships with interested parties, agencies, and nonfarmworkers, such as farmers, applicators, and the Highway Patrol. He mentions workers, but again he is referring to individual workers. He is not willing to interact with workers as a group or via their chosen organization. This is an example of how people are "regulated for" in opposition to workers' efforts to empower themselves in order to control the adverse circumstances surrounding them. Agribusiness knew that if workers organized effectively and demanded changes in pesticide use this militance could spread to other aspects of agribusiness. Regulators knew their objective interests lay with agribusiness and sought to protect grower hegemony.

Regulators were in the position of the "fox watching the hen." Due to their close relationship with growers, many rules were not enforced. Agencies usually sided with agribusiness, but not always. At times, regulators clamped down on issues of blatant public concern, or on growers who adopted unrealistic positions. Henry Voss, the current CDFA director, recently explained the agency's approach to enforcement, or the perceived lack of it. "You have to decide whether you're trying to build a record of catching people and fining people or whether you're trying to assure a safe use of chemicals. And if you're looking for a safe use of chemicals, then I think education and working with industry in the long term will be a lot more productive . . . than having stiff penalties" (Voss in Paddock 1990, A19).

In short, both agribusiness and pesticide regulators had a fairly similar position and set of attitudes towards pesticides. Agricultural chemicals presented only a minor set of problems (usually not having to do with workers but with other aspects of the environment), that supposedly could be handled in a rational and cautious way.

The UFWOC and Pesticides

Not surprisingly, the UFWOC had a very different perspective on pesticides. According to early union participants (Huerta 1991; E. Medina 1991; A. Medina 1991; Cohen 1991), pesticides were an issue from the start. People involved in farmwork recognized that pesticides, or *la medicina,* caused certain acute symptoms. Chronic problems were less understood. Those living in the area at the time tell of watching pesticide clouds roll over the landscape (Huerta 1991) or of applying sulfur without gloves and how it affected their skin (E. Medina 1991). Anecdotal knowledge was supplemented by systematic information provided by the union health clinic, where doctors and nurses learned the full extent of pesticide poisoning (Huerta 1991; Moses 1991).

Worker safety was the UFWOC's point of entry into pesticides. Given insufficient information, the absence of a regulatory framework, and the basic powerlessness of farmworkers, the UFWOC adopted a multipronged strategy to address the problem. Their objective was unionization in order to provide better wages, security, and working conditions, as well as to ensure the health and safety of field-workers. While fighting for this objective, they discovered that pesticides served as an important leverage against growers, by creating bad publicity for them. Poisoning already exploited and oppressed workers was a strategic representation, but it also served to attract the support of those who otherwise may not have supported the UFWOC (E. Medina 1991). Pesticides were both a demand and a tool in the struggle.

The centerpiece of the UFWOC strategy was the union contract. Only a contract could ensure safe working conditions because it was enforceable. The court system in the southern San Joaquin Valley, and particularly Kern County, was notorious for supporting growers' interests and could not be relied upon to interpret legal questions in favor of workers.[17] Nor could the legislative process be counted on, as rural legislators were disproportionately influential and attuned to agribusiness needs. Even if the legislature acted with good intent, the union knew enforcement would be negligible due to the lack of resources, the dispersed nature of agriculture, and the political realities. For these reasons, the contract was the instrument that was thought to provide the greatest power and protection to workers. Legislation and the courts were not abandoned; indeed, the UFWOC carefully exploited all possibilities while focusing on the contract. The struggle over pesticides could not be separated from the struggle for free and fair elections, since pesticides were seen as an important worker demand that the contract should address, similar to wages, health insurance, and hiring procedures.

But unlike wages, where the problem and remedies were identifiable, pesticides presented a far more complicated issue. Although individual workers had personal knowledge and experience with pesticide exposure, they lacked a forum by which they could realize the collective nature of the problem (Segur 1991). Before the clinic, workers felt they had little choice but to accept pesticides as an occupational hazard (E. Medina 1991; Segur 1991).

Marion Moses, a volunteer nurse, became particularly interested in pesticides, but could find only sparse medical and scientific information. With the support of Chavez and other union leaders, Moses assembled a group of knowledgeable individuals to serve as an advisory board to the Union, known as the Health and Safety Committee (A. Medina 1991; Moses 1991). The committee was comprised of a physician, a dentist, and an occupational health and safety specialist, Anastacio Medina (Moses and Padilla 1966). Their job was to build a database pertaining to all health and safety matters for the union. By 1967 the UFWOC knew it wanted to formulate a health and safety clause for the contract but lacked the necessary information. According to occupational health and safety specialist Anastacio Medina (1991), the union sent him pesticide studies, contract proposals, poisoning episodes, and other occupational health materials to review. In 1970 the committee ceased to exist because it was no longer needed. Its objective of educating the union had been met. Union members were proficient in health and safety issues, including pesticides, and the battle then shifted to the courts, to the boycott, and to negotiations.

A long term UFWOC agenda was ironed out in January 1968 at a union and California Rural Legal Assistance (CRLA) retreat. The CRLA, whose mission it was to provide legal services to the rural poor, could not file suits on behalf of itself, so farmworkers and the union were frequently its clients. The CRLA worked with the union, but there was tension between the two groups, not only because they claimed the same constituency (the rural poor), but also because of conflicts between the autonomy and the ambitions of each organization (Abascal 1991). Though the UFWOC had a dedicated legal staff, the CRLA was needed to deal with long-term legislative changes, such as banning DDT on the federal level and filing class action suits. Given limited resources, UFWOC attorneys had their hands full with contract negotiations, and with suing and defending themselves against local growers.

At the January meeting a set of critical issues were identified and the CRLA was charged with bringing about legal reform. Pesticides arose as a key problem facing workers, and Ralph Abascal, a CRLA lawyer, was assigned to work on the issue. At the same time, pesticides became more central to the union's struggle from that point on (UFWOC 1969d; Abascal 1991; Averbuck 1991).

Escalation of the pesticide campaign can be seen in several ways, including lawsuits, the boycott, the elevated role of pesticides in negotiations, and the contract. As previously mentioned, the UFWOC's struggle was not about better wages but about power. Only through a position of power could farmworkers attain better working conditions, wages, and opportunities. Clearly, farmworkers' position vis-à-vis pesticides was an intimate and vulnerable one. Although they were the "yellow canaries" for the environment as a whole, they were least able to marshal the necessary resources to protect themselves, their communities, the food supply, and the local environment.

Environmentalists and Pesticides

Although environmentalists are frequently associated with pesticide activism, they in fact had little to do with this struggle because of their positionality and the historical development of environmentalism. They approached pesticides from a totally different perspective, one that was not connected to agricultural production. Instead, their activism focused on other arenas of pesticide use, such as in national parks, attesting to the mainstream movement's concern with quality-of-life issues — issues in which they were not directly threatened. During this period conservationists were only beginning to consider pollution issues. The lack of concern on the part of mainstream environmental groups, and the outright opposition from some (Jukes 1971), reflects both the history of the larger environmental movement and the conservative tone of an agriculturally based region.

The locus of national environmental pesticide reform was the Environmental Defense Fund (EDF), and to a lesser extent, the Audubon Society (Clement 1972). EDF was born in New York in 1967 from a group of scientists, lawyers, and others interested in ecology (Rogers 1990). That year, Victor Yannacone, a brash young lawyer, sued the Suffolk County Mosquito Control Commission against their continued use of DDT. The case went so well that Yannacone and his partners began using litigation as a tool for protecting the environment (Rogers 1990, 53–59), a strategy known as "Sue the bastards!" (Graham 1990, 231). The EDF filed suits that banned DDT in Michigan, Wisconsin, and ultimately, nationally.[18]

The activist lawyers attempted to serve as the legal arm of the Audubon Society (Graham 1990, 226), which had earlier (1959) sought to stop the use of heptachlor in ant eradication efforts in the South (Clement 1972). The board approved the idea but could not support the lawyers' call for the removal of DDT because the board contained chemical company executives who opposed the move (Rogers 1990, 53).

> How conservative National Audubon's board could be at the time was shown by its reluctance to go on record against the use of DDT. Staff members since John Baker's day had been in the forefront of those clamoring to have the chemical banned, yet the board held back an official resolution for fear of offending certain well-to-do contributors who had interests in finance, industry, and agriculture and did not want to be part of what they considered a direct assault on corporate profits. (Graham 1990, 231–32)

Although the EDF was not adverse to working with industry (Rogers 1990, 63), they were far more radical than Audubon, which played the role of the "gray lady" of conservation (Graham 1990, 231). During the mid-1960s, Audubon membership grew tremendously as people were attracted to both conservation and environmental issues (Graham 1990, 228). Although Audubon benefited from their long history as a conservation force, this growth was partially attributable to their mainstream tactics and positions. Through moderation and a high level of credibility, they were able to explore pesticides through their magazine, *Audubon* (Graham 1990, 227), without ever questioning the exploitive and racist character of an agricultural system that promoted pesticide use.

Given the conservative nature of the San Joaquin Valley, it is not surprising that environmentalism was not widespread. There was, however, a Sierra Club. The Kern-Kaweah chapter was established in 1953, and Fresno had a Tehipite chapter. Both were heavily involved in conservation and preservation issues and were instrumental in providing an alternative set of uses and values to the traditional logging and mining of the Sierras (Sierra Club 1961). The emphases of the chapters were recreation and educating the public to the virtues of wilderness, particularly the Sierras. One possible reason the local club did not espouse a social justice orientation was the demographics of the group, coupled with the politics of an agricultural region. The membership roster of the 1960s contains no Spanish surnames, and the profiles of the membership indicate the majority were college-educated and professional individuals (Sierra Club 1957).

Interestingly, Jack Zaninovich, a large grower in the region, was a member. This is not contradictory, however, because the chapter did not address pollution or urban and social issues until the 1970s. In the late 1950s and early 1960s most people joined because they were interested in conservation.[19] The Kern-Kaweah newsletter, *The Road Runner*, did not feature a real discussion of pollution until May 1969. The publication's coverage of pesticides, which was minimal until the mid-1970s was confined to discussions of gardening with reduced pesticides (Sierra Club 1957; 1961; 1969; 1970, 6). This refusal to acknowledge pollution, and in particular pesticides, is fairly remarkable given their intensive use in the valley. It demonstrates how important positionality is both in defining an issue and in recognizing the political and environmental consequences of agribusiness hegemony.

Although the San Joaquin chapters were hesitant to address pesticides, the San Francisco Bay chapters were not. The Sierra Club's first pesticide action in California was to oppose the National Park Service's spraying of Tuolumne Meadows in Yosemite National Park (Siri 1979, 34). It was reluctant to challenge pesticides, partly because the membership did not feel well informed, preferring to leave such technical matters to the experts (Siri 1979, 34). It also had members who supported pesticide use, such as Thomas Jukes, a chemical company engineer who worked diligently on behalf of DDT (Jukes 1971). Feeling a formal position was necessary, the Sierra Club eventually fashioned a policy that opposed pesticide use in wilderness areas but did not advocate banning DDT until years later (Siri 1979, 35). This contradiction is a stark example of how narrowly mainstream environmentalists approached pesticides; their consciousness was limited to National Park land, and they ignored the environmental and human destruction going on in the larger community.

Subsequently, many environmentalists have become involved in pesticide matters and have been an important force in pressuring agri-business to consider alternatives to pesticides, such as integrated pest management (IPM), defined as "a strategy of pest containment which seeks to maximize natural control forces such as predators and para-sites, and to utilize other tactics only as needed and with a minimum of environmental disturbance. It is a concept, not a fixed technique" (Glass in Davis and McMurtry 1979, i). It includes mechanical and biological control, as well as cultural practices (Andres, Oatman, and Simpson 1979, 3; Bishop, David, and Watson 1979, 61– 66). IPM does not mean the abandonment of pesticides, only that they become one of several tools to combat any particular pest.

Pesticides are increasingly less effective, but their use continues to rise (Villarejo 1994). Greater exposure to a chemical promotes greater tolerance so that species develop an immunity over several generations. This was dramatically seen in a recent pest infestation in California's Imperial Valley (DeVoss 1987). Immunity is exacerbated by monocul-ture, the practice of cultivating a single species over a large area, which "eliminat[es] the mosaic of habitats which supported many predators and parasites and stabilized pest populations" (Andres, Oatman, and Simpson 1979, 1). Thus, monoculture and immunity both contrib-ute to ever increasing pesticide use, a cycle known as the "pesticide treadmill."

IPM is still in a fledgling state. Because each technique is applicable to only a limited number of pests, a great deal of ecological knowledge is necessary to develop an effective IPM plan. Unfortunately, few resources have been directed toward this research. The lack of IPM knowledge is a systemic problem, reflective of the priorities of agribusiness, extension, the universities, and farmers. While it may be tempting for the public to condemn farmers for not adopting alternative control methods, it is unrealistic to expect them to forsake pesticides when a more solid option is not available (Runsten 1991).

In the early 1960s IPM was practically unknown. There was sparse public awareness of pesticides, let alone a framework for dealing with occupational injuries. The UFWOC helped create public awareness of pesticides as a public health issue, and prompted the state to develop a regulatory framework and enforcement mechanism. The UFWOC in-creased public consciousness by testifying at hearings, filing lawsuits, linking pesticides to consumer residues and the environment via the boycott, and through their contract negotiations.

The Pesticide Campaign

In looking at how the UFWOC mobilized, linking the goal of unionization to the issue of pesticides, two distinct areas of activity can be identified: (1) lawsuits and administrative actions, and (2) the boycott, negotiations, and contracts. The legal undertakings were defensive actions intended both to harass and to impinge upon agribusiness as well as to achieve substantive improvements in worker and community exposure through pesticide reduction. The second category was geared toward mobilizing supporters, building a movement, and translating collective power into victories at the bargaining table.

Laws and Administrative Policies

The UFWOC was involved in a large number of lawsuits. Their legal activities can be divided into those providing services to workers, supporting the union's structure, engaging in legal defense, and improving labor law and working conditions (Alvarez 1973, 224). Pesticide reform is in the last group. Jerry Cohen, chief counsel for the union during the 1960s and 1970s, explained the obsessive litigation, particularly in terms of pesticides, as necessary for two reasons: (1) the union lacked an alternative due to the absence of a regulatory mechanism, and (2) suits became bargaining chips in negotiations with growers (1991).[20] Because there were so many demands and issues on each side, using lawsuits as bargaining chips was an important part of their strategy (Cohen 1991; Huerta 1991). Legal action went both ways, however, and growers sued the union rampantly, often for fabulous sums of money.[21]

At the heart of the UFWOC's pesticide lawsuit strategy was an effort to expand the rights and protection of workers and local residents. They knew pesticides poisoned workers, caused environmental degradation, and left residues on food. They wanted a union contract to combat clear-cut problems and achieve specific objectives. The UFWOC was not fighting bad policy or laws; there were no policies to fight. The issue had never come up, forcing activists to make a case against pesticides; therefore, growers did not consider pesticides a legitimate union concern, feeling it had only been raised to harass them (Wall 1969; *Pacific Business* 1971). The growers were partially correct in their belief that the union was capitalizing on pesticides. As pesticides became a liability for growers, the UFWOC fully exploited this vulnerability in order to enhance their position (see fig. 3.3).

Pesticides presented Chavez with an ideal organizing issue, one that would have both an external and internal impact (Averbuck 1991). Pesticides had an internal impact by providing an opportunity to organize workers through educating them as to their rights. Pesticides had an external impact on growers by instilling a great deal of fear.[22] Chavez realized the matter required careful handling. He wanted workers to have safe, union jobs, not to face unemployment in the grape industry. For this reason, he did not act as fast on the issue as other union leaders might have wished (Huerta 1991; Averbuck 1991).

The UFWOC filed two types of lawsuits against pesticides: (1) those seeking to change the conditions under which pesticides were used (procedural), and (2) those seeking to ban specific pesticides.

Procedural Lawsuits. One of the UFWOC's first pesticide lawsuits centered on access to application records.[23] In order to reduce pesticide exposure via the contract, the union needed detailed pesticide application information to enhance diagnosis as well as to facilitate the development of labor contract safeguards (UFWOC 1969f). Though the clinic was seeing numerous poisoning cases, they did not know which pesticides were responsible for which injuries, and neither field-workers nor the general public had access to those records.

Jerry Cohen asked to review the Kern County pesticide application records on August 20, 1968. After repeatedly denying him permission, the agricultural commissioner, Thomas Morley, contacted local professional sprayers who were required to submit such information, and together, they convinced a judge to issue a temporary restraining order against Cohen. The defendants acknowledged an uncertain legal basis for their request, but argued, "[S]urely it can harm no one to prevent this at least for the few days involved" (*Atwood Aviation v. Morley* 1968). The plaintiffs and their attorney, Stephen Wall, could not

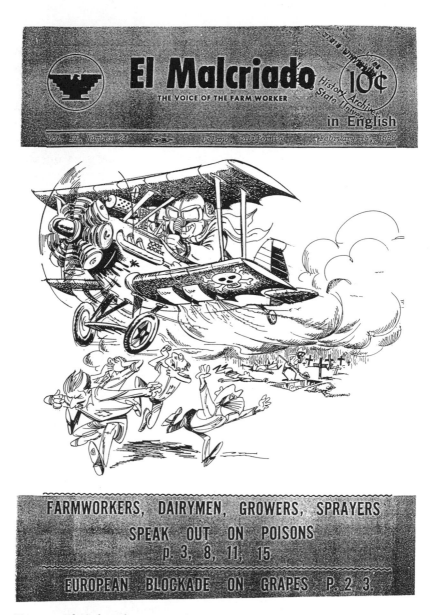

Fig. 3.3. *El Malcriado* cover, February 15, 1969. *United Farm Workers of America,* AFL-CIO *Archives, Walter P. Reuther Library, Wayne State University.*

conceive of why the union would need such information if not for harassment. "Obviously these people who are putting the pressure on Mr. Morley seek to use the information for their own purposes" (*Atwood Aviation v. Morley* 1968).

In October 1968 the UFWOC challenged the legality of the restraining order. They had hoped to avoid a lengthy factual disclosure by an appellate judge reversing the decision. The UFWOC argued that not only was the situation urgent, due to worker poisonings, but the judge was prejudiced, as indicated by his immediate signing of the restraining order. The appellate judge, however, did not feel the situation was urgent, thus forcing the UFWOC to take their case to the Superior Court. The case was scheduled for January 1969, but the UFWOC sought to settle out of court. They called for a detailed inventory of each pesticide application, including what was sprayed, when, and where, the amount, the crop, the wind conditions, the method of application, and who sprayed it. In addition, they requested three days notification before a poison was sprayed, with written warnings in both Spanish and English (UFWOC 1969f).

This may have been the most sweeping demand ever made in terms of pesticides. Especially noteworthy was that it extended disclosure from professional sprayers to all farmers who used injurious materials, thereby bringing an entirely unregulated set of applicators into the regulatory fold. In a letter to Stephen Wall, the plaintiffs' attorney, Cohen conveyed the union's demands and rationale.

> The most pressing problem which faces us as of now is the ever-increasing danger to farmworker health and safety which arises from the use of dangerous pesticides in the vineyards. The enclosed proposal is an initial step in insuring adequate protection to farmworkers. . . . [We] are attempting to obtain information not only from spray applicators who are required to maintain records with the Agricultural Commissioner, but also from growers who are not required to submit any information to the Agricultural Commissioner. The reasons for this are as follows: . . . As Mr. Griffin [a professional sprayer] stated to us, he has developed a certain expertise in the application of dangerous materials. This case will force him to disclose to the United Farm Workers Organizing Committee certain information concerning the use of pesticides. It is ironic that growers who do not possess the expertise which Mr. Griffin possesses do not have to disclose information to

the Agricultural Commissioner. We are fully aware that one possible result of the case will be the ever-increasing use by growers of their own equipment which would inevitably lessen business for more responsible applicators. Therefore, we are anxious to put covered spray applicators as well as non-covered growers under the terms of this agreement. Section 4 which requires growers to post written warnings in the fields where injurious materials have been applied is a minimum safety requirement which I am sure you will fully support in light of your expressed concern for the health and safety of agricultural workers. (Cohen 1969a)

Attorney Wall completely rejected the UFWOC's proposal.

It is obvious either that we completely failed to communicate or else you are trying to be funny. . . . It was my thought that if you would demonstrate at least some degree of reasonableness and good faith by not now insisting upon receiving the privileged information such as specific descriptions of properties and names of persons and companies, which incidentally could be useful to you only in contemplated activity such as filing nuisance law-suits for propaganda purposes related to your so-called table grape boycott, then perhaps this present litigation might be settled. . . . But here is what you came back with: You want the name of the grower, the name of the airplane pilot, the name of the material and the dosage used, the legal description of the property treated, and the exact date of the treatment, and so on. . . . These you intend to use in connection with your Delano Clinic or in negotia-tion of future contracts? (Wall 1969)

The UFWOC made a final overture to the growers before the trial date by inviting them to meet solely on pesticides. The letter, written by Cha-vez, stated that if the growers were not willing to talk, then the UFWOC would escalate the boycott, since their only recourse was to appeal to the "conscience of the American people" (Chavez 1969a). Parts of the letter, those stating Chavez's concern for the health and safety of work-ers, became famous throughout UFW literature.

There is one critical issue of such overriding importance that it demands immediate attention, even if other labor relations problems have to wait. I mean the harmful effects of spraying grapes with pesticides, or economic poisons, as they are called. We have recently become more aware of this problem through an increasing number of cases coming into our clinic. . . . We will not tolerate the systematic poisoning of our people. Even if we cannot get together on other problems, we will be damned — and we should be—if we will permit human beings to sustain permanent damage to their health from economic poisons. (Chavez 1969a)

The growers did not respond. The boycott escalated and the case went to trial before the Kern County Superior Court where Wall argued that the documents were protected as trade secrets. The UFWOC insisted they were public records and disclosure was in the public interest because of the hazardousness of pesticides (*Atwood Aviation v. Morley* 1969a, b). Although the judge concurred that the records were trade-secrets, the real question became, was it in the public interest to release the information? On this point, the judge issued a resounding "no" (*Atwood Aviation v. Morley* 1969c), as he did not see how the information could be of use to the UFWOC, and even if it was, he did not see it as the court's duty to assist in the matter.

> It is difficult to understand . . . how the information in these records would assist in such bargaining and further, even assuming that such information could be helpful, it does not appear to the court to be a proper function of this court to require the opening of these records for this purpose. . . . Such a policy is fully justified including the fact that requiring the disclosure of this information would seriously hamper the essential cooperation existing between all segments of the pesticide industry and the farmers on the one hand with commissioner on the other. (*Atwood Aviation v. Morley* 1969a, 9, 10)

The judge's opinion illustrates not only his identification with agribusiness but also the complete erasure of farmworkers from the public and state consciousness. Farmworkers were not even considered in "the essential cooperation between all segments of the pesticide industry!" (*Atwood Aviation v. Morley* 1969a, 10).

The UFWOC appealed the decision, but while on appeal a similar case was underway in Riverside County. Amalia Uribe, an eighteen-year-old Mexican immigrant, became ill while working in a field. Her doctor could not accurately diagnose the injury because of inadequate information concerning her exposure, and although the Riverside Agricultural Commissioner Robert Howie allowed Uribe to examine the annual summary report, it was entirely too general to assist in the diagnosis (*Uribe v. Howie* 1971). They needed the specific pesticide reports. The case went to trial on August 21, 1969. Uribe and the UFWOC seemed to have a solid case with the Bureau of Occupational

Disease testifying that it would be "extremely desirable" for farmworkers to have access to pesticide records because it was essential for diagnosis (*El Malcriado* 1969c, 7). Even the California attorney general intervened. Since at least one thousand Californians suffered pesticide illness in 1968, Charles O'Brien, chief deputy of the attorney general's office, felt the "life and death" of future Californians was at stake (Harner 1969, 137). Unfortunately, Judge Neblett ruled against disclosure. His decision was based on four separate grounds, but the key element was the status of the reports as trade secrets (*Uribe v. Howie* 1971).

The attorney general's office appealed the case, arguing that the reports were public records not trade secrets and that the public interest required disclosure. Judge Gardner of the Appellate Court agreed and overturned the previous decision. He argued the reports were not trade secrets and thus not protected from disclosure, but even if they were, the public interest was best served by disclosure.

> Even if the information in the spray reports does contain trade secrets, we believe that the public interest is far better served by disclosure than by the converse. . . . Against this must be measured the interest of the public in having access to the contents of the spray reports. There was testimony presented that the information contained in the reports is important to the study of the effect of pesticides on man.
>
> Moreover . . . the information in the reports would be most helpful to entomologists attempting to devise even more effective pesticide programs. The perfection of such programs would be of commercial benefit to the growers, who would be able to increase productivity and to the consumer, who would be able to obtain produce at reduced prices. These considerations far outweigh the interests of pesticide spray applicators in barring inspection of the spray reports by the public. (*Uribe v. Howie* 1971)[24]

Even though the judge finally acknowledged the public's right to such information, his perspective was, once again, aligned with the interests of growers and consumers. While the decision was contrary to the interests of agribusiness, the state was intervening in a way that ensured the industry's long-term viability with only minimal regard for the most impacted segment of the population — workers.

With the Riverside ruling, the UFWOC's appeal in Kern County was allowed to lapse (*Atwood Aviation v. Morley* 1971), and all pesticide reports became public documents.[25] This was one of the first cases in which the public acquired access to information on private production with immense social consequences. Right-to-know laws are considered essential to any environmental battle, yet it was not long ago that activists lacked these rights. This is a little known but important part of environmental history that not only demonstrates the power of agribusiness and the marginalization of farmworkers, but also how the union chose to intervene in the dominant power arrangements. The lawsuit put agribusiness on alert that the UFWOC was serious both about pesticides and about curbing their power. An editorial from the UFWOC's magazine, *El Malcriado,*[26] summarized their position.

> The public has a right to know what pesticides are being used on what food crops, in what amounts and strengths, at what time of the year. The public has a right to know the extent of industry testing of a new poison before it is approved for use, both for its effects on "pests" and side effects on other life, on the environment, on man himself. Only then can the public develop programs to protect itself, setting amounts of poisonous residues allowable on foods, regulating or banning the poisons, writing safety codes to protect workers involved in applying the poisons or working in proximity to them.
>
> As long as the present policy of secrecy is maintained, the government agencies will remain servants of the oil, chemical and agribusiness industries, profits will take precedence over public safety, and America's food supply will be subject to increasing contamination and poisoning. It's time to end this horror story and take control of the poisons. (*El Malcriado* 1969d, 4)

Administrative Actions and Lawsuits to Ban Pesticides. The UFWOC also filed a set of lawsuits aimed at banning particular pesticides (table 3.3). Case reconstruction was difficult because most had lapsed with little explanatory documentation in the court files. Even union members involved in the cases could not recall the outcomes. The goal of many of these suits was not only to create substantive changes in worker conditions through the elimination of certain hazardous substances but also to harass the opposition. Court action was seen as better than no action. The UFWOC, however, was aware of the court's

Table 3.3. Administrative Actions and Lawsuits Aimed at Banning Pesticides

Action/Case	Objective	Date	Venue	Outcome
Repeal DDT tolerance	Ban DDT	October 1969	FDA	No response
Request zero tolerance	Ban DDT	October 1969	HEW	Denied
Ponce v. Fielder et al.	Ban DDT plus 11 pesticides	1969	U.S. District Court Ninth Circuit	Lapsed
Ponce v. Fielder et al.	Ban DDT	1969	Superior Court of Sacramento	CDFA limited DDT on 47 crops
Solis and Torres v. Fielder	Ban organophosphates	1970	Superior Court of Fresno	Fielder began enforcing laws

Source: Compiled from Averbuck 1991; Getze 1969; Lopez et al. 1969b; *Ponce v. Fielder et al.* 1969a, b; *Ponce v. Fielder et al.* 1969a, b; and *Solis and Torres v. Fielder* 1970a, b.

limitations, particularly in rural California. Most cases lapsed either because the law was changed, the law was enforced, demands were met in the contract, or the union offered the withdrawal of a lawsuit as a concession to aid negotiations (Abascal 1991; Cohen 1991).

During this period, Rachel Carson's book *Silent Spring* made DDT highly visible by revealing how, as a persistent toxin, it accumulated and persisted in both the environment and animals, producing long-term consequences. The Environmental Defense Fund (EDF) was tackling DDT in the Midwest and along the East Coast, but California was slow to seriously oppose DDT, partly because of agribusiness power. Due to the severity of its health and environmental impacts, the UFWOC pursued its banning at both the federal and state levels.

In October 1969, the CRLA, charged with carrying out legislative reform on pesticides, requested on the behalf of six individuals and the EDF that the Food and Drug Administration (FDA) repeal the DDT tolerance on raw agricultural commodities (Lopez et al. 1969a). According to Ralph Abascal, the CRLA attorney who filed the case, the EDF was included to enhance credibility (Abascal 1991). It was uncertain how the FDA would respond to an administrative action undertaken by a group of marginalized, unknown persons that included Chicanas, mothers, and farmworkers. The participants were carefully chosen. Five of the six petitioners were nursing mothers, which was important because DDT accumulates in breast milk. Indeed, one petitioner found her breast milk contained .20 ppm of DDT. Given their nursing status, these women clearly were interested persons. Other claimants included a farmworker and two women married to farmworkers (Lopez et al. 1969a).

As anticipated, the FDA did not act on the petition, deciding to "defer consideration of the serious allegations that were made" (Lopez et al. 1969b). On October 31 the CRLA rebutted with a more forceful petition that was directed at the department of Health, Education, and Welfare (HEW), which had ultimate jurisdiction over the FDA. The request called for zero tolerance of DDT on all raw agricultural commodities, which was, in effect, asking for a ban on DDT (Lopez et al. 1969b). Just days earlier, Finch, then director of HEW, had banned cyclamates — not because they were a human carcinogen but because they were an animal carcinogen:

[L]et me emphasize in the strongest possible terms that we have no evidence at this point that cyclamates have indeed caused cancer in humans.

Thus, my decision to remove cyclamates from the list of approved substances in no sense should be interpreted as a "life-saving" or emergency measure. I have acted under the provisions of law because it is imperative to follow a prudent course in all matters concerning public health. (Lopez et al. 1969b)

Given DDT's carcinogenic nature, and Finch's emphasis on "prudence," it appeared the DDT ban would be approved. The case was significant because it could potentially unleash a flood of challenges to other pesticides (Green 1969). The situation was complicated, however, by the fact that Finch was under pressure to oppose the CRLA because then Governor Ronald Reagan and California Congressman George Murphy were waging a vendetta against it.[27]

Finch denied the CRLA's appeal. He reasoned that DDT was not a food additive (as were cyclamates) and therefore not subject to the Delaney Clause, which the CRLA had invoked. The CRLA then turned the case over to the EDF, who appealed the case to the United States Court of Appeals. This appeal led to a lengthy hearing before the United States Environmental Protection Agency (EPA), and eventually led to a national ban on DDT (Wurster 1991).

This case is instructive in several respects. First, the fact that Finch denied the appeal largely due to political pressure (despite the fact that society in general and farmworkers in particular were exposed to this carcinogen) attests to agribusiness's and the state's commitment to pesticides, and their power to stifle resistance. Pesticides, while an important issue in their own right, became a metaphor for the larger power struggle. That such a subaltern group as farmworkers had the audacity to challenge agribusiness's methods of production was inconceivable. It was perceived as a loss of control to a subordinate group. Farmworker powerlessness when confronting the entrenched power of dominant institutionalized forces prompted the UFWOC to pursue the paths of contract negotiations and the boycott in order to build public pressure and support. Increased public support aided their legal strategy.

Besides the FDA request, the UFWOC filed two lawsuits to ban DDT, one against the State of California and the federal government and the other to ban organophosphates in California only. David Averbuck, the

UFWOC attorney who filed the two DDT suits on behalf of Vicente Ponce, a Coachella grape picker, said they were filed because the growers refused to discuss pesticides. "The growers and sprayers have refused even to discuss the problem of the use of DDT and other economic poisons. . . . They haven't even answered our letters, even though the UFWOC has agreed to divorce the subject utterly from its fight for union recognition and collective bargaining" (Getze 1969).

The federal suit was a class action on behalf of all consumers, the general public, and farmworkers. The defendants included Jerry Fielder (director of CDFA), Robert Howie (Riverside Agricultural Commissioner), and numerous Riverside County agribusiness firms. The suit claimed the defendants had violated the civil rights of farmworkers and a Mexican treaty that protected migratory birds and mammals (50 Stat. 1311 in *Ponce v. Fielder et al.* 1969a). Because growers (and their regulators) would not discuss the possibility of pesticide reduction, and because Fielder and Howie were continuing to grant permits to recklessly spray DDT, the UFWOC had no alternative but to turn to the courts.

> [B]ecause of the failure of the Defendants JERRY FIELDER and ROBERT M. HOWIE, to control the users of economic poisons, Plaintiff is threatened with continued spraying by growers while working as a farm worker. That for years, the State of California has lost wildlife, natural resources and beauty because of the reckless disregard by Defendants in the control and use of the economic poison DDT.
>
> That the exact location of the vineyards owned by said Defendants and the dosage of application of DDT are in records held by Defendant ROBERT M. HOWIE, but said Agricultural Commissioner has refused and continues to refuse to show these records to the general public, and therefore description of the properties sprayed with DDT cannot be pleaded with greater specificity. That said Defendants have acted in flagrant disregard for the protection of human life and natural resources of Plaintiffs. (*Ponce v. Fielder et al.* 1969a)

This complaint, although an attempt to ban DDT, obviously resonates with the earlier lawsuit to disclose spraying records. In short, the UFWOC found a second way to attack the problem of closed spraying records, in conjunction with the problem posed by DDT itself. Although the complaint was subsequently amended to ban eleven additional pesticides,[28] the suit was allowed to lapse for several reasons. First, by June 1970 the UFWOC had begun winning contracts that through their health and safety clause banned many of the specified chemicals on union ranches. Second, by 1972 DDT was banned both in the state and nationally.

The state suit to ban DDT was identical to the federal one, except it was filed in the Superior Court of Sacramento (*Ponce v. Fielder* 1969a, b). No further action was taken after the initial filing. According to Averbuck, who filed the case, within seventy-two hours of filing, the CDFA had proposed limited reductions of DDT on forty-seven crops including "forage crops, fly control, control of pests of chicken, cattle, horses, swine, and turkeys, in dust form on any crop, and for common household use" (Gillam 1969). Averbuck was confident this was a direct response to the suit (1991).

Unfortunately, this was only a partial reduction, and it did not apply to produce, a primary path of exposure for workers. By December, the CDFA had proposed a more comprehensive phaseout of DDT, but Fielder rejected any suggestion that the action was related to the UFWOC's suit. Instead, he attributed it to research progress: "The University of California has confirmed that 'suitable substitutes' are now available for DDT and DDD on grapes, olives, walnuts, and cherries" (Gillam 1969).

Both the strategy of banning and the focus on DDT itself merit some elaboration, as they are important to understanding the complex relationship between issue identification, pollution control, and subalternity. Until fairly recently, the majority of U.S. pollution-control efforts have emphasized mitigating the resultant waste product or pollution. Much of the philosophy underlying policy is derived from our experience with smokestack pollution control. The phrase *pollution control* is indicative of a larger philosophical orientation that has been slow to recognize that all pollution must go somewhere: we can change its form and disposal site (land, air, or water), but it must go somewhere. Implicit in this approach is the belief that pollutants are safe as long as they are adequately controlled. Public faith in technology, ignorance of the biophysical impacts of pollution, and disregard of inconsequential populations, such as farmworkers, allowed regulators to believe pesticides, like DDT, could be safely handled. Moreover, even if there had been a concerted effort in the 1960s to develop real safety standards for the use of pesticides, to what extent would the needs of farmworkers have been taken into account? How would such regulations have been enforced? Who could have enforced them, given the local political economy? There was no mechanism, institution, or person in place to defend workers' rights.

For all of these reasons, the UFWOC sought a total ban on undesirable pesticides. This was essentially the only way of ensuring safe working (and community) conditions in terms of agricultural chemicals. The UFWOC's strategy of banning (like the EDF's) shifted the debate from pollution control to source reduction, which, as Barry Commoner (1990) persuasively argued, is the only real way of eliminating certain pollutants (as illustrated in the case of leaded gasoline). Banning eliminates the pollution problem and protects the most vulnerable who may fall beyond the purview of regulatory protection, no matter how well intentioned that protection may seem.

Also of significance was the focus on the pesticide DDT itself. Because of its very serious ecological problems, and because it was so widely and intensively used, it understandably and rightfully attracted the attention of not only Rachel Carson but of mainstream environmental groups as well as the UFWOC. Here was an issue upon which diverse populations could agree; yet, because of varying groups' different positions, it became a contradictory issue. Once DDT was banned, mainstream environmental groups retreated from the issue of pesticides for a number of years, thinking the problem was solved.

The demise of DDT, however, actually led to a different set of pesticide problems, especially the heavy use of organophosphates. Since the hallmark of DDT was its longevity, an alternative set of pesticides that rapidly lost their toxicity was sought. It was thought that organophosphates would solve the problem because they are acutely toxic for only a short period of time, causing less long-term ecological damage and less severe food residues. Acute worker exposure, however, actually increased. It rose because workers who came in direct contact with fields and produce after spraying were being exposed to a much more acute poison. Yet despite this alarming problem, environmental groups did not renew their interest in pesticides until the 1980s.

Faced with the growing problem of organophosphates, farmworkers Robert Solis and Lazaro Torres filed a suit to ban organophosphates in the Fresno Superior Court in June 1970 (*Solis and Torres v. Fielder* 1970b). Jerry Fielder of the CDFA was charged with not enforcing elements of the California Agricultural Code that would have protected them and other workers from potential harm. The California Agricultural Code charges the director of CDFA with controlling and regulating any pesticide injurious to the environment, humans, animals, or crops (Section 14001). After sufficient hearings and investigation, the director must then develop adequate regulations to address when, where, and how an injurious pesticide may be used, including the possibility of banning a pesticide if that is necessary to prevent injury (Sections 14005 and 14006). Although Fielder had classified some organophosphates as "injurious materials," many others, such as demeton, delnav, and dibrom, were not regulated (*Solis and Torres v. Fielder* 1970b, 2). Hence, the petition asked Fielder to begin enforcing the law by declaring all organophosphates to be injurious materials (*Solis and Torres v. Fielder* 1970b, 5). Once declared injurious, they could be fully regulated, thereby setting the stage for regulated use, limited use, or even a ban. In a surprise move, the judge issued the mandate that day, instructing Fielder to enforce the law immediately or show cause why he should not (*Solis and Torres v. Fielder* 1970a, 2).

In all of these legal actions we can see how pesticides assumed multiple meanings, as evidenced in their role in shaping oppressive conditions or in shaping the course of struggle. Pesticides were a very real problem and threat to farmworkers, rural communities, and the local environment, and because the UFWOC was interested in much more than just wages, pesticides inevitably became an issue. Pesticides, from the UFWOC's perspective, posed a moral, political, health, and ecological problem. But because pesticide use was embedded in a web of power relations, and because public consciousness was high, pesticides also became a multipronged tool to use against agribusiness on several levels. On one level, lawsuits were an extreme annoyance and could be a real form of harassment. Depending on the court process and the ultimate ruling, they could also be expensive. Most important, the political message contained within the legal action demanded a voice for farmworkers not only in production but in any other matter affecting their well-being. The days of complete agribusiness hegemony were numbered.

Conversely, lawsuits can potentially pose an obstacle to movement building. As a mobilization and empowerment strategy, legal action is today being critically reevaluated (Cole 1992). While, as we have seen, legal action can produce real reform and results, it is in many ways an elitist approach. By employing legal strategies, the subaltern (or any other disadvantaged group) surrender their power to lawyers. In mounting a movement for social change, activists must weigh the potential benefits of lawsuits against the power of mobilizing people themselves. The UFWOC never lost sight of this and was careful to balance legal action and mobilization efforts. Building a movement means working with and developing a core of committed individuals, a process achieved one-by-one and household-by-household. It is a long and tedious process to convince individuals to commit to *la causa,* and at times to experience serious hardship and self-sacrifice. During this period, the UFWOC built a phenomenal movement, and the issue of pesticides played a major role in shaping that movement.

The Boycott, Negotiations, and Contracts

The Boycott

Just as the UFWOC's pesticide litigation increased in 1968, so too did pesticide's role in the boycott. Marion Moses began a tour in 1968 to teach UFWOC organizers about pesticides (E. Medina 1991; UFWOC n.d. b) and initiated outreach to individuals and organizations sympathetic to the union's concern with "economic poisons." She targeted such activists as Ralph Nader (Moses 1968c), Charles Wurster of the Environmental Defense Fund (Moses 1968b), Tony Mazocchi of the Oil, Chemical, and Atomic Workers Union, and the Scientific Institute for Public Information (SIPI), headed by Barry Commoner (Moses 1968a).

Through outreach by Moses and other organizers, the UFWOC brought to the public's attention the problems associated with field work and pesticides. As one organizer explained, "now they had two messages with which to hook people: first, the exploitation of farmworkers in general, but if that did not appeal to them, they could then appeal to either their ecological concerns, or self-preservation" (E. Medina 1991). Though the UFWOC portrayed workers as dying in the fields (fig. 3.3), they carefully linked pesticides to consumer food residues

WARNING:

EATING GRAPES MAY BE HAZARDOUS TO YOUR HEALTH

POISON

NOT FOR INTERNAL USE

All California grapes are sprayed with poisonous pesticides. Neither washing nor cooking can completely destroy pesticide residues. As U.S. Senator Murphy recently testified in Congress, the following poisonous residues are found on this year's grape crop:

DDT	Parathion (nerve gas)
DDE, DDD	Sulfur
Aldrin	Kelthane
Dieldrin	Toxaphene
Endrin	See Congressional Record, 8/12/69

DO YOU KNOW THE DANGERS OF PESTICIDES?

Any pesticide residues are injurious to man. DDT, and related pesticides are chemical compounds which do not break down. They are stored in the cells of plants, animals, and humans.

The build-up of DDT has been scientifically connected to the death of fish, sterilization of birds, and cancer in mammals. Doctors and scientists are deeply concerned about the long-range effects of DDT on human beings, both on the living and on those yet to be born.

More than 100 million lbs. of pesticides are dumped on California fields every year. This year there were over 35,000 pesticide applications in the Delano table grape area alone.

Grape growers refuse to talk with the farm workers' union about protecting workers and consumers from pesticides.

PROTECT YOURSELF FROM THE DANGEROUS HIDDEN EFFECTS OF PESTICIDES!

Only a Union Contract Can Protect Farmworkers & Consumers From Dangers of POISONOUS PESTICIDES
DON'T EAT GRAPES

UFWOC
P.O. Box 130
Delano, Ca. 93215

Fig. 3.4. Pesticide warning prepared by the United Farm Workers Organizing Committee. *United Farm Workers of America, AFL-CIO Archives, Walter P. Reuther Library, Wayne State University.*

(fig. 3.4), since some were not sufficiently moved at the thought of worker exposure. By emphasizing their vulnerability, and that of their children, the UFWOC cast pesticides in a new light which allowed them to connect with a more powerful group — consumers.

The UFWOC ensured their organizers were equipped to convey the pesticide message. In addition to Moses' tour, the legal staff regularly disseminated pesticide updates (Legal Department 1968; Legal Office 1969; UFWOC 1969a). These information sheets included results of laboratory analyses of grape residues (Legal Office 1969), how many pounds of various chemicals were used in a given year (Farnsworth 1971), legal updates (Legal Department 1968), strategies and tactics for pressuring markets to remove grapes (Board Members 1969), and articles and stories highlighting the dangers of pesticides to consumers and workers (UFWOC 1969a and 1969e; UFWOC n.d., c and d; *Chicago Daily News* 1969; Farm Workers Action Committee n.d.; *Fresno Bee* 1969b; Green 1969; *Los Angeles Times* 1969; Taylor 1969a).

One collection of news excerpts, for example, carried the caption, "A strong farm workers union means cleaner healthier fruits and vegetables for *you* and *your* family!" (J. Brown n.d.). Another information sheet intended for public circulation bore the headline, "California grape workers are killed and maimed every year by the pesticides you are eating. DON'T EAT GRAPES" (UFWOC n.d., a). One leaflet, intended for boycotters, contained a story in which a government agency accused the agriculture department of not adequately protecting the public from pesticides. The UFWOC concluded, "This is all the more evidence why only union contracts can protect workers and consumers from pesticide poisoning. USE IT!" (*Los Angeles Times* 1969).

Of greater importance than the union's propaganda sheets were their strategy sheets. One board meeting agenda was entitled "Safeway Escalation–Possible Techniques" (Board Members 1969). The document lists methods for boycotters to pressure Safeway into not selling grapes. These techniques included the use of petitions, card mailings, picketing, shop-ins, balloon-ins, sit-ins, fasts, sanitary suits, phone harassment, and other strategies for applying high-level pressure to the Safeway corporation. Another option was to prepare a very strong pesticide leaflet, with a skull and crossbones, entitled "Choice Tidbits" — meaning stories of people who suffered from pesticide poisonings. The leaflet could be distributed in neighborhoods, stores, and newspapers. Other actions included testing local grapes for DDT residues and publicizing the results. Boycotters were urged to test Coachella Valley grapes because of the region's high DDT use. Finally, one could find a consumer (preferably a nursing mother) willing to sue a local market chain that sold grapes with pesticide residues. The instructions stated, "Find a local volunteer lawyer who will be willing to file the suit. When you find the hip lawyer and the hip consumer — call Delano for further information" (J. Brown 1969).

The UFWOC also made presentations to organizations interested in learning more about farmworkers and pesticides. Their newspaper, *El Malcriado*, carried a tremendous number of pesticide stories, especially in 1969. This diversity of tactics was one of the more brilliant aspects of the UFWOC's strategy. They offered something for everyone and for every pocketbook. That enabled them to build a large, broad-based movement. Each level of commitment was accompanied by its own method and degree of contribution. For those mildly concerned, they could boycott grapes. Those wanting to do slightly more could join a letter-writing campaign or picket a local market. Especially dedicated individuals could become organizers. Finally, for those with limited time, there always existed the option of simply donating money to *la causa*. With such wide-ranging options, the UFWOC built a coalition of individuals from all walks of life across the United States.

The boycott tactics of the UFWOC are perhaps the most familiar of the pesticide campaign. The boycott was supported by almost all organizations that could even remotely be labeled liberal. A high level of political agreement is not necessary to support the unionization of highly marginalized farmworkers, particularly when other social justice movements, such as Civil Rights and the War on Poverty, were underway. The UFWOC's success in spreading the word and gaining support was partly attributable to the strategic way it used culture, ethnic identity, and pesticides. By emphasizing the various identities of farmworkers and the different facets of the struggle (often in a skillful way), the UFWOC was able to build the image of an oppressed and exploited racial and ethnic minority struggling against ruthless and greedy Anglo growers.

Accordingly, their rhetoric at times emphasized the racist nature of this conflict that was causing the death of Chicano workers. This appealed to those concerned with Chicano empowerment. Other times, they stressed how the power of capitalism and the state served to oppress highly marginalized workers (see fig. 3.5), appealing to those on the left and to labor. By using rich cultural symbolism such as the image of revolutionary hero Emiliano Zapata (fig. 3.6), the UFWOC not only inspired farmworkers, it also drew other Chicanos/Mexicanos looking for an affirmation of their identity and those Anglos who wished to stand in solidarity with an oppressed cultural and ethnic group.

Together, this group of boycotting consumers, university activists, Chicanos, labor groups, and others concerned with social justice managed to apply enough pressure upon the state and agribusiness to begin negotiations with the UFWOC.

Negotiations

In January 1969 Chavez announced an escalation of the pesticide campaign as a result of growers' refusal to meet with the UFWOC (Chavez 1969a; *Fresno Bee* 1969a; UFWOC 1969d). The growers referred to this new phase as the UFWOC's "Rule or Ruin" strategy, in which the UFWOC intended to "acquaint the public with the problems raised by the wholesale use of economic poisons" (*The Packer* 1969, 22b). Because of mounting economic pressure, a few growers did respond to the UFWOC's invitation to talk, and secret negotiations were held in the spring of 1969. Significant obstacles precluded a resolution — these included the participating growers' fear of industry reprisals and their concerns over how the UFWOC could wage a partial boycott, encouraging the public to buy union grapes and boycott nonunion growers (Cohen 1969b; Hartmire 1969). Talks broke off, and the general boycott continued. On June 3, 1969, Chavez wrote a letter to all the growers, chiding them for not caring enough to discuss the problems of pesticides, health, and safety.

> Gentlemen, I fear you have missed the point. We wanted to discuss with you the use of *poison*: DDT, parathion, TEPP, dieldrin, etc., the use of nitrates as fertilizers, and even the side effects attached to the use of [the] plant hormone, gibbrellin. As producers of food you must be aware of your social responsibility to the workers and consumers to insure their health and safety.

DELANO, CALIFORNIA   VOL. III, No. 14, October 15 - 31, 1969

PESTICIDE RESEARCH

AND THE POLITICS OF POISONING FOR PROFITS

SEE EDITORIAL, PAGE 4

Fig. 3.5. *El Malcriado* cover, October 15, 1969. *United Farm Workers of America,* AFL-CIO *Archives, Walter P. Reuther Library, Wayne State University.*

Fig. 3.6. Ad for Zapata buttons. *United Farm Workers of America,* AFL-CIO *Archives, Walter P. Reuther Library, Wayne State University.*

Surely, California table grape growers are not so interested in profit from the sales of grapes that they would willfully do harm to unsuspecting workers and consumers. Surely, as members of the California Farm Bureau Federation, an organization whose primary goal seems to be the destruction of our Union, you have been officially informed of their request for a Statewide moratorium on the use of DDT and other crop chemicals that might prove harmful to consumers. Surely you have read in your trade journals of the scientific and medical research linking these economic poisons to the destruction of fish and wildlife, the pollution of water, and even to cancer. These and similar matters would have been on our agenda for the proposed meeting. What could have been the harm of such a private and frank discussion of how best we could promote good health, safety, a balanced ecology, and a clean environment in the production of table grapes? What could we as a union have personally gained by such a meeting? What as table grape growers would you have lost?

And what has been the result? Again, this grape season the indiscriminate use of DDT and another wholesale slug from the arsenal of economic poisons dumped on the grapes—enough poison to destroy the balance of nature for generations to come. The most efficient, inexpensive, and expedient way to produce the damn grape seems to be the only touchstone of morality in your industry. Our city water, our streams and rivers, our ocean, our atmosphere and environment, our fish and wildlife — indeed, our very health and well-being as consumers and workers seem to have no place in the grape market. (Chavez 1969b, emphasis in original)

This forceful letter generated some results. Approximately ten growers began negotiations aided by the Federal Mediation Service (Hartmire 1969). Talks began on June 13, 1969, and no sooner had they begun when non-negotiating growers, along with Governor Reagan and California Congressman George Murphy, began attacking both the union and the negotiations (Hartmire 1969). Talks lapsed on July 3, 1969. Many important issues were discussed including union recognition, wages, the hiring hall, the successor clause, and pesticides (UFWOC 1969c). The issue of pesticides was, perhaps, the central topic of discussion. Not only was the boycott generating negative pesticide publicity, but the union was making specific and unprecedented contractual demands on the issue. These two facts — negative publicity and contract demands — largely shaped the concerns and demands articulated by each side.

A major problem for growers centered around the question of how the UFWOC could differentiate union grapes from nonunion grapes in terms of the boycott. The growers correctly pointed out that, even if the boycott was called off, the public was still left with the image of all grapes being poisonous. The UFWOC's response was to declare union grapes as "clean" by using the union label as an indicator. This was not adequate, however, because as the mediator explained, by July 3, 1969, pesticides had already been applied to the coming fall crop. How could those grapes be declared clean (UFWOC 1969c, 5)? This was a serious problem that the UFWOC was never able to successfully resolve. It highlights the contradictions in a strategy that uses pesticides as both a demand and a weapon. Moreover, it reveals the problems inherent in waging an industry-wide campaign versus one aimed at individual growers. The UFWOC's willingness to declare grapes clean when they were not further illustrates their readiness to compromise on pesticide issues if that would facilitate the union's goal of securing a contract. This led many to believe that the UFWOC was simply exploiting pesticides as an issue, thereby eroding their moral authority. On the other hand, one could argue that this deception, lasting only one season, was a small price to pay in return for a strong contract that would offer far greater protection to workers, to consumers, and, ultimately, to the environment.

Another point of contention between growers and the UFWOC was how they defined the pesticide problem. Growers focused on consumer food residues that from their perspective were linked to negative publicity, "Kovakovich [a grower] wanted to make clear that their concern was regarding the public aspects of the pesticide program — 'We can set aside the affect on the worker' " (UFWOC 1969c, 2). The growers wanted the pesticide campaign stopped in order to save the good name of grapes. They agreed to abide by all federal and state laws regarding pesticides, and suggested that they unite and urge the government to better address the problem even if that entailed more stringent regulation.

In contrast, Dolores Huerta, lead union negotiator, insisted that the prime concern was the worker, and that the effect on workers could not be set aside (UFWOC 1969c, 2). She also rejected the suggestion of invoking the government, since it could not be relied upon to effectively protect workers from pesticides (UFWOC 1969c, 2), as evidenced by the federal government's initial refusal to ban DDT and the CDFA's reluctance to enforce laws unless threatened. Relatedly, the growers were simply not willing to concede that pesticides were an arena open to worker control. Pesticides were an issue only to the extent that they generated negative publicity and to the extent that growers were willing or not willing to follow existing laws. Nonetheless, Cohen insisted that pesticide management should be an area of joint responsibility, both because of regulatory shortcomings and, as Chavez had eloquently stated, because pesticides were part of working conditions that were subject to contractual control.

Each side's contractual proposals were worlds apart in many regards, but one of the biggest chasms was over pesticides. The growers' proposal stated that "the Union agrees that it will not harass any Employer regarding the use of pesticides as long as the Employer agrees to abide by the regulations heretofore referred to. The Union agrees that it will not embark upon any program regarding pesticides that can in any way be detrimental or harmful to the Industry in which the Employer belongs" (Growers 1969). Chavez interpreted this as an effort to muzzle the union, and insisted that any contract would apply to individual growers and not to the entire industry. "On the question of pesticides we quite frankly don't want to compromise when the health and safety of the workers (and consumers) are at stake. If non-union grape growers continue to use pesticides in a dangerous manner, the union will continue to publicize the fact" (Hartmire 1969).

This, again, suggests how pesticides became a double-edged sword. Negative publicity was one of the UFWOC's strongest weapons, and they rejected any proposal intended to silence them on the issue. At one point the UFWOC offered to suspend the pesticide campaign in exchange for an acceptable contract; the growers rejected this offer. The UFWOC figured that if an acceptable contract was signed, it would inevitably contain strong pesticide language and would protect workers (Cohen 1969d). Thus, the UFWOC would forfeit the negative publicity to reach their contract objective.

After negotiations collapsed, the rhetoric and aggressiveness of each side escalated. The growers hired the public relations firm of Whitaker and Baxter to counter the negative publicity of the boycott (Taylor 1969b).[29]

In August 1969 a series of hearings on the status of migratory workers was held in Washington, D.C. Senator Walter Mondale of Minnesota was instrumental in coordinating hearings entitled "Migrant and Seasonal Farmworker Powerlessness." Three days were devoted to the topic of pesticides and farmworkers, handing the UFWOC a national forum from which to publicize their struggle. Being the talented strategists they were, the UFWOC seized the moment by describing in detail how many chemicals were used in California, the extent of pesticide poisoning, what happened to injured workers, the degree to which the growers controlled the courts, the union's proposed solutions, and growers' refusal to negotiate (Cohen 1969c; United States Congress 1970). This was an important step in building public awareness and support.

Contracts

While the hearings were being conducted, Chavez appealed again to growers by saying that the UFWOC was willing to reconsider wage, but not health and safety, demands (*El Malcriado* 1969a). As the strategy of the growers' public relations firm stressed no compromise, the growers took the offensive, stressing consumer rights and how the union was denying the public their freedom of choice (Consumers' Rights Committee 1969). An *El Malcriado* editorial characterized growers' latest move as "a new campaign of smear and insinuation, implying that there is no danger from pesticides and that the union's concern over pesticides is a hoax; insinuating that the union is embarking on a campaign of arson and violence to terrorize rural California; and of course assuring America that there is no strike, and no 'real' farm workers are members of the Union" (*El Malcriado* 1969b). Despite this "fight to the bitter end" mentality, one wine grape grower signed. Wine grape growers had signed in the past, but the Perelli-Minetti and Sons contract, signed September 18, 1969, was the first contract to contain the historic health and safety clause. Previous contracts had elements of the new health and safety clause, but none were as comprehensive as the Perelli-Minetti contract. It provided for a health and safety committee, comprised of an equal number of union and ranch representatives who would advise and be informed on all pesticide matters. In addition, it prohibited the use of DDT, aldrin, dieldrin, endrin, and it restricted the use of chlorinated hydrocarbons. A cholinesterase test was also required whenever organophosphates were used.[30]

This was the first contract in which growers recognized the union's right to participate in pesticide regulation. Opponents and some supporters considered the union unreasonable in their pesticide demands. A manager with Freshpict commented on the pesticide provisions.

> Then there's the insecticide control clause. The UFWOC health and safety committee has the right to determine what insecticides will be used, where and for what purpose. . . . You just can't have a committee that is emotionally involved determine that. It is not qualified. Those decisions should be made by experts to protect the workers and if regulations are not strong enough, the laws should be changed. . . . Health and safety committees are fine, and most unions have them. *But their job is to make sure state and federal laws are upheld.* If the employer is not adhering to regulations, the committee has the right to make the company abide by legal requirements. (Arnold in *Pacific Business*, 1971, 39, emphasis added)

On the surface Arnold's suggestion of changing the law reflects an un-
familiarity with both fieldwork and agribusiness politics. Farmworkers
could not realistically hope for effective pesticide regulation because
agribusiness controlled the courts and legislature.

Far more revealing is how this excerpt illuminates prevailing attitudes towards science, nature, and environmental regulation — a topic
that is a rallying point for the contemporary environmental-justice
movement. The belief that health and safety regulations are the province of experts indicates the extent to which policy and management
are rife with rationality and modernity. The notion that those who are
most affected and emotionally involved (in this case farmworkers; in
others, women, native people, and children) are not qualified to determine what are appropriate working conditions underscores the elitism
and exclusionary practices of conventional environmental and occupational regulations. It also, of course, denies the validity of local knowledge, or the insights that farmworkers bring to the hazards of agricultural production. This is, again, a clear example of how environmental
regulatory practices rendered farmworkers invisible. Further, because
mainstream unions had all but surrendered their voice in management
decisions, content to ensure compliance with existing laws, it seemed
all the more radical that a subaltern group, like farmworkers, would
demand such rights. The UFWOC had taught workers who were emotionally involved all about pesticides. This was crucial to empowering
workers by allowing them to participate in ensuring their own safety.

The contrast between this strategy of worker organizing and that of
legal intervention should be apparent. While one set of actions rests
with lawyers, the other seeks to create the conditions whereby the
worker is able to exercise his or her voice. The process of producing
those conditions is twofold, not only must the power relation be altered
(by building a movement), but the worker must be ready to assume
leadership and responsibility, which usually is the end product of intensive political and personal development.[31]

Although the Perelli-Minetti contract was an important victory,
the wine grape growers were not the prize; table grape growers were.
The boycott continued full strength through the winter of 1970. That
spring, the UFWOC tasted their first major victory with Lionel Steinberg and David Freedman of the Coachella Valley. The contract, signed

on March 31, 1970, represented a more sophisticated version of the Perelli-Minetti contract. After the signing of the Wonder Palms Ranch contract, as Steinberg and Freedman's operation was called, others began signing as the economic pressure grew (Girard 1970). In mid-July a large group of Delano area growers began serious negotiations and on the 29th twenty-six major growers signed. It was an historic occasion with more than eight hundred people watching. This was the union's real victory. Although from 25 to 30 percent of the grape crop was not yet covered, it was only a matter of time. The holdouts were mostly in northern Tulare County, as well as Fresno and Lodi (Girard 1970). Southern San Joaquin growers, their staunchest opponents, had signed.

The workers actually won only a five-cent increase in their hourly wage, which rose from $1.75 to $1.80, while their box incentive pay declined from $.25 to $.20. The higher base wage was intended to assist workers who were not superb pickers, and annual wage increases were scheduled throughout the three year contract. The real gains were in terms of benefits and rights. For each hour worked, the grower contributed $.10 to the Kennedy health and welfare program, and $.02 to the social development fund. Other changes associated with unionization were seniority, the right to be excused for union business, camp housing, job security, leaves of absence, and vacation pay. Most importantly, the union had the right to represent workers in the grievance process around issues of hiring, discharging, disciplining, and accessing records. For their part, the union was prohibited from striking. The substance and context of the contract provisions underscore how pesticides, as an environmental issue, were comparable to other equally important problems, such as housing, wages, and job security, by their incorporation into the contract. Since most facets of farmworkers' lives were shaped by inequality and powerlessness, unionization and the contract opened the door to more power and dignity, including a reduced vulnerability to pesticides.

The health and safety clause represented a somewhat unique set of rights. It sought to protect workers from pesticide abuses, provide access to information, give workers a voice in pesticide management, protect workers who disagreed with management, and guarantee workers the right to refuse work considered dangerous.

Section 18. Health and Safety

Company and the United Farm Workers Organizing Committee, AFL-CIO recognize the need to protect and conserve human life, water, soil and vegetation. Economic poisons, when used incorrectly by a grower in agriculture in any crop, create grave dangers to farmworkers and to consumers, disrupt the earth's ecology and do not properly serve the farmers. In the hope of developing, with the help of Federal, State and University consultants, new, imaginative and creative approaches to the problem of conserving our natural resources, and in hope of taking progressive steps to protect the health of farm workers, and consumers, Company and Union agree that the subject of economic poisons is a necessary and desirable subject for this collective bargaining agreement. Company and Union agree as follows:

A. Union shall cause to be formed a Health and Safety Committee (the "Committee") comprised of workers' representatives. Members of the Committee shall have free access to all records concerning the use of economic poisons. The Committee shall participate in the formulation of rules and practices relating to the health and safety of workers including, but not limited to, the following: use of economic poisons; the use of garments, materials, tools and equipment as they may affect the health and safety of the workers; and sanitation conditions.

B. DDT, ALDRIN, DIELDRIN, ENDRIN, PARATHION, TEPP and other economic poisons which are extremely dangerous to farm workers, consumers and the environment, shall not be used.

C. The Committee shall approve the use of organophosphates. Company will notify Committee at least seven (7) days prior to the application of organophosphate material. Such notice shall contain the information set forth in paragraph D, below. The Committee shall determine the length of time during which farm workers will not be permitted to enter a sprayed field following the application of an organophosphate pesticide. One baseline cholinesterase test and other additional tests shall be taken at the expense of Company when organophosphates are used. The results of said tests shall be given to Committee immediately, and, if requested, to an authorized Union representative.

D. The following records shall be kept and made available to the Committee and to any other authorized Union representative:

1. A plan showing the size and location of fields and a list of the crops or plants being grown.

2. Pesticides and economic poisons used including brand names plus active ingredients, registration number on the label and manufacturer's batch

or lot number. (a) Dates and time applied or to be applied (b) Location of crops or plants treated or to be treated (c) Amount of each application (d) Formula (e) Method of application (f) Person who applied the pesticide (g) Date of harvest

E. No worker under this agreement will be required to work when in good faith he believes that to do so would immediately endanger his health or safety.

F. There shall be adequate toilet facilities, separate for men and women in the field readily accessible to workers, that will be maintained at the ratio of one for every forty workers or fraction thereof.

G. Each place where there is work being performed shall be provided with suitable, cool, potable, drinking water convenient to workers. Individual paper drinking cups shall be provided.

H. Workers will have two (2) rest periods of ten (10) minutes which insofar as practical shall be in the middle of each work period.

I. Tools and equipment and protective garments necessary to perform the work and/or to safeguard the health of or to prevent injury to a worker's person shall be provided, maintained and paid for by company, such as, but not limited to: grape knives, rain gear, gloves, pruning shears, and umbrella for tractor drives. Workers shall be responsible for returning all such equipment that was checked out to them, but shall not be responsible for breakage.

J. Adequate first aid supplies shall be provided and kept in clean and sanitary dust proof containers. (Chavez and Steinberg 1970, emphasis in original)

This new contract provided significantly more rights and opportunities to participate in meaningful decision making than the Perelli-Minetti contract. The clause differed structurally in that the preamble placed pesticides within the context of natural resources, merged the sanitation clause with health and safety, thus reflecting the attitude that pesticides were closely related to sanitation (Huerta 1991; A. Medina 1991; E. Medina 1991).

A few provisions were far reaching. For example, the health and safety committee was composed solely of persons of the union's choice, not the company's. Previously, the committee had advised in reentry decisions, now they determined reentry periods. This was critical because premature reentry was a primary means of poisoning. The contract could not prevent poisoning, as much was still unknown, but it ensured decisions were based on the best available information and workers' interests were fully considered. The contract protected workers' right to refuse dangerous work, an important victory since fear of job loss was a major impediment to challenging unsafe conditions.

Other provisions pertained directly to ranch pesticide use. Parathion and TEPP were banned in addition to DDT, aldrin, dieldrin, and endrin, and the union reserved the right to ban future pesticides. When organophosphates were applied, the company was required to give the committee seven days' notice instead of the previous "as soon as possible." Finally, the company was required to provide adequate first aid, tools, and equipment that workers needed, as well as items that made the job more tolerable, such as rain gear and umbrellas for tractor drivers. In addition to increased protections and rights, workers also had a greater responsibility to ensure the safe, and increasingly limited, use of pesticides. Contracts varied slightly depending on the crop. For example, lettuce contracts prohibited DDD and the herbicides 2,4-D and 2,4,5-T (Dalzell and Teller 1973). Despite these variations, most 1970 and 1973 contracts contained similar provisions.

Obviously, this was an unprecedented achievement that placed farmworkers in a somewhat more equal relationship. It has been suggested that the union's accomplishments were not sufficiently meaningful because they did not create pesticide legislation (Taylor 1991). This raises an important question as to the efficacy of the union's strategy. If a worker was not under a union contract, he or she was not protected (although many reforms were subsequently adopted by nonunion ranches, if only to avoid the threat of unionization). On the other hand, had they implemented legislative changes, the problem of enforcement would still exist. Filing a complaint with the county agricultural commissioner rarely brought results.[32] Though many contract stipulations were not followed (Cohen 1991), the contract did provide a mechanism for dealing with them through dispute resolution, arbitration, and the collective power of organized workers.

The UFWOC's Legacy and Contemporary Field Conditions

The UFWOC, one of the most important forces for change to ever hit California agriculture, has left a mixed legacy. On one level, the UFWOC was ultimately responsible for breaking the chains under which growers had long held California farmworkers, and set in motion the wheels of both social and environmental change. We are finally beginning to reap the benefits of the UFWOC's efforts to raise both the public's and the growers' consciousness of the consequences of pesticides. Growers are exploring less chemically intensive farming systems (DeVoss 1987; Corwin 1989; LaGanga 1989; Sector 1990), and California pesticide regulation has finally been shifted to the relatively new CAL-EPA (California Environmental Protection Agency 1992). Reentry standards have been instituted, and the University of California claims a commitment to sustainable agriculture in their research and extension activities (Lyons and Zalon 1990). The UFWOC was the first to open the door for this change.

Despite these developments the UFWOC was unable to achieve lasting changes in fieldwork. Due to the antilabor position adopted by both the state and federal governments, the increasing internationalization of the global economy, and the declining power of the UFW itself, field conditions today have regressed over the past twenty years. In 1973 the Teamsters, who have a history of trying to undercut agricultural organizing initiatives, began competing with the UFWOC to represent farmworkers.[33] Growers, increasingly unhappy with the UFWOC because of their inability to effectively administer a union, openly turned to the Teamsters who epitomized traditional labor and were far less militant than the UFWOC. While willing to pursue conventional union demands over wages and seniority, they were not committed to pursuing workers' rights, participation, and empowerment (Taylor 1975; Levy 1975). Nor did their membership include social justice advocates, Chicano activists, and clergy — all of whom made it quite difficult for growers to deal with the UFWOC. By 1975 many growers had made a conscious decision to disengage themselves from the UFW however they could (Villarejo 1991a). Due to Teamsters' aggressiveness, growers' contempt for the UFW, poor performance (in particular the inability to make the transformation from a social movement to a functioning union), and increased immigration, the UFW started losing contracts. The decline began in 1975 and continued until 1994.

As of 1986 only 10 percent of the work force was unionized (Martin, Vaupel, and Egan 1986, 11). Throughout the 1980s the UFW existed as a political organization but ceased to exist as a union organizing workers. One reason for the change in strategy was that the California Agricultural Relations Board was so proagribusiness that organizing was futile since elections and other prounion activities would be challenged and subverted. Instead, the UFW continued to pursue the boycott, hoping it would work once again (C. Chavez 1991, 1989b; Campbell 1990; Forter 1989; Otten 1989a; Pandol 1989; Connell 1984). It seems, however, that it had lost much of its shock value.

Public support for the UFW also dwindled because some have felt the union was exploiting pesticide abuses (Tatarian 1989; Runsten 1991), as demonstrated in its focus on consumer residues — a minor nuisance compared to worker exposure (Moses 1991).[34] A final episode that made many question the UFW's motives was the McFarland cancer cluster, which emerged in the early 1980s in southern San Joaquin (R. Taylor 1987; Scott 1988). Some felt the UFW tried to cash in on the cancer cluster publicity by depicting it in their video, *The Wrath of Grapes* (Connell 1987; C. Chavez 1989a; Forter 1989; Otten 1989b; Roderick 1989).

In accounting for the downward spiral of farmworker organizing, however, any shortcomings of the UFW are far outweighed by the processes of internationalization. Economic integration has resulted in greater competition with Mexican producers, exerting a continual downward pressure on California farm wages. Throughout the 1980s, due to the debt crisis and civil strife in Mexico and Central America, there was a continuous surplus of farm laborers. Not only are many of these workers undocumented, but a significant number are indigenous people who speak neither Spanish nor English. Some critics have charged that the UFW still identifies itself primarily as a Chicano union when, in reality, most farmworkers are no longer Chicano but Mexticos (Zabin et al. 1993), Oaxaquenos, and Central Americans, requiring a new organizing strategy. This new generation of highly vulnerable farmworkers is indeed facing oppressive conditions, but there are signs of growing activism and organization.[35]

In June 1993 the UFW was faced with the sudden and tragic death of Cesar Chavez. This terrible loss has also presented a new set of challenges to the union (Proffitt 1993). Arturo Rodriguez, Chavez's son-in-law, is now president. He is committed to organizing once again. Reminiscent of a similar action twenty-eight years ago, the UFW led ten thousand on a march from Delano to Sacramento in April 1994 to signify their return to the fields. In addition to organizing and holding ranch elections, the UFW is now offering union membership to any farmworker who would like to join in order to take advantage of union benefits and services (Proffitt 1993). It is not, however, this recent innovation that appears most promising. Instead, it seems the ranch organizing itself is headed in the right direction since the UFW has won four elections as of the spring of 1995 (UFW 1995; Arax 1994). Only time will tell how the organizing will proceed.

The ambiguity of the UFWOC's pesticide campaign is perhaps a common feature of subaltern environmental struggles. For poor people, environmental problems and struggles do not exist by themselves. If they did, it would be easy to identify, analyze, and solve the problem. But as can be seen, farmworkers did not encounter pesticides in the abstract. Instead, those experiences were shaped by power and economic relations that served not only to expose workers to hazards but to present them with a limited range of options to effect change. Because of their marginality, the UFWOC had little choice but to use pesticides as both a demand and a weapon.

Although during the period under investigation, agribusiness insisted the UFWOC's campaign was a hoax, that simply was not true. If the UFWOC wanted solely to exploit the issue they would have spent all their energies on the boycott and negative publicity, the strategies that ultimately brought the growers to the table. The UFWOC never hesitated to publicize growers' disregard for workers and pesticides. If exploitation had been their sole objective, however, they would not have developed such an elaborate health and safety clause or refused to negotiate on pesticides. Instead, the UFWOC would have suggested a more simple health and safety clause, similar to the one put forth by the Teamsters.[36]

The pesticide campaign also demonstrates the fundamental connections between the environment, economic activity, social relations, and material well-being. The process of transforming nature in the production of food is both an environmental and economic activity. It is the nature of this production system, in conjunction with uneven international development and racism, to produce subaltern communities who are heavily impacted by pesticides but who have little faith in pursuing established channels. Farmworkers' relationship, or position, to pesticides is obviously an intimate one of extreme vulnerability, both physically and socially, quite different from that of mainstream environmentalists. Therefore, because of their different positions, subaltern and environmental groups do not attempt to solve environmental problems in the same way. Pesticide issues are only a part of the UFWOC's larger struggle to gain more control for members over their lives — socially, economically, and environmentally. Finally, while these characteristics and patterns may be common to all subaltern struggles, they are played out somewhat differently in resource-based communities, as the next chapter demonstrates.

4

Ganados del Valle:
Resource Management as Contested Terrain

De la tierra fui formada
La tierra me da de comer
La tierra me ha sostenido
Y el fin yo tierra he de ser

New Mexican Proverb[1]

The scholarship and political activism of the environmental justice movement have focused on documenting and remedying environmental racism largely within the context of urban land use and pollution issues. While resource management is a prominent theme in many Third World struggles, natural resource use has not attracted the same attention among marginal U.S. activists. In fact, it is routinely dismissed as a mainstream concern, since middle-class environmentalists have articulated wilderness and the preservation of nonhuman environments in an elitist fashion. If these issues are approached from a subaltern perspective, however, it becomes vividly apparent that resource use is but another lens through which to view inequality. Moreover, investigating natural resource use illuminates the systematic way in which environmental relations are structured by various forms of power — in the case of Ganados, by economic marginalization and racism. At the same time, a significant portion of this conflict is also over identity and meaning.

Ganados del Valle is a community development group trying to

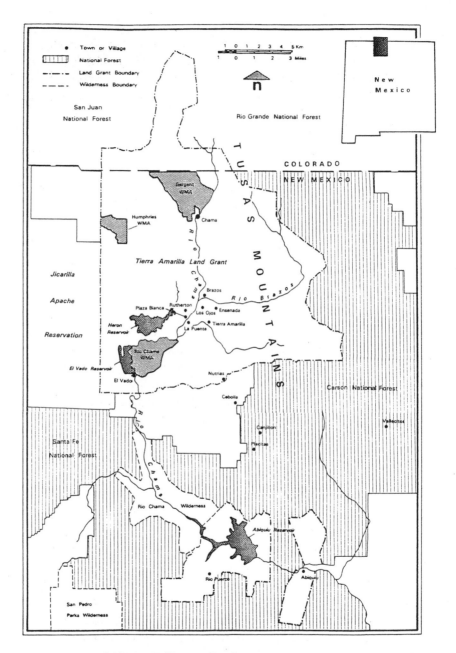

Fig. 4.1. Map of Chama Valley, Rio Arriba County, New Mexico. *Drawn by Tom Do, adapted from a map by Duane Griffin.*

forge a culturally and ecologically viable set of economic activities in a region suffering from sparse economic development and racially defined social groups. Although a good number of Hispanos, as the local Spanish-speaking population is known,[2] have achieved prominence in the state, many northern Hispanos still live in deep poverty. Although their culture is celebrated in local architecture, restaurants, and Christmas rituals, for many — particularly the monolingual Spanish-speaking with limited education who live in isolated rural areas — life can be a constant struggle.

Juxtaposed against this population has been a steady influx of wealthy and middle-class Anglos who are changing the character of northern New Mexico. The incoming Anglo population is largely urban, educated, and attracted to mainstream environmental values that often conflict with the values and needs of poor rural Hispanos (L. Taylor 1988).

Ganados is comprised of a group of low-income Hispano households trying to create a vertically integrated series of businesses built on sheep, wool, and fine woven products. Due to a lack of accessible grazing land, Ganados has sought to graze in a highly controlled manner on local wildlife lands, known as Wildlife Management Areas (WMAS), originally intended for elk (fig. 4.1). The state resource agency responsible for the WMAS, the New Mexico Department of Game and Fish (NMDGF), hunters, and local environmentalists have opposed Ganados' initiatives, arguing that the land is for wildlife, specifically for elk and elk hunting. The conflict reveals not only how a group's social and ideological position contributes to specific understandings of environmentalism, but also how differential power allows certain conceptions of resource use to become hegemonic, thereby masking any inequities they may perpetuate.

Though Hispanos can be conceptualized as subaltern, the dominant-subordinate relations are not as firmly drawn as in the case of farmworkers. One reason for the blurred lines is what Stuart Hall (1992) has noted as the element of desire, which creates far more complex and ambiguous categories and identities. Desire may be expressed through rendering a group as exotic, appropriating elements of their culture, or by imitating them. In this case, structural inequality is somewhat masked because the dominant group has interpreted aspects of Hispano life and culture in a positive light. Nevertheless, it is clear that the Anglo population is far more powerful, allowing their vision of land and resource use, whether it be a Taos ski resort or a wilderness preserve, to prevail over that of rural Hispanos.

Being subaltern includes lack of voice (Spivak 1988), or at best, a voice that is barely audible. Woods (1993), in a highly original study, has sought to uncover the voices of poor, rural, southern blacks, in terms of their vision of regional planning, through a textual analysis of the blues. Despite such methodological innovations, we rarely have a clear grasp of any subaltern group's vision of resource use, precisely because their peripheral position prevents their ideas from reaching a larger audience. Moments of mobilization and uprising are then openings that allow us to interrogate those visions, to discern their various components, to analyze what they are about, and to explore what they mean to the subaltern.

Ganados' grazing conflict is one such instance. Although this story centers on grazing, it also concerns wilderness, wildlife, resource management, and economic development. Once again, this is a multidimensional oppositional resource struggle that is centered on various lines of power. Because of the poverty of the region, racism, and local cultural patterns, Hispanos lack economic, social, and political power. They encounter many resource problems through a subordinated status, whether it be in terms of state agencies or powerful ranching interests. The only way the prevailing social arrangement can be altered is to become more powerful. The strategy is not the union contract, as in the case of the UFWOC, but the building of an economic base and the fostering of a strong ethnic and place-based Hispano identity.

There is a rich dialectic between identity and economic development; the membership of Ganados has pursued this particular project because it reinforces a desirable cultural identity, but it is the economic project that makes a Hispano pastoral identity more than a myth. Cultivating this identity is not only a source of personal and group fulfillment, it also enables Ganados to achieve both political and economic power. By acquiring more power, they can fight for their vision of resource use, which does not emphasize preservation but sustainable environmentalism directed at developing rural people so that they can care for the land (Varela 1994).

Given their marginal economic status, it is essential that Ganados use local resources to contribute toward their livelihood and therefore they seek to use the local rangeland in a highly controlled way. Regardless of how Hispanos' historical attachment to the land is often equated with good stewardship, that is not enough to ensure that they will engage in a careful and appropriate use of rangeland. Precisely because of their desire to maintain and reinvent a particular identity and a desirable way of life, however, Ganados are credible in their efforts to carry out an ecologically sound grazing program. Their need to affirm a Hispano pastoral identity and to recreate a particular quality of life, coupled with a well-thought-out economic and community-development plan, has enabled them to articulate a viable subaltern vision of resource use.

Opposition has come from environmentalists and professional resource managers who favor preservation, which does little to address rural Hispanos' needs for community development. It is ultimately a short-sighted view. If Ganados' project does not succeed, locals will either emigrate to the city or be more willing to support extractive industries or polluting manufacturing activities. "Sustainable environmentalism . . . values and takes great stock in the observations and experiences of rural people who live on and watch the land. It creates partnerships from within and outside the community in order to bring the best thinking possible to solve problems. . . . This is a lot harder than leaving for the city or leaving everything up to the outside expert who will 'give' us jobs" (Varela 1994, 59). Ganados' quest to move beyond marginalization recognizes the centrality of poverty, the racialized nature of their condition and the fact that their long-term economic viability is tied to the ecological well-being of the land. Thus, their strategy involves undertaking economic development, gaining social and political power, and cultivating an appropriate cultural identity.

La Vida in Northern New Mexico

New Mexico's biggest selling point, both historically and today, is its scenic landscape and cultural diversity. The physical and social attractions of the state draw both visitors and new residents, inviting new forms of economic activity (e.g., tourism) while casting an opaque glow over deep economic and social inequalities. People fleeing the large urban centers of California, New York, and the Midwest have relocated to New Mexico because of its beauty, ethnic diversity, slow pace, and casual lifestyle. Accelerated growth has brought escalating real estate prices (Rio Grande Sun 1991a) but limited real economic and community development. Northern New Mexico's legacy of Hispano poverty, which has existed for almost one hundred years, has been altered only slightly by the influx of wealthy Anglos and the resultant increase in seasonal tourism and construction jobs. By examining the history and contemporary situation of northern New Mexico, we can see how a subaltern population has been created, how they intersect with environmental concerns, and how they seek to improve their situation. While this is very much an economic struggle, it also demonstrates how marginalized communities can be committed to achieving both an affirming identity and a particular quality of life.

Northern New Mexico is located in the Rio Grande River basin and is carved by rivers that emerge from the Colorado Rockies and local ranges, resulting in a dramatic landscape of plateaus, valleys, mountains, and canyons.[3] Ganados is based in the Chama Valley in Rio Arriba County (fig. 4.1). With an annual average precipitation of fourteen inches, the valley, like all semiarid environments, experiences sporadic drought. Lowland vegetation is characterized by scrub, chamisa, big sagebrush, and pinyon-juniper woodland, while irrigated plots, in contrast, appear lush and green. The mountains contain grasslands, ponderosa pine, juniper, and mixed conifers, depending on the elevation (Griffin 1991, 2). The three WMAs in Rio Arriba County encompass both lowlands and highlands with grasses that are considered premium rangeland. In general, northern New Mexico is sparsely populated and the Chama Valley is no exception, with the population scattered throughout a series of small villages (fig. 4.2).[4]

Under the Spanish crown, European, Indian and mestizo explorers entered New Mexico in 1540 in their search for gold. Early attempts to colonize the Indians failed (Dunbar Ortiz 1980), preventing effective Spanish settlement until the early 1690s when they approached the Indians in a more conciliatory manner. The area was settled through a system of Spanish and later Mexican *mercedes* (land grants). Ganados is located on what was once the Tierra Amarilla Land Grant.[5]

Fig. 4.2. Los Ojos, one of the small villages typical of the Chama Valley. *Photograph by the author.*

Early Hispanos lived in villages adjacent to water sources, and used the commons for timber, grazing, herbs, and other resources. Although the commons were not privately owned, use was controlled by usufruct rights (Peña 1991b). Originally engaged in a pastoral economy dependent on extensive land holdings, Hispanos were subsistence oriented, participating in limited commercial activities. With the Treaty of Guadalupe Hidalgo (1848) and growing Anglo infiltration, many Hispanos lost their lands, particularly communal ones that were crucial to their system of grazing.[6] As a result of these changes and increased population growth, Hispanos were forced either to migrate or to become grazing sharecroppers, known as *parteros* (Baxter 1987), or if they were fortunate, become wage laborers.

In response to these conditions the region has a long history of resistance, rebellion, and violence, initially directed at individual Anglos and later at state agencies. This resistance, which never really congealed into a full-fledged movement to take back New Mexico, was largely directed at the perceived cause of Hispano problems — loss of grant lands and the imposition of Anglo-American control (Rosenbaum 1986). It is crucial to understand that there was, and is, a burning resentment over both the inability to make a living and the perceived cause of this inability: loss of communal lands.[7] The inability of many households to reproduce themselves has driven a large number of the political projects, and consequently, has shaped environmental conflicts. While these political projects are a response to racialized economic and social marginalization, they also exacerbate antagonisms between Anglos and Hispanos, thereby perpetuating and intensifying the racialization of the region.

Widespread unemployment during the Great Depression caused many Hispanos to return to their villages. They eventually sought government aid, thus beginning the process of dependency (Forrest 1989). There have been many well-intentioned efforts to improve economic conditions in the area, including Protestant missionaries (Deutsch 1987), comprehensive studies (Harper, Cordova, and Oberg 1943; Weigle 1975), and attempts to create a "craft economy" (Forrest 1989).

During the 1960s, Hispano resistance reasserted itself, this time with a connection to both the broader Chicano struggle of the Southwest and the larger antipoverty movement that was surfacing in the United

States. Feelings of injustice reemerged under the provocation of Reies Lopez Tijerina, who led the formation of La Alianza, an organization that fought for the return of grant lands.[8] This unrest caused northern New Mexico to again become a focal point for government intervention both through the War on Poverty and through private initiatives, including the Ford Foundation and the American Friends Service Committee (Burma and Williams 1960; Wagon Mound Redevelopment Agency 1964; North Central New Mexico Economic Development District 1977, 1975; 1973–74). These planning schemes, however, routinely failed because they ignored cultural differences, focused heavily on rational economic programs, disregarded the loss of a land base upon which a prosperous rural society is dependent, and refused to align themselves to the needs and aspirations of Hispanos (Knowlton 1964).

Over the years a large portion of the Hispano land base fell into the hands of the federal government, primarily the United States Forest Service (USFS). Because of this perceived injustice, the USFS (and, to a lesser extent, other agencies) has been the target of Hispano resistance efforts. The relationship between Hispanos and the USFS is a complex and troubled one in several respects (de Buys 1989; Peña 1991a). At first glance, it is plain to see that Hispanos believe the USFS stole their land. Second, since the USFS is the authorized resource manager in the area, it has implemented its vision of resource use — one that has often run counter to the needs and aspirations of rural Hispanos. Finally, there is a long history of complaints about the way the USFS and its personnel treat locals, including hiring of few Hispanos, advocating policies that disadvantage them, and slighting their culture and traditions. In short, there is a general climate of disrespect and distrust between rural Hispanos and public resource agencies (see Wilmsen 1994; Garcia 1990; James 1990; Sandoval 1990; G. Vigil 1990).

For many reasons, Hispanos have been unable to build a prosperous rural economy based upon either the local resources or agriculture, causing northern New Mexico to rank as a region of deep poverty.[9] With an Hispano per capita income of $7,496 (United States Bureau of the Census 1990a), Rio Arriba ranks as the twenty-ninth poorest county out of thirty-three in the state of New Mexico. Countywide, 28 percent of the population is living below the poverty line, but in the

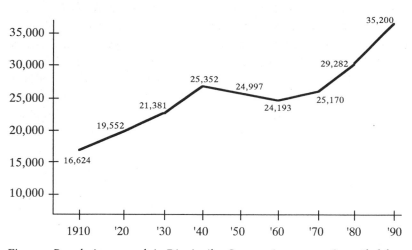

Fig. 4.3. Population growth in Rio Arriba County since 1910. *Compiled from Bureau of Business and Economic Research 1989, 84–88.*

Chama Valley vicinity that figure is 39 percent (United States Bureau of the Census 1990b). The annual average unemployment rate is 16.2 percent, which obscures seasonal swings ranging from 13.1 percent to 18.9 percent (New Mexico Department of Labor 1991, 5, 6; Sunwest Financial Services 1990).

Rio Arriba County has been undergoing steady population growth since the late 1970s (fig. 4.3). The majority of the increase has been due to Anglo in-migration, or Hispanos returning to the homeland (Carlson 1990). Out of a total population of 34,365, Hispanos still constitute a full 72.6 percent (United States Bureau of the Census 1990c), but the Anglo presence is felt far beyond their numbers because they tend to be more affluent and able to buy land, thereby driving up the cost of real estate. Since this is a rural area, land is especially critical to economic activity. Therefore, it is not just a question of a new group moving in, but a group that acts to undermine the ability of many natives to sustain themselves.

Due to their relatively long history in the region, the tightly knit nature of village life, and the historic isolation of the villages, Anglos and Hispanos define themselves in opposition to the other. This social distance, along with the larger racialization of the Spanish-speaking

and Anglo populations, has resulted in Hispanos and Anglos considering each other to be separate 'races'. This skeletal racial structure is
fleshed out by an alignment of 'race' and culture, in which each 'race' is
associated with a particular language, history, and culture. Within the
local racial structure, as throughout the southwestern United States,
Anglos are dominant and considered superior, while other 'races' (defined by their Spanish language and historical connection to Mexico),
are subordinate, considered inferior, and seen to deviate from the general norm (as defined by hegemonic Anglos).

There is also the additional element of desire. Although Hispanos
are considered inferior, Anglos, intrigued with the exotic, yearn for
Hispanos' strong sense of place and envy what appear to be strong
family ties among Hispanos. This paradox illustrates the complex and,
at times, contradictory nature of racism. Because of this alignment and
the history of the region, racial categories are less marked by the idea of
phenotype than they are by cultural identity as signified by language,
history, residence, and culture.

As always, care must be taken not to create a unified image of the
subaltern. Many Hispanos have migrated from northern New Mexico
to the cities, particularly Albuquerque, and there exists a significant
number of Anglos native to the north. Thus, there is not a complete
fit between "racial" groups and spatial histories. While some Anglos
struggle to make a living, many are entrepreneurs or professionals. This
racialized class and division of labor is evidenced in an Anglo per capita
income of $11,979 as opposed to a Hispano per capita income of
$7,496 (United States Bureau of the Census 1990a).

Since year-round, full-time employment is not readily available,
most Hispanos' lives consist of a complex set of strategies designed to
provide at least a minimal year-round cash flow. This usually includes
seasonal wage labor, transfer payments, subsistence activities, and perhaps entrepreneurial efforts. The heterogeneity of economic activities
precludes an easy class categorization of Hispanos. Instead, their economic marginality must be seen in the context of regional poverty:
northern New Mexico suffers from a lack of employment opportunities
due to limited capital investment, exacerbated by a racially and ethnically defined community.

In 1986 the entire county reported only 6,780 salaried, nonagricul-

Table 4.1. Gross Receipts and Employment by Major Sector for Rio Arriba County, 1986

Sector	Receipts	Employment
Agriculture	na	na
Mining	$16,871.20	49
Construction	36,334.00	476
Manufacturing	3,907.70	170
Transportation, Communications, and Utilities	30,733.50	410*
Wholesale and Retail	3,787.60	1,241
Finance, Insurance, and Real Estate	8,104.40	219
Services	22,250.50	1,986
Government	na	2,229
TOTAL	$222,443.30	6,780

Source: Bureau of Business and Economic Research 1989, 192.
*Employment figure does not include communications.

tural jobs. Most workers were employed, often on a part-time basis, in government (2,229), services (1,986), and wholesale and retail trade (1,241) (see table 4.1).[10] As elsewhere, service jobs are low wage, female dominated, and because of the tourist orientation of the area, often seasonal. Government transfer payments are the single largest source of personal income. However, this category includes public construction projects that typically provide summer employment for men. Private construction has also increased due to the region's population growth and secondary home business.

Hispano poverty is therefore a function of both underemployment and unemployment caused by the region's lack of economic development. Moreover, the better-paying jobs and entrepreneurial opportunities are largely filled by Anglos, due to their higher level of formal education and access to capital. In this case, Hispano poverty and relative powerlessness are caused by uneven development, the division of labor, and class position.

Hispanos live in nonfarm rural communities, which are rural areas lacking a significant agricultural economy. In 1989 only seventy-one people reported being employed in the agricultural sector (table 4.2). Ironically, many men would like to make a living in agriculture and continue to identify themselves as ranchers (Kutsche and Van Ness 1981, 45), but this is a distorted view of reality.[11] This incongruity between economic reality and professed identity is a testament to how strong the role of identity is to all people, even the poor and marginalized. It testifies as well to its complexity. Invoking this pastoral identity is essentially nostalgic, but it obviously looms large in rural Hispanos' collective history and identity. Its significance helps us understand perhaps one reason why past economic development projects have failed, and why Ganados, thus far, has succeeded. Hispanos neither identify with nor want to be good Protestant homemakers or simple craft producers. They identify as pastoral people and desire to reclaim that lifestyle. This is an excellent example not only of how our identities are a blend of the past and the present (Rutherford 1990), but also of how poor people's needs cannot be reduced to economics. Instead, economic needs and activities result from an engagement with culture, in this specific instance with identity. In effect, ranching and grazing have multiple meanings. Although both are economic activities, both also symbolize a particular quality of life and meaningful identity.

De Buys (1989) has pointed out that shepherding and ranching allow Hispanos to have an "authentic" interaction with nature. It should be realized that, due to the short growing season, ranching is the primary form of agriculture in the north. Those who do have sufficient grazing land, either through inheritance or leasing, overwhelmingly raise cattle. The sheep industry has been in decline for decades; prices for lamb and wool have fallen in comparison to cattle and beef (*New Mexico Stockman* 1988, 3, 51). Further aggravating the disparity between the two crops, the federal government recently announced the cessation of the wool subsidy program.

There are, however, valid economic reasons why Ganados is built on sheep and not cattle ranching. For one, cattle are far more expensive than sheep, so it would be more capital intensive to start an operation.[12] Secondly, sheep provide more job opportunities. The process of producing and marketing wool and woven products is extremely labor intensive, and Ganados is about economic development. Finally, the

Table 4.2. Employment by Major Industry in Rio Arriba County, 1981–89

Industry	Year								
	1981	1982	1983	1984	1985	1986	1987	1988	1989
Government	2735	2741	2786	2865	2744	2599	2614	2531	2600
Services	1914	1891	2073	2255	2496	2589	2723	2888	3001
Retail	1215	1281	1322	1359	1436	1476	1464	1436	1479
Construction	391	461	465	571	607	701	635	587	750
Manufacturing	271	184	178	186	182	230	263	265	234
Finance, Insurance, and Real Estate	301	327	311	323	338	340	364	383	401
Wholesale	125	128	110	107	120	128	131	150	135
Agriculture, Forest, Fish	122	137	128	140	95	77	63	59	71
Mining	32	32	38	39	62	65	67	65	58

Source: Bureau of Economic Analysis 1991.

local Hispanos have experience with wool production and crafts (although these skills were almost extinct). In contrast, there is only a limited tradition of leather production in the region. Also, it is questionable if leather could provide as diverse a set of economic options as does wool. Wool provides a wide spectrum of job opportunities for diverse groups. For example, although most people involved in Ganados are adults in their prime working years, the children also learn to weave, and the elderly are able to earn money by performing relatively light tasks, such as washing and drying the wool.

Another key obstacle to widespread cattle ranching is land scarcity and cost. One local landowner with large holdings recently explained that there is plenty of grazing land but the lease rates are linked to the cattle market, not the sheep (Mundy in Hales 1991). However, many locals dispute this claim, stating that they find it difficult to secure a lease even with cattle. Exacerbating this situation for local Hispanos is the competition with large cattle operations from Texas and southern New Mexico that transport their livestock to graze on the area's exceptional grasslands (R. Serrano 1990b).

Regardless of the price, there is not a lot of land readily available for lease or purchase because only 28 percent of the county is privately owned. Over 50 percent of the area is held by the federal government in the form of two national forests, 17 percent is held by the Jicarilla Apache, and 2 percent is owned by the state. Although Forest Service land can be grazed outside of wilderness areas, it is necessary to have base land in order to qualify for a lease. Those opposed to Ganados' grazing often cite the fact that the state owns only 2 percent of the land in the county. This masks the fact, however, that they own 20 percent of the land in the immediate Chama Valley area (Ganados n.d.), effectively diminishing the available grazing base.

In addition to land availability, several land-use patterns and customs mitigate against the development of a healthy rural economy (Weber 1991; Carlson 1990). Most importantly, many Hispanos own very small plots that cannot support a viable economic operation. Related to this is the problem of fragmented landownership, reflecting not only the loss of grant lands but the practice of equal inheritance, which has had severe consequences for rural economic development. As a result, it becomes extremely difficult to piece together a viable parcel

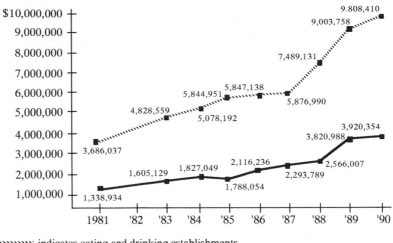

··········· indicates eating and drinking establishments
———— indicates lodging

Fig. 4.4. Income from tourism in Rio Arriba County from 1981 to 1990.
Compiled from State of New Mexico, Taxation and Revenue Dept. 1991.

for grazing, ranching, or cultivation. Furthermore, many plots are not cultivated because the owners are too busy commuting to work in wage labor, or they no longer live in the area (P. Torres 1990).

An extra burden facing small farmers is the difficulty of finding buyers, since their harvests are small and of varied quality (P. Torres 1990). Most supermarkets prefer to deal with fewer, large-scale growers. Access to land and economic development are also constrained by urban Hispanos who own USFS grazing permits. An urban worker in Albuquerque, for example, may continue to graze a few head of cattle because of his or her attachment to the land and animals. While understandable, this does nothing to help rural Hispanos who are trying to make a living in northern New Mexico.

In contrast to the patterns of small holdings, a few people have acquired very large parcels either for speculation or recreational uses. Thus, the region is characterized by somewhat polarized landownership, with many Hispanos no longer able to buy land in their "homeland."

Given the lack of agricultural opportunities and the scenic nature of the region, it has become a de facto tourist area. People are attracted to the area's beauty, hunting, recreation opportunities, and the so-called "quaint" Hispano culture. According to the Bureau of Business and Economic Research (1989), tourism revenues have shown consistent growth over the past decade (fig. 4.4). The Economic Development and Tourism Department[13] has worked diligently to develop the tourism potential of New Mexico (New Mexico Economic Development and Tourism Department 1990a, b; New Mexico Department of Tourism 1991).[14] Even though the city of Albuquerque generates one-half of all tourist revenues in the state (New Mexico Economic Development and Tourism Department 1988, 38), the northern part of the state is seen as a potential gold mine that is beginning to pay. Indicators of expanding tourism in Rio Arriba County include the growing use of state parks (fig. 4.5), significantly increasing visitor inquiries, increasing revenue from lodging taxes, and the quadrupling of membership in the Chama Valley Chamber of Commerce (*Rio Grande Sun* 1991c, B1).

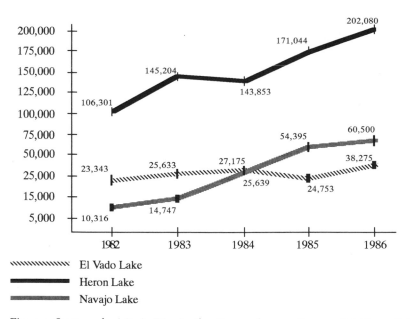

Fig. 4.5. State park visits in Rio Arriba County from 1982 to 1986. *Compiled from Bureau of Business and Economic Research 1989, 128.*

Tourism is contentious for several reasons, primarily because it is often unplanned (*New Mexican* 1989, A8), haphazard, and illegal (Miller and Potter 1986). Local residents have little input into the planning and development process, which allows developers to operate fairly autonomously and with minimal community or regulatory input. Another reason people react strongly to tourism is frustration with the fact that there simply is no other proactive development occurring.[15] One could argue that the growing role of tourism reflects larger market forces, but one could also argue that tourism simply represents the easiest course to pursue, as it has thus far required little planning while adding money directly to the state coffers (Richardson 1990). Tourism, including environmental and ethnic tourism, has recently caught the attention of scholars and policy makers (Van den Berghe 1994; Varela 1990a). Despite the fact that many places depend heavily on tourism, it can sow the seeds of its own demise and lead to other contradictions. This is particularly the case in ethnic tourism, where local people themselves become the spectacle.

Varela (1990a), in an effort to promote a more dignified form of tourism that ensures that the local peoples will reap some of the economic benefits, has distinguished between what she calls "resort tourism" and "visitor tourism." Resort tourism is characterized by "theme parks, slick resorts, large shopping malls or franchise motels and restaurants," while visitor tourism seeks to develop and highlight the skills and resources of the local community. Aside from the Ganados project, most tourism in the region has fallen into the first category (e.g., Taos and Santa Fe) in which outside interests and newcomers with capital benefit most. In describing the dominant tourism that has developed in the Chama area, one public official derisively noted that the top job opportunity for female Hispanos seems to be cleaning toilets (Humphries 1990). This is not the kind of tourism many Hispanos favor, and Ganados provides a dramatic alternative.

Residents' differing visions for the region came to a head in the early 1980s when a ski resort was proposed. Investors pointed out that agriculture no longer serves as the region's economic base and that a resort economy, with skiing, golf, and related recreation, was the best alternative (Hales 1991). Local boosters insisted the project would be well planned, but many were skeptical. Caution was indeed warranted because nothing in the history of the county would lead one to believe that it would be carefully planned. Despite widespread underemployment, local Hispanos were suspicious of the types of jobs that would be created. Others pointed to Taos and Santa Fe, where despite phenomenal tourist growth, Hispanos remain impoverished (Selcraig 1993). It was widely believed that contractors would bring their own work crews, further depriving residents of better paying construction jobs (User Surveys of Land Development Regulations and Review Process n.d.). Concerns over water contamination, land speculation, low-paying jobs, and haphazard development led many to oppose the plan. Many others, including middle-class Hispanos, supported it.

The ski resort is a microcosm of planning problems facing the Chama Valley, and illustrate the larger social and environmental challenges associated with resource-based tourism. As developers continue to open up new subdivisions, the demand to live in the area drives the price of land up to the point where local people cannot afford to buy it, further rendering agriculture a nonviable economic activity. Likewise, the tax burden has become impossible for some people, particularly the elderly, to meet.

A second set of problems caused by development is environmental. Because so much activity goes on either without the county's supervision or knowledge (illegally), subdivisions do not adequately consider groundwater levels, proper sewage, and drainage (Miller and Potter 1986). The result has been serious groundwater contamination, which is a threat to the region because many depend on the water for both personal and agricultural use.[16]

An equally important but overlooked environmental consequence of leapfrogging subdivisions is the loss of habitat. Habitat loss is the chief cause of decreasing biodiversity—a point basic to understanding the precarious status of many threatened and endangered species. It should be pointed out that it is not rural Hispanos buying these lots; rather it is urban folks and newcomers. Ganados and environmentalists, as well as other segments of the community, have worked together to oppose haphazard development and to strengthen land use and development regulations in order to protect both habitat and agricultural land (Rio Arriba County Policies Planning Task Force 1987, 3–6).

The county is currently at a juncture. Due to a lack of leadership, the more powerful forces of an unregulated market are reshaping the region physically, culturally, economically, and socially. The current crisis has been brewing for years, and although leaving the area has become the norm, it should not be construed as a happy acquiescence. Rather, there is a bitterness in the irony that the Hispanos who remain live in mobile homes on inherited land, while incoming Anglos can afford to build new adobe homes.[17]

While many Hispanos and Anglos are friends, and there is intermarriage, there is no escaping the fact that many Hispanos attribute their economic hardship to the loss of grant lands plus Anglo land usurpation. Local analyses range from the belief that Anglos simply make better financial managers to the conspiracy theories that center on the state's desire to remove all Hispanos in order to pursue full-scale tourist development. Consequently, many Hispanos have a romanticized view of the opportunities that regaining their land would provide. Many commented that if they could simply regain their land all their problems would be solved. But few are fully aware of the complexities of the modern economy and the near impossibility of ever becoming economically independent, even with a sizable land base (Morales 1990; Valdez Martinez 1990; Aguilar 1991; A. Serrano 1990; S. Martinez 1991). In reality, many lack the skills and knowledge necessary to effectively compete in today's market economy. Their attitudes toward land and activities such as grazing, farming, and forestry are rooted in the economic realities of an earlier generation and time (Weber 1991). The reality of modern economic development is far more complex.

The roots of Ganados can be traced to La Alianza, which, as previously mentioned, was formed in the 1960s. Although anchored in the struggle to recover lost grant lands, La Alianza provided many with their first taste of political activism through its several community development institutions, including the Abiquiu Corporation, and La Cooperativa, an agricultural enterprise. After the demise of La Alianza, a group of core activists established La Clinica, a community health clinic near Los Ojos. Over time, activists realized that the clinic, while important, was only addressing the symptoms of rural poverty, since much of the illness they saw was caused by the stress of economic uncertainty. Ganados' early leaders knew the community needed a form of economic development that would improve rural households and income, offer dignified work, allow people to develop their various talents and skills, and resonate both with the cultural heritage of Hispanos and with their desire to rejuvenate a pastoral cultural identity. Thus was born the idea behind Ganados del Valle. Although that idea may appear simple, community and economic development never materialize simply out of good intentions. A great deal of skill, planning, and knowledge are necessary to put together what may appear to be a relatively easy development strategy. This was certainly the case with Ganados del Valle—while they drew on their cultural heritage, they remained firmly rooted in the late twentieth century.

The Politics of Public Land Use

In the western United States, approximately one-third of all land is publicly owned, making it the focal point of many environmental struggles in the region. The emergence of the industrial West has brought a thriving service economy and an urban-oriented, educated population—two harbingers of contemporary environmentalism. At the same time, the historically important role of resource use and extractive activities is still quite visible, especially beyond the large urban centers.

Though the West is a towering symbol of freedom and opportunity in our national consciousness, this is a highly racialized image that mostly celebrates the achievement of white males (Limerick 1988). Erased from the collective memory are both the contributions of all women and subordinated nonwhite groups, as well as the extent to which much of the West has been developed on the backs and resources of subaltern populations. Moreover, many of these communities have routinely been denied the fruits of their labors. A similar set of prejudices and biases can be seen in public land policy and professional resource management. Both are modern phenomena in that they presume a singular public and work under the guise of scientific objectivity, all the while promoting policies that favor dominant groups and ignore both the reality of inequality and the existence of cultural differences.

While not wanting to suggest that there is consensus among the dominant groups involved in public land issues — and there is not — it is true that few of these groups or individual actors have sought to understand or articulate public land and resource issues from a subaltern point of view. There are, of course, very serious problems plaguing public land policy in the western United States — problems that would exist regardless of social inequalities. Charles Wilkinson (1992) has observed that much of our resource policy and law is rooted in another era, reflecting the needs and objectives of a young nation caught up in western expansionism (imperialism). This has left us with such relics as the 1872 Hardrock Mining Law.

Another factor contributing to fractious debate is the number and diversity of actors involved in public land issues. Obviously, the environmentalist has a different vision of resource use and management than the resource user. Typically, western resource conflicts center on land use: What will the land be used for? Will it be used for ecological preservation, landscape and scenery enjoyment, hunting, logging, grazing, or some combination of the above? Various political and economic interests lead to different positions, and because of their role and status, environmentalists, resource managers, and large resource users have emerged as the legitimate voices and participants in public land struggles.

Minority communities and small resource users, in contrast, rarely participate in these debates, and are not considered political actors in this arena. In short, the resource views and positions of mainstream environmentalists, state resource managers, and organized resource users (such as hunters), have become hegemonic. Because of its subordinate status, Ganados' participation and vision of resource use are viewed as oppositional. This particular struggle is articulated as a choice between grazing and wildlife, but clearly it is much more complex. It is an example not only of how a seemingly benign and objective resource policy ignores the needs and concerns of the subaltern by assuming there is a single public, but of how such policy can actually undermine a low-income community's efforts to make a living and carry out equally sound environmental strategies.

Grazing

Ranchers and Environmentalists. Few can deny the contentious nature of grazing in the West. On the one hand, there is no hiding the ecological destruction that grazing has left in its wake (Ferguson and Ferguson

1983). On the other hand, ranchers vigorously defend their livelihood and lifestyle. That grazing has come to be considered an environmentally offensive activity in and of itself is unfortunate but understandable (Moffatt 1990; Krueger 1988, 4). Environmentalists' opposition to grazing is an inevitable response to the poor way it has been managed. It also reveals underlying biases inherent in the definition of an environmentalist that preclude the ecologically conscientious rancher from being considered a legitimate one.

[Environmentalists consider grazing to be a quality-of-life issue, being concerned in this case with the quality of rangeland hours or days away from their, usually urban, home. This is not intended to delegitimize environmentalists' position or participation, but to stress that they are *personally* detached from grazing itself. This detachment stems from their geographic location (urban and suburban versus rural), their economic position (privileged and secure versus poor), and their economic location (service sector versus manufacturing or primary). Their position allows them to adopt such a perspective, accords them the luxury to be involved in an issue not immediately affecting them, and enables them to promote wilderness at the expense of resource use.] Preservation is essential at times, but we must also recognize that it is the easier path. It does not require fundamental social change by all of us. In contrast, Dobson has pointed out that this is one of the great shortcomings of mainstream, or managerial, environmentalism; it does not work to change the options available to people. Preservation — an example of managerial environmentalism — simply bans certain activities in a given place. This is not necessarily the most effective or meaningful way of altering our societal response to environmental degradation.

The opening of the West by Europeans can be seen as a series of booms and busts with severe ecological consequences that environmentalists for the most part have responded to with managerial environmentalism. Upon acquisition of the West, public ownership of land was not seen as the purview of the U.S. government, so it was distributed to encourage people to develop it (Petulla 1977, 84). Ultimately, this led to chaotic and conflicting patterns of land use resulting in widespread overgrazing and damage to the range. The Taylor Grazing Act was passed in 1934 in response to the ecological and social consequences of uncontrolled grazing (Fleming 1933),[18] and created local districts to set carrying capacities and manage permitted grazing. Unfortunately, the local boards charged with regulating grazing have been dominated by rancher interests (New Mexico People and Energy 1980, 5; Eastman and Gray 1987, 35), and as a result, the range has suffered. A 1979 Bureau of Land Management (BLM) study indicated that close to 80 percent of the range was in "fair condition or worse" (in Limerick 1988, 156). Yet, in the face of such facts, neither the stocking rate nor grazing policy was significantly reduced or modified.

Realizing that the public range was not well managed and that grazing fees were far below market, environmentalists have pressured for reform (Ferguson and Ferguson 1983). They have fought for increased grazing fees, lower stocking rates, and consideration of the role of wilderness by BLM, as a multiuse agency. There has been a gradual shift in the orientation of the BLM, but certainly not to the degree environmentalists would like. For example, under the Federal Land Management and Planning Act, the BLM has designated some lands as suitable for wilderness (Foreman 1986), but the adequacy of this proposal has been challenged (Fish 1987). In other developments, BLM allotment management plans must now be accompanied by an environmental impact statement (Fowler and Gray 1980, 1), and the federal government has succeeded in raising the price of grazing permits.

While these are feeble reform efforts to environmentalists, to ranchers these recent policy changes "can only be described as anti-livestock" (Moody in Torell and Doll 1990, 29). Both sides paint the other in the worst possible light, often to the point of the absurd, hoping to strengthen their own point of view. "The greatest unfairness of all is that the American public is having its lands and water and wildlife and other public resources depleted for this and future generations by an absolutely obdurate, selfish, greedy aristocracy" (Calkin 1990). Ranchers believe there is great merit in what they do, and they should be allowed to continue converting "otherwise worthless public forage into red meat and a desirable way of life" (Torell, Ghosh, and Fowler 1988, 1). Indeed, the situation is so bad that some environmentalists believe the term *managed grazing* is an oxymoron (Calkin 1990).

The conflict itself, however, goes beyond grazing. Grazing is simply the manifestation or embodiment of conflicting ideas and values. Ranchers resent environmentalists not only because they perceive them to be outsiders intervening in their ranching activities, but also because they feel they collide with traditional American values. Ranching organizations and institutions are devotees of private property and consider the existence of public land an attack on freedom.[19] "Freedom cannot be maintained without the right to own property. . . . Meanwhile, the United States government owns almost one-third of the nation's land, but that apparently is not enough. We are told by the 'safety' mongers that the government must acquire more land, because free people suddenly cannot be trusted to properly care for it. The government, we are told, can 'care' for it better" (Price 1990, 34).

A few ranchers have made significant efforts to introduce conservation into their operations. This has necessitated that they rethink their entire approach to grazing — not an easy task. One group of Oregon ranchers, committed to creating more ecologically sound ranching, found they had to change their entire operation, altering such practices as continuous rather than seasonal calving, reducing their use of hormones, paying close attention to the ecology of their ranch, and working in cooperation with other ranchers — none of which currently characterizes contemporary ranching (Marston 1992).

When discussing the ecological consequences of grazing, there is a tendency to concentrate on grass management and the condition of the range. But ranchers also intersect with environmentalism in the area of wildlife. Two-thirds of our country's wildlife is located on private land (Miller 1987), which leads to endless clashes. Ranchers commonly complain that wildlife costs them by eating forage. One rancher told the New Mexico Department of Game and Fish, "Over-grazing of wildlife on public lands leased by the ranchers constituted a taking of their private property rights" (Welsome 1990, 3). The rancher wanted compensation for what wildlife ate on public lands! While some ranchers espouse wildlife concerns and promote wildlife through watering holes and other improvements, most generally oppose wilderness laws, environmental initiatives, and government intervention (Burgess 1990, 32; Eppers 1990, 6; *New Mexico Stockman* 1989a, 32; Mocho 1987, 6; G. Price 1990, 34).

Ranching, to environmentalists and much of the public, represents all that is wrong with resource policy in the United States. First, there is no denying that the livestock industry has effectively coopted its regulator, the BLM. Because of this conflict of interest, insult is added to the injury of land degradation by the government subsidies, given to ranchers, that result in the public footing of the bill for rangeland destruction (Ferguson and Ferguson 1983) — an important point to remember when ranchers wax on about the American Way and free markets.

Though New Mexico has an expanding and diverse economy, including high technology industries, primary activities still comprise more than 10 percent of the state's economy (Sunwest Financial Services 1990, 21). Because New Mexico, until fairly recently, has identified as a rural state, mainstream environmentalism is a recent phenomenon. In fact, New Mexico's shift to an urban industrial orientation has been rather sudden, which helps to explain the existence of highly contrasting positions. Though mainstream environmentalism is relatively new to New Mexico (Kimball 1991), already diverse organizations exist. The Sierra Club, The Audubon Society, National Wildlife Federation, Wilderness Society, The Nature Conservancy, and Earth First! are all established.[20] The Sierra Club is the largest environmental organization in New Mexico with more than 5,500 members (Flint 1990, 1).

The membership of the organizations involved in the grazing conflict was composed predominantly of Anglo, middle-class individuals.[21] One environmentalist described his organization in the following way: "Audubon is a predominantly White group. I think it's more of a class issue than a race one. People with the money, time, and interests, people who don't have to be concerned with making a living" (Jervis 1990). This quote illustrates the position of environmentalists and how they might clash with those who do "have to be concerned with making a living." It is, of course, conceivable that people with "money, time, and interests" would advocate an environmentalism that seeks to incorporate the needs of the rural poor, but for the most part they have not. This is largely a function of mainstream environmentalism's narrow articulation of environmental concerns, exacerbated by nonwhites' suspicion of, and at times, outright rejection of, Anglo environmentalists.

Certainly there are cases of cooperation, such as the large number of Hispanos and environmentalists who united to oppose mining in the community of Questa (Martinez 1993), but these cases are in the minority. More often, conflicts arise over power, resources, and minority rights—important issues that must be openly confronted and discussed if mainstream environmentalists and subaltern communities are ever going to work together.

Both sides are complicit in portraying and interpreting these real points of friction as shallow cultural differences articulated in a manner devoid of their economic and political context. Both Anglos and non-whites may reify cultural differences to the point where they obscure other points of conflict, such as the economic needs of subaltern communities and unequal power relations. "In the eyes of land-based people, the environment is an ecosystem in which the people exist as one part of a harmonious whole, deriving food and materials, as needed, for their continued social, cultural, and economic existence. In the eyes of environmentalists, the same land may represent an area that should be protected for its own sake, for its beauty and pristine qualities, for wildlife habitat, or for recreation" (Taylor 1988, 91). This practice of using cultural differences as a code for power differences is understandable within the context of New Mexico's tourist economy, which is based on the marketing of cultural mystique and diversity. It does not, however, advance a nuanced understanding of how differential power and wealth create various approaches to resource use and environmentalism.

Since much of New Mexico is publicly owned, and because many environmentalists are drawn to the landscape and recreational opportunities that the state has to offer, it is not surprising that environmentalists should concentrate on public land issues. At present there is a strong trend towards preservation among environmentalists, whether the issue is logging, hunting, road building, or grazing. Grazing as a traditional resource use is generally opposed by environmentalists who, as one activist explained, "tend to have a knee-jerk reaction to it" (Freeman 1990). Though grazing is a constant concern to all environmentalists in New Mexico, various groups have adopted a broad range of positions. Some local groups, such as the Public Lands Action Network (PLAN), support a total ban on all public land grazing. The Sierra Club's position has been mixed as they have sought to devise innovative policy solutions to encourage ranchers to take better care of the land while penalizing those who do not. The National Wildlife Federation opposes a total ban on grazing. "Wildlife interests are not a part of the

'Beef Free by '93' campaigns of such radical groups as Earth First!"
(Griffith 1990, 11).

Different positions reflect varied organizational philosophies, which
in turn mirror the interests of different social and political groups. The
National Wildlife Federation, for example, attracts a much more conservative and economically mixed constituency because of its hunting
antecedents. In some ways, the NWF is more inclusive and diverse than
the Nature Conservancy, which attracts a well-educated, professionally
oriented membership who are more likely to espouse preservation.[22]

Indeed, the primary purpose of the Nature Conservancy is preservation, as they specialize in acquiring endangered or threatened habitat.
Formally begun in 1917, the Nature Conservancy has saved more than
3 million acres (Scheffer 1991, 5). Its revenues in 1985 were $83.7
million, making it one of the wealthiest environmental organizations in
the world (Tober 1989, 40). While the strategy of the Nature Conservancy recognizes the link between wildlife and habitat, it does not
explore the links between the needs of rural communities, economic
development, and social justice. Indeed, the Nature Conservancy representative involved in the grazing conflict did not think the three WMAS
were a significant issue because they constituted such a small percentage of the local land base. By distancing themselves from any challenge
to the prevailing power arrangement, the Nature Conservancy has become one of corporate America's favorite environmental causes — not
only because they "exude moderation and balance," but because they
"validate the existing distribution of property rights" (Tober 1989, 45).

Environmentalists are an increasingly important force in New Mexico because of their numbers, influence, political power, and economic
strength. Because of this, the NMDGF has sought to cultivate a new
constituency among environmentalists in order to broaden their base of
support (Evans 1990a). Consequently, environmentalists have exerted
a growing influence on the policies and politics of the NMDGF, forcing
the agency to broaden its mandate beyond hunting in order to consider
other expressions of environmental concern. "As people from New
York come in, they may not be interested in hunting or fishing, but they
like to go somewhere where they can be assured that they can see an elk
or deer" (Montoya 1990).

Given their emphases and membership demographics, it is not surprising that New Mexican environmentalists have not embraced a social justice agenda or sought to align themselves with the subaltern. While they do not wish to oppose or harm marginalized communities — in fact, individual environmentalists were all too aware of the existing disparities within the region — none seem able to incorporate subaltern needs into their programs. As a case in point, in 1970 the Sierra Club Foundation was given a one hundred thousand dollar donation to assist rural Hispanos in buying land for summer grazing in an effort "to develop projects that combined environmental and social goals" (Suro 1992, A16). Somehow, the land was never bought. This seems to be rather typical of mainstream environmentalism — it realizes the need to make connections with poor and nonwhite communities but finds it difficult and often problematic.

In New Mexico, while some politically progressive groups such as the Southwest Research and Information Center actively work with subordinated communities, the most the majority can do is to hope they do not have to oppose such communities. This ambivalence was displayed when I interviewed members of mainstream groups and asked if and how they should be concerned with the social justice implications of environmental policy and ideas, such as sustainable development. While concurring that it was an important topic, the general response was that their organizations lacked the resources to pursue such work and that it was up to someone else to do (Waldman 1990; Jervis 1990). In short, by choosing not to become involved in a more redistributive environmental program, one that challenges the boundaries of the mainstream movement, environmentalists have contributed to the continued peripheralization and subordination of subaltern groups. With their power and status they have the ability to change the nature of environmentalism, but they have not done so.

Hunters. Hunters are similar to environmentalists in that they too are an interest group. They have a somewhat different perspective on grazing because they are more akin to traditional resource users. Hunters, by and large, tend to have mixed attitudes towards grazing. They oppose grazing that is ecologically destructive or that competes with hunting opportunities, but they are not philosophically opposed to it per se. Though hunters and environmentalists do have some common interests, the two view each other with suspicion. Environmentalists sometimes derisively label hunting and wildlife organizations as "rod and gun" clubs, objecting to their close attachment to guns and the National Rifle Association. Sporting organizations often consider environmentalists too radical, priding themselves on their less confrontational tactics (Weingarten 1990).

As a group, hunters have contributed significantly to both conservation and environmentalism (Reiger 1986). Early organizations such as the Izaak Walton League, the Boone and Crockett Club, and the National Wildlife Federation were established not only for camaraderie, but encouraged recognition that wildlife was a resource in need of protection. Initially concerned solely with wildlife, hunters later began to address habitat in general, which enabled them to be included within the environmental fold (Reiger 1986, 22).

Overall, hunting has increased in the United States since the 1920s, but began a decline in 1980 that was expected to continue, due to social and demographic changes (Heberlein 1987, 6, 31). Officials from the NMDGF (Evans 1990a) reported that hunting in New Mexico was ebbing, but recent statistics indicate that between 1980 and 1985 hunters increased from 114,400 to 150,000 in the state (*New Mexico Wildlife* 1989b, 13). This discrepancy could be due to the fact that New Mexico is effectively attracting the dwindling number of sport hunters from other states but still recognizes the larger downward trend among state residents.

Most hunters, both historically and in the 1980s are white males. Approximately 10 percent of the male population hunts, in contrast to only 2 percent of the female population (Heberlein 1987, 6). They also have above-average incomes and are disproportionately college educated (Heberlein 1987, 8). But hunters are more diverse than aggregate statistics suggest. Certainly there are great differences between those who hunt for food because they are poor, and those who enjoy the pursuit, guns, competition, and domination of animals (Kellert 1978).

Despite their somewhat mixed membership, hunters tend to be conservative, and while they often see preservation as too severe a policy tool, they do not espouse a social justice agenda. This is an important distinction that often gets confused and distorted in the public mind. All too often those who support preservation are considered *radical*—a term equated with the politics of the left. Preservationist and leftist politics are not the same. Similarly, hunters' and conservationists' opposition to preservation does not make them supporters of subaltern communities. Although these groups may at times share the same position on an issue, a very different set of politics is at work. Marginalized communities are interested in changing the power relationships in which they are embedded, not just in fixing an environmental problem.

Hunters, on the other hand, do not necessarily share the same liberal understandings that environmentalists do. For example, when asked about his organization's nonwhite membership and participation, one hunter simply responded that their bylaws prohibit discrimination (Weingarten 1990), thereby illustrating a rather shallow understanding of the arguments surrounding discrimination, social difference, inequality, and participation. In contrast, most environmentalists are capable of launching into a detailed analysis of the causes and consequences of racialized poverty in the state, the historical inequities nonwhite New Mexicans have endured, and the tangled nature of struggles between environmentalists and oppressed communities. Thus, while hunters may appear to be more socially progressive in certain respects, their motivation and values are highly conservative.

Hunters, it must be understood, are a powerful special interest group. Few organized interests can boast their accomplishments: establishment of a national wildlife refuge system, implementation of hunting restrictions, passage of the Pittman-Robertson and Dingell-Johnson Acts,[23] and improvement of both game and nongame habitat (Heberlein 1987, 6). As a growing environmental consciousness has penetrated society, hunters have joined with regulatory agencies and conservation groups to form what Tober calls the "wilderness industry," which he describes as "the constellation of organizations and individuals that institutionalize the relationships between humans and wild animals. This is a complex industry. . . . It is an industry substantially influenced by the interests, passions, and deeply held beliefs of millions of people — of elected and appointed officials, of political activists, sport hunters, and bird watchers, scientists, and philosophers" (Tober 1989, ix).

It is worth pausing to consider this industry because it is indicative of how we have structured our relationship with nondomesticated animals. The existence of an industry attests to our concern with wildlife as well as to the fact that we are willing to actively intervene in order to manage this resource as we see fit, which is in keeping with our larger desire to manage and control nature. The industry does this not only through its management techniques (e.g., hunting permits and stocking fish), but also through the images it presents of wildlife (such as cuddly bears or majestic elk versus fungus or flies). The creation of the wildlife industry also reveals the inability of our economic and cultural institutions, in and of themselves, to adequately protect wildlife. If we truly valued wildlife both as a society and individually, there would be no need for such an elaborate industry because we would change our practices to better meet the needs of wildlife (e.g., through our land development practices).[24]

Moreover, by building an hegemonic discourse surrounding wildlife, the various actors involved successfully legitimize and institutionalize their role and interests. Hunters, for example, are now considered germane to any wildlife management system simply because we have eliminated most predators. In the same way, the dominant discourse has given rise to new forms of wildlife interaction (such as bird watching, photography, whale watching, and wildlife feeding) that the industry encourages through community presentations, wildlife contributions via tax forms, and NMDGF's attractive magazine *New Mexico Wildlife*. Ultimately, by forging an alliance among wildlife enthusiasts (hunters, environmentalists, government, and the general public), the wildlife industry is ensured legitimacy, continued support, and funding (Tober 1989). This strategy has worked well in New Mexico. In 1985 hunters spent $66.9 million while nonhunting wildlife enthusiasts spent $365 million (*New Mexico Wildlife* 1989b, 13). This success could only have come about through the active participation and promotion of wildlife by mainstream environmentalists.

Resource Agencies. Perhaps the best window into the evolving nature of public land-use conflicts are resource agencies themselves, since they are the sites of contestation. Whether it be the National Park Service, the United States Fish and Wildlife Service, or New Mexico Department of Game and Fish, these organizations respond to the various pressures exerted by special interest groups, not the concerns of the poor and marginalized. In fact, NMDGF policy takes pains to distance itself from political considerations, framing its decisions in terms of science and the law. Shrouding itself in the objectivity offered by science, however, does not mean that the policy is fair, just, or non-ideological.

The NMDGF is comprised of wildlife professionals charged with protecting the game and wildlife of New Mexico. Although subject to different and often competing pressures, it enjoys an unusual degree of autonomy because only a portion of its revenues are derived from the state's general fund. Instead, most monies come from user fees, and federal sources.[25] Because of the shifting demographic and social characteristics of New Mexico, the agenda of the department has changed over the years. Originally created to enhance hunting opportunities and to conserve wildlife, law enforcement played a large role in carrying out the agency's early policy objectives (Montoya 1990; NMDGF *Annual Reports,* 1915–16). Even though the NMDGF has changed considerably, this image remains with many Hispanos.

Over time the state realized that hunting and tourism could generate large revenues (NMDGF *Annual Reports,* 1912–14), and it has taken a number of measures to promote such activities. The department hired its first nongame biologist in 1971, signaling its philosophical shift from providing large game for hunting to caring for all species and ecosystems. The NMDGF has become more environmentally conscious since then, and words like ecology, ecosystem, and ecological community are sprinkled throughout its publications. This change was a result of antihunting sentiment as well as the rise of modern environmentalism (NMDGF *Annual Reports,* 1969–74).

In the mid-1990s, NMDGF workers see themselves as resource managers and insist they manage ecosystems for all species. There clearly remains a commitment to charismatic mega-fauna and to managing the resources so as to ensure the financial and political viability of the agency (similar to other bureaucracies) — all of which can be seen in its elk management strategy. Since 1910 the NMDGF has sought to replenish elk in the north. Today elk are found far beyond their historic range (Gonzales 1987, 6). Several resource professionals (Harris 1990; Sandoval 1990), including the director of the NMDGF (Montoya 1990), have acknowledged a surplus elk population, and small landowners have pressured the agency to harvest more elk (Kaemper 1990), both indicative of a problem with current management. Some residents asserted that the WMA grasses are so poorly managed that elk are forced to graze on local farm and cropland. Local conservation professionals felt that NMDGF did not work to improve the habitat, concentrating instead on big game rather than the ecosystem (Harris 1990). Others echoed the contention that NMDGF's sole concern was big game and not the larger regional environment, and certainly not the local people (Sandoval 1990).

Director Montoya rejected the charge that NMDGF did not properly manage habitat. He conceded that the elk population had grown. "In the last ten years we've probably tripled our elk herd in places we never had elk before" (Montoya 1990). Moreover, he admitted it was necessary to "entice elk into" the WMAs, because they ventured onto adjacent lands. The NMDGF's solution was to increase elk hunting permits by three thousand. Montoya interpreted the situation as follows: "Well, that's the first time I've been criticized for doing a good job. My job is to have elk available for the public, whether it be for hunting, viewing aesthetics, or whatever. That's my job, I'd like to have lots of deer. . . . I'd like to be accused of having too much wildlife. I'd like sportsmen to say, 'Mr. Montoya, you have too many deer, too many elk, too many bears, too many peregrine falcons, and bald eagles.' That would tickle me to death, because that's my job" (Montoya 1990). This is not the attitude of someone committed either to all species or to all New Mexicans. Rather, Montoya's words reveal his devotion both to large game species and to hunters — the two major concerns that frame his environmental commitment.

Although NMDGF employees saw a great distance between themselves and other conservationists (including the Soil Conservation Service, ranchers, and private hunting interests, such as the Chama Land and Cattle Company), there are more similarities than a first glance would suggest. Both sets of resource professionals are in the business of managing resources. The resource conservationists seek to create a productive and diverse range for a variety of users. They are not preservationists. NMDGF is in the business of providing large animals "whether it be for hunting, viewing aesthetics, or whatever" (Montoya 1990).

The public often assumes incorrectly that WMAs are wilderness areas where nature is allowed to be free. Montoya himself dispels such myths

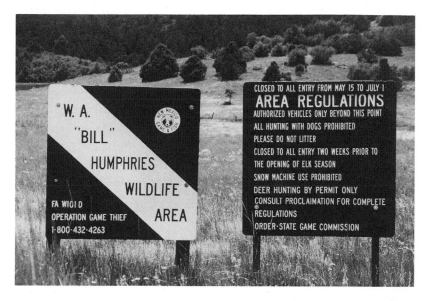

Fig. 4.6. Signs at the Bill Humphries Wildlife Area. *Photograph by the author.*

by noting that he intended to increase elk-hunting permits in order to keep the population in check. These are managed lands—managed for different constituencies that are not overly concerned with the needs of subaltern communities (fig. 4.6). Obviously, hunting is conceivably of great significance to low-income communities as a potential source of food. In fact, NMDGF officials did mention turning over poached animals to poor households for meat, but in no way do their policies or objectives systematically address social justice concerns.

The subject position of the various voices involved in resource management, as well as the many competing visions of nature, force us to look critically at the very concepts of wilderness and wilderness preserves. Rio Arriba County has three WMAs—Sargent, Humphries, and Rio Chama—all of which were once part of the Tierra Amarilla Land Grant. The Rio Chama and Humphries WMAs were purchased in the 1960s, and the Sargent in the 1970s. All were bought with the explicit purpose of increasing public elk-hunting opportunities. "Most of the land in the Tierra Amarilla Land Grant is controlled by large private ranches. They use the land for livestock grazing and big game hunting

by sportsmen who pay a high trespass fee. The Little Chama Valley
Ranch . . . would provide approximately a ten-fold increase in the
hunting opportunity over that now offered on the property" (NMDGF
n.d., a).[26] This quote comes from the application to acquire the Sargent
WMA, but similar language exists in the program narratives and management plans for both the Humphries and Rio Chama (NMDGF 1980,
1984).

Each WMA was purchased in a similar manner, but with some variations. The first step in establishing a WMA is for the NMDGF, as the
lead agency, to decide that additional land is necessary to carry out
a management objective and to select a parcel or parcels. Once the
state approves the purchase, NMDGF approaches United States Fish and
Wildlife Service (USFWS) for approval and funds. Through the Pittman-
Robertson Act (PR), money is available to purchase and improve hunting and wildlife areas. But because it is a federal funding source, the
USFWS must approve major transactions involving lands acquired with
PR funds. According to an USFWS administrator in New Mexico, there
was a time when the USFWS closely supervised the NMDGF because
it lacked adequately trained personnel. Over time, however, it has
evolved into a highly professional organization, and the USFWS simply
rubberstamps most NMDGF decisions (Parsons 1990).

The purpose and scope of WMAs can be altered subsequent to acquisition. For instance, in 1977 an additional two tracts of land were
added to the Humphries because they were needed to "increase the
carrying capacity of the Humphries Wildlife Area for big game species
and increase hunting opportunity on the area" (NMDGF 1977b). Another improvement was an airstrip in 1964 on the Rio Chama Wildlife
and Fishing Area. Approximately seventy acres of land were cleared
for the airstrip, but NMDGF did not "anticipate that this development
would adversely affect the development or administration of this area
for wildlife" (NMDGF 1964). These examples illustrate not only the
breadth of activities that have and do occur on WMAs, and the political
winds to which the NMDGF has been subjected, but also reveal that the
very idea of nature and wilderness is socially constructed and subject to
the meanings and values humans impose on them.

Despite the very real problems associated with grazing, and the complex relationship between environmentalists, resource agencies and

ranchers, grazing should not be dismissed. It is a potentially renewable economic activity. The fact that we as a society (along with much of the human population) engage in overgrazing is a function of the local political economic system, culture, and grazing practices (Eastman and Gray 1987). The fact that people have engaged in sustainable forms of grazing indicates that it is not simply human nature which creates such problems. People have the choice to become conscious of their relationship to the land. While some environmentalists would like to see an end to all grazing, I do not believe that is necessary. Renewable economic activities, in contrast to nonrenewable, are precisely the type we should be encouraging.

There is no escaping the fact that rural people must support themselves. The question is, How will they support themselves? Environmentalists are quick to oppose polluting industry, mining activities, and sprawling resorts, yet what options do poor, rural people have? The hard work of environmentalism is not the creating of a wilderness, but the devising of new methods to achieve more ecologically and socially sustainable economic activities.

A positive step in this direction are the recent reforms adopted for grazing on public lands. Whereas grazing permits had been allocated with no consideration of the quality of grazing management, new leases will be contingent upon the quality of the range, thus instilling in ranchers a motive to care for the land. While this is a notable improvement in and of itself, it should be clear that such a policy adjustment will not necessarily speak to the needs and concerns of marginalized populations.

Within the rhetoric of environmentalism and environmental justice, it is often implied that the same forces responsible for social injustice also cause environmental degradation. "It doesn't take a Ph.D. to see that the political and economic system that destroys the earth is the same system that exploits workers" (Erickson 1990, 5). This may be true, but as Chantal Mouffe and Ernesto Laclau have pointed out, these connections are not inevitably made (1985). Instead, they must be explicitly articulated. The history of dominant environmentalism in the United States bears out this point, since environmentalism and social justice have not been closely aligned or integrated. Thus, when speaking of subaltern communities, we must first recognize what their needs are, and then consider the larger power relations in which they are located. Taking these factors into account, subaltern groups will almost always favor using the environment over preserving it.

Their chosen path of resource use may stem from historical and current patterns of resource management, such as rubber-tapping in the Amazon, or from innovative efforts to create an economic base that draws on a variety of strategies (Paarlberg 1994). This is the case with Ganados. Although grazing has historical antecedents, their plan is informed by some of the latest thinking and technology in the areas of grazing, marketing, weaving, and animal care. Though subaltern groups have clear economic goals, the process of fulfilling them is both social and cultural. When we say that Hispanos have a cultural attachment to the land, they do; but that relationship is also an economic one. The fact that the land holds a special cultural significance, however, does not necessarily translate into an ecologically sustainable set of practices. Nor does reference to the past or the renewal of grazing activities signal either the maintenance of culture or a cultural renaissance. It is precisely because a particular culture, or way of life, is passing away that such issues become symbolically important. In the case of Ganados, however, the possibility exists that grazing may transcend symbolism and once again become a significant economic activity. It is that possibility, I would argue, that motivates Ganados, and perhaps other subaltern resource-dependent communities, to adopt a serious environmental consciousness.

This environmental consciousness can never be divorced from the community's quest for economic and political empowerment and their desire to assert a specific cultural identity. This is what Ganados mean when they describe themselves as supporters of sustainable environmentalism. They never lose sight of the connections between the land, culture, and economy. Sustainable environmentalism is distinguished from conservation and environmentalism in that they both are concerned with counting numbers — How many species can be saved? How many board feet of wood can be harvested? — without consideration of the larger social-ecological linkages, ignoring the role of frontline rural communities as the guardians of local resource use.

Unfortunately, environmentalists and resource management agencies, in this case the NMDGF, often have a narrow vision of what constitutes appropriate resource management. The rise of the single-purpose agency stems from several factors; the dominant environmental paradigm that seeks to separate environmental and economic concerns, the activism of politically powerful environmentalists, and the disregard most resource users have exhibited toward the land. In response to these realities, environmentalists have insisted that the only way to protect wildlife is through a single-purpose agency, an agenda not distracted by other concerns. But this framework denies that humans are part of nature, treats wildlife as if it existed in a void, and distances itself from any connection to social justice. In reality, wildlife exists within the context of communities, and policy must deal with those linkages.

Grazing as Contested Terrain

Ganados' perspective on grazing is largely structured by their poverty. Because of emphasis on preservation and the separation of economic concerns and environmentalism, resource users are not considered environmentalists by the mainstream movement. But by the same token, ranchers often state that they are the real environmentalists due to their intimate interaction with nature and dependency on resources. Of course, this ignores a long history during which resource users exhausted resources, creating vast ecological destruction (Lewis 1992), which shows that there is little that automatically makes one an environmentalist.

As I have mentioned, Ganados' environmental ethic has little to do with an essentialized Hispano identity; rather, it stems from an informed and conscious decision to create a viable and long-term economic project. Ganados' planners know that depleting resources will only lead to economic demise, through the diminishing of both the range and tourists — both of which are instrumental to its project. Such a rationale, however, is not enough to ensure that Ganados will not overgraze. In stressful times, such as drought or economic difficulties, it is entirely possible that Ganados might suspend their long-term vision in order to provide a temporary solution, rationalizing their actions as being in the best interests of the group. This potential problem must be anticipated and addressed both through written policy and through discussion with other interested parties. Aside from this potential problem,

Ganados have one of the most ecologically sound agricultural operations in the region, and this is precisely the type of project that should be supported. Ganados' vision of resource use, however, was disparaged and blocked by the dominant powers because it came from a subaltern viewpoint. In effect, Ganados' proposal was a challenge to the hegemonic vision of resource management, and its attempt to address explicitly the needs of marginalized communities was rejected.

Ganados del Valle

Ganados was born in the early 1980s, but its philosophy was formed over a long period of time. Activist Maria Varela, along with a local math teacher, Gumercindo Salazar, and struggling rancher Antonio Manzanares, initiated the grazing cooperative and corporation now known as Ganados del Valle. Low-income Hispanos individually could not build a successful agricultural operation. By pulling their meager resources together, they collectively could compete in an environment of escalating land prices. Their objective was to build a vertically integrated business that not only would produce jobs (keeping dollars in the area), but also would empower people (building upon their cultural and ecological history).

The first project of the cooperative was an effort to protect sheep herds with guard dogs instead of the more commonly used pesticides. After the initial success of the guard-dog program, Salazar, Manzanares, and Varela utilized telemarketing, receiving better prices for their lamb. Around 1983 the activists sought to involve more locals. Many were hesitant to join due to previous cooperative failures, but a few signed on (Salazar 1991). Manzanares ran the grazing operation, which included arranging summer grazing and making flock management decisions such as which animals to cull or how many could be fed over the winter. Varela contacted funding organizations such as the New Mexico Community Foundation (NMCF), to locate support for the fledgling group (Cassutt 1990; Salazar 1991).

During the early 1980s, nuns at the Los Ojos convent offered weaving instruction to local women, most of whom considered it recreational. Varela introduced the women to weaving master Rachel Brown, who expanded their knowledge of weaving and instituted Ganados' apprentice weaving program. These weavers and their products constituted the basis of Tierra Wools, the first business. By 1983 Ganados del Valle had incorporated and sold eleven thousand dollars worth of merchandise in its first six months.

In subsequent years, Ganados grew in both size and diversity. In the mid-1990s Ganados had four businesses and several community-development programs. The businesses included Tierra Wools, the weaving operation and store; Pastores Feed and General Store (fig. 4.7); Pastores Lamb, which markets organically grown specialty lamb; and the Rio Arriba Wool Washing plant. The community programs include a livestock shares program, which enables members to increase their individual flocks; the Milagro Fund, which provides seed money to other rural cooperatives; a summer arts program for local children; and the Churro Breeding program, aimed at increasing the number of churro. The churro is a breed brought over from Spain that has almost become extinct in the United States. It is noteworthy for its hardy character and short hair, ideal for craft use, but it was almost completely displaced by the merino and other species during the industrialization of sheep and wool production. In addition to revitalizing the churro, Ganados have sought to be environmentally conscious throughout their operation by using only natural dyes, drying their wool in a solar space, exploring ways to recycle tires, and working in the community to prevent haphazard development.

Ganados is structured around the four businesses. Members of Ganados pay nominal dues, participate in any program, and rotate responsibility for running each facet of the business. In 1990 there were approximately twenty-five weavers and fifteen growers, although the weavers are not required to be cooperative members. Each weaver works at her own pace, makes her own designs, and is paid by the piece. The demand for Tierra Wools' goods is so great the weavers have a hard time keeping up. Tierra Wools also hires other types of workers, such as local teenagers to work the store counter (members must also take turns at this task).

The sheep growers' structure is somewhat simpler. Ganados itself owns a flock, but the majority of the sheep belong to individual members who graze and manage their sheep cooperatively. An agricultural marketing specialist oversees lamb production, a challenging job even

Fig. 4.7. Pastores Feed and General Store in Los Ojos. *Photograph by the author.*

for the most experienced individual. In order to assure quality control, all growers must adhere to the same guidelines. Previously, most had managed their flocks in a less systematic manner and were not consistent with important management practices, such as regular use of vaccines or proper winter feed (Quintana 1990).

By most measures, Ganados del Valle is an economic development miracle that has captured national attention (Puleston Fleming 1985; Christensen 1988; Charland 1989; Jackson 1991). In 1993 the four businesses had combined sales of almost five hundred thousand dollars and employed forty people (mostly women), directly increasing the income of more than 150 rural households (Ganados 1993). Equally as important as the revenues Ganados has generated is the opportunity it has provided for people to grow. Women who previously saw themselves as housewives with limited efficacy have developed diverse skills and greatly expanded their horizons. They have a sense of ownership in Ganados. That, more than anything, means hope for the future.

At this point Ganados is continuing to expand, but it is limited by a lack of grazing land. They have a cooperative herd of about two thousand sheep, 25 percent of which are churro. During the summer, growers plant feed crops while the animals graze in the high country. In the fall, the animals return to the valley and are fed the crops. If the crop is lost or insufficient, however, the grower must buy feed, which can be quite expensive (Quintana n.d.).

Ideally, Ganados would like to have their own grazing land, but buying a ranch is nearly impossible. As one ex-rancher put it, "If you went out to buy it now, you couldn't pay the interest on it if you lived a hundred years" (Puleston Fleming 1985, 40). The other option is to lease, but leasing would be a very expensive proposition for Ganados because sheep simply do not realize cattle's rate of return, and as previously mentioned, sheep offer numerous employment opportunities.

The Struggle to Graze

Soon after the grazing cooperative was formed, Ganados faced the problem of patching together sufficient summer grazing land. Because of the proximity and size of the WMAS, Ganados approached NMDGF about the possibility of limited summer grazing on the Sargent WMA.

This was not an unheard-of proposal, since grazing has occurred on WMAs throughout New Mexico as well as on the Sargent (Olson 1983; NMDGF 1978–81).

The Sargent had been grazed by its former owner, Virginia Binkley, who deeded it to the Nature Conservancy who, in turn, sold it to NMDGF to be used for habitat. From 1978 to 1981, subsequent to its designation as a WMA, Binkley was allowed to graze cattle on the land (NMDGF 1978–81). The reason given for allowing Binkley to graze was to see "if grazing can be used to improve the quality and quantity of forage for elk" (Olson 1983). The grazing, however, was terribly mismanaged and had disastrous effects on the land (C. Sanchez 1982) and on future policy decisions.

NMDGF was not enthusiastic about Ganados' idea, immediately citing legal and political obstacles that precluded their grazing. Nevertheless, it did inquire through normal channels as to the feasibility of Ganados grazing.[27] It is important to note that NMDGF undertook no similar inquiries when Binkley sought grazing rights. NMDGF has the authority to determine such matters, assuming it does not act "capriciously" (Evans 1990a) and chose to exercise its autonomy in the case of Binkley. In the case of Ganados, however, they chose to consult with all related agencies and authorities.

Because of the recent grazing disaster by Binkley, the USFWS, involved because federal monies contributed to the purchase of the lands, opposed the grazing initiative (Spear 1985; Fjetland 1983). Soon after, NMDGF prepared a new management plan for the Sargent that suspended all grazing until the land had been rehabilitated. In the interim, Ganados revised its grazing strategy to include other WMAs and sought support from both the governor of New Mexico and local politicians (Varela 1988, 1987). The proposal was placed within the context of failed development plans. "Over the last thirty years, the State of New Mexico has been unable to mount effective and enduring development programs in the isolated rural communities in northern New Mexico. . . . Research done by the organization has indicated that with a sound management plan, under daily supervision of a shepherd, grazing sheep on game lands can improve the pasture for wildlife" (Ganados del Valle 1984, 2).

Manzanares formally asked the game commission for permission to graze on the Sargent and Humphries WMAs in July 1985. He proposed that NMDGF "appoint a Task Force to permit a pilot project of grazing from mid-June to September for a minimum of (3) years, preferably five (5)" (NMDGF 1985). At this point, the full extent of NMDGF's opposition became clear. The commission opposed the plan, and although the chairman did establish a committee to study the matter, the committee never convened. In September the commission voted to place a moratorium on grazing on the WMAs. "The proposal was totally unacceptable to the department and the commission. The amount of grazing they would be doing would have meant that in a short period of time there wouldn't be anything left." Chairman Koch also mentioned that USFWS "wouldn't allow such grazing, since Federal funds are used to maintain the area" (Koch in Schein 1985), despite the fact that a representative from the Department of the Interior supported obtaining a new direction on WMA land use, should there be any administrative or legal concerns (a procedure that previously had been used in the case of the airstrip).

Ganados continued to press for the grazing proposal through political outreach and research, but the NMDGF issued a resounding "no" in May 1988. "The bottom line appears to be that we are unwilling to consider any project being conducted on the wildlife areas when we can not be assured that it is beneficial to our management of the areas. Unless there is some significant change in what we have seen in the past proposals and evaluations, we see no reason to discuss the issue further" (Olson 1988). According to NMDGF policy, new projects or techniques can only be entertained if a management problem is identified or if a change can be proven to enhance the area in terms of the management objectives.

As the predominantly Anglo institution denied the predominantly Hispano proposal, the issue became ethnically and racially charged. Grazing was allowed on other WMAs. Why should Ganados be treated differently? Surely it was not a case of protecting an endangered species since, by NMDGF's own admission, elk were more than plentiful in the region. "They don't like our accusations of prejudice — but when you couple this decision with the information that for the past five years they have permitted livestock grazing on two wildlife areas in the southern part of the state, prejudice against northern New Mexico communities is a plausible conclusion" (Varela 1989, A9). The chairman of the NMDGF commission replied, "The charge of prejudice is of particular concern to me, not only because it is utterly baseless but because it damages the credibility of legitimate claims. It is clearly a case of crying wolf, when you consider that a Maestas of northern New Mexico chairs the Commission, and a Montoya from Las Cruces heads the Department, claims of prejudice by Ms. Varela strain credibility" (Maestas 1990).

The fact that two Hispanos were involved in the decisions offers a valuable opportunity to more closely examine the different conceptions of racism at work. From the perspective of the NMDGF, it was not a racist organization because it had allowed a few nonwhites to achieve positions of power. This particular articulation of racism is one based on discriminatory acts against nonwhites. In this form of racism, nonwhite persons are discriminated against, therefore it is antiracist to hire, promote, or include them. This conceptualization of racism can be seen throughout the country through such mechanisms as affirmative action, and by the environmental justice movement's demands that the mainstream movement hire more people of color. While an essential component of an antiracist strategy, this understanding of racism does not begin to include the many features embedded in the current discourse of racism, and the practice of exclusion (see the discussion in chapter 2). It denies questions of power, inequality, and the frequent equating of culture, 'race', history, and ethnicity.

Ganados' perspective was based on a different operationalization of racism, one that saw Hispanos as an unequal community based on 'race' and ethnicity, history, culture, and political institutions. Their understanding of racism shows us that just because persons are of a particular heritage and "racial group," it does not necessarily mean they will be more sympathetic to their community of origin. In the words of British author Paul Gilroy (1993), "It ain't where you're from, it's where you're at" that matters.

The civil rights community has recently discovered this, and it is an important lesson for environmental justice activists. These different ideas of racism allow society to differentiate between individual and institutionalized racism. Institutionalized racism can be seen in the goals, procedures, and values of the NMDGF, which are elitist and racist because they do not take into account the resource needs and objectives of poor Hispano communities, therefore working to their detriment.

The ideology and practice of the NMDGF takes its cue from dominant environmentalism and value-free science. Because of the legitimacy and power that are imbued in science and environmental management, we do not see them as racist, even though the outcome of their policies may be racially inequitable. At one point NMDGF Commission Chairman Maestas stated that if they were to allow grazing, they should not unduly favor a subaltern group. "It is not the legality that I have a problem with, but the fairness or lack thereof. I personally do not see why Ganados should have any more right to use those areas than any other entity. If we are ever going to allow grazing, it should be available to everyone" (Maestas 1990). While a number of environmentalists can readily distinguish between allowing Ganados or a large corporation to graze, Maestas cannot see why Ganados should be given special preference. "If you want to maintain your culture, that's fine, just do it on your own hoof" (Maestas in Kernberger 1990). Poverty, social justice, and cultural considerations were irrelevant to Maestas. His position may appear to be fair and unbiased, but this overlooks how dominant Anglo cultural values have been incorporated into policy and practice. Both institutionalized hunting and preservation are examples of how rules and policies maintain the dominant Anglo culture and forms of economic organization. It is only when nonwhite people with distinctive cultures make special claims that we must all play fair.

Faced with the continued rejection of its proposal, Ganados, like the UFWOC and other groups of limited power, decided to go public with their story in the hope that public opinion could be brought to bear on the NMDGF. Ganados' first step was to introduce a significantly changed proposal. With assistance from the Soil Conservation Service, Ganados' agricultural marketing specialist studied the Sargent, Humphries, and Rio Chama WMAs to better understand the local ecology and devise a more effective grazing plan based on the work of Alan Savory, who has advocated short-term grazing. The new plan, *A Proposal to Improve Wildlife Habitat on the Rio Chama, Humphries and Sargent Wildlife Areas* (Ganados del Valle 1989a), emphasized the ecological contributions of grazing (table 4.3).

The proposal laid out several assumptions. First, a complete man-

Table 4.3. Grazing Schedule for the Proposal to Improve Wildlife Habitat on the Rio Chama, Humphries, and Sargent Wildlife Areas

Dates	WMA	Acreage Grazed	AUM* Consumed	AUM Remaining
5–14 to 6–15	Rio Chama	8,400–14,000	400	720
6–16 to 8–15	Humphries	7,330–10,470	400	843
8–15 to 10–5	Sargent	7,800–20,400	400	640

Source: Compiled from Tapia and Silvers 1990; Ganados del Valle 1989a.
*An AUM (Animal Unit Month) is the amount of forage required by an adult cow or its equivalent per month.

agement plan would require grazing as well as other methods. Second, as existing forage had increased invader species and deteriorated the nutritive value and palatability of the undergrazed sites, highly controlled grazing would eliminate invader species and increase the quality and quantity of vegetation. Third, the improved forage would attract more elk, decreasing the number wandering onto adjacent ranches because of the more desirable forage. At each site, management would focus on a particular habitat problem. For example, grazing on the Humphries WMA would focus on eradicating rabbit brush, while on the Sargent it would concentrate on the thatch problem.

There were, of course, a host of other issues, some of which were resolved and some not. For one, both the Rio Chama and Humphries lacked adequate water facilities that Ganados was willing to provide. In contrast, a more troublesome issue was posed by the Sargent's resident elk herd, which totaled about 560, and its migratory herd, which ranged from 600 to 800. The plan sought to reduce any interaction between elk and sheep by ensuring that a shepherd or shepherds would be present at all times, moving the sheep if they were grazing too heavily in one place, directing them to areas in need of grazing. In addition, all elk calving sites would be excluded from any grazing activity. The plan was timed for minimal overlap between the two species, because as the elk moved toward higher elevations, the sheep would be moved to lower ones (Tapia and Silvers 1990). Nevertheless, the possibility of interaction remained a concern to some.

Ganados packaged the plan as a proposal to enhance the WMAS because that is what the NMDGF had said was necessary to graze: a plan that would improve the habitat. Because limited research has been conducted on sheep grazing in geographic areas comparable to the WMAS, only contradictory evidence was available from the literature and other states' departments of game and fish (Hershcopf 1988; Polenz 1988; Reinecker 1988; Smith 1988; Tsukamoto 1988). While Ganados was convinced, based on its analysis and research, that the plan would enhance the vegetation, the NMDGF insisted there was no problem in the first place.[28]

Ganados briefly discussed the new proposal with the NMDGF in July, who in turn consulted with the Nature Conservancy, since they had deeded the land. The deed contained several restrictions that were continually used by the NMDGF to justify why Ganados could not graze:

> The premises hereby conveyed shall forever be held solely as wildlife habitat and shall be utilized in accordance with sound wildlife management practices, PROVIDED, HOWEVER, that the continued use of no more than 200 acres, located in the southern portion of Binkley Release Areas No. 4, by snowmobiles, may be permitted, PROVIDED, that overnight camping shall only be permitted at areas designated by the New Mexico State Game Commission in accordance with its duly adopted regulations AND PROVIDED FURTHER, that timber may be removed in accordance with accepted practices for improvement of wildlife habitat. (The Nature Conservancy 1975, emphasis in original)

The deed restrictions themselves are interesting because of what they reveal about contemporary environmentalism. Although this land (once part of the Tierra Amarilla Land Grant) was located in a region of deep poverty, Binkley was willing to allow snowmobiling and camping (activities conforming to environmentalists' and others' quality-of-life and recreational needs), but only limited timber removal, and no grazing. Despite these restrictions, Binkley grazed the land after it become a WMA, although the New Mexico Nature Conservancy claimed no knowledge of such grazing (Waldman 1991). Moreover, the NMDGF had previously allowed grazing on the WMA, and wrote the Sargent management plan so as not to exclude grazing by recognizing its possible benefits. "Areas grazed by livestock remove vegetation and allows a more desirable vegetation to come back in the Spring" (NMDGF 1980, 8). Regardless of the deed restrictions, the actual actions and policies of the NMDGF were far more ambiguous.

On July 29, 1989, Salazar testified before a United States House Interior Oversight Subcommittee hearing. Ganados was facing a crisis because its lease at the time (with the Jicarilla Apache) would soon expire. He eloquently expressed why he felt the NMDGF should try to work with them:

> It is important for environmentalists and conservationists to understand that a wildlife refuge cannot be torn from the economic, social and physical fabric of a community. If you want a healthy wildlife refuge then you must pay attention to the economic needs of the surrounding community. We offer one solution to deteriorating wildlife habitat and a declining economy. We also offer an opportunity for the state and federal agencies charged with the responsibility of conserving wildlife to develop a productive and cooperative partnership with a local community.
>
> Elk is not an endangered species, the churro is, so is the Hispanic pastoral culture of northern New Mexico. If we can work together to solve this problem the wildlife will benefit, the churro will be preserved and our children will inherit a strong culture and economic future. (Salazar 1989)

Salazar's quote illustrates an important dynamic in this conflict: though Ganados' struggle is often labeled a culture clash or an effort to preserve a dying culture, the reality is far more complex than such simple (but effective) cultural arguments may imply. First, we must note that Ganados employs cultural arguments because the dominant environmental paradigm does not allow for economic considerations. Economic arguments are not considered legitimate by the environmental and resource community; the thought of a declining culture is. Ganados has marketed itself in such a way as to gain support. Second, it is worth looking critically at the particular concept of culture invoked by Salazar (and many others). It is based on a problematic model. By casting the Hispano pastoral culture as endangered, it presumes that the culture is static and essential. The fact is, for most Hispanos a viable pastoral culture no longer exists and, therefore, cannot be saved. It died when the pastoral economy became a thing of the past. However, culture and identity are not unidirectional; they are far more complex, contradictory, and multidimensional. Culture and identity are in a continuous state of process. While they are informed by the past, they are also a response to the dominant culture, and contemporary political economy. As Stuart Hall (1992) has observed, "There can . . . be no 'return' or 'recovery' of the ancestral past which is not re-experienced through the categories of the present: no base for creative enunciation in a simple reproduction of traditional forms which are not transformed by the technologies and the identities of the present" (p. 258).

Ganados is trying to create the space in which to bring together the necessary elements (e.g., grazing, animals, and weaving) that will allow the reconstruction of an Hispano pastoral identity (fig. 4.8). This is a new creation, a product of the late twentieth century, not a remnant of the nineteenth — although it is, of course, informed by the past. The role of identity in the Ganados project is paramount and must be properly understood. At times Ganados and the Hispano pastoral culture may be seen in essentialist terms — what is called strategic essentialism (Fuss 1989), as members reify their cultural history and attachment to the land. We must, however, differentiate between rhetoric and reality. Ganados is taking elements of a treasured past and refashioning them into something that can facilitate the political and economic empowerment of the group. What is important is the maintenance of a connection to the group past, and Ganados allows for this link.

It is crucial to understand the significance of history, particularly romanticized histories, to those subject to historical erasure. "Those left behind by capitalism have no option but to collectively create a 'remembered' village and economy that serve(s) as an ideological backdrop against which to deplore the present" (Scott in Guha 1990, 92–93). Certainly, a large part of Ganados' appeal for both Hispanos and outside supporters is the creation of a remembered village, but unlike previous representations, this one is not built solely on dreams and romanticization; it is firmly rooted in a clear and realistic political vision.

Things became more heated on August 18, 1989, when Ganados was prepared to make a presentation at a NMDGF commission meeting. Chairman Maestas stated that no action could be taken because

GANADOS DEL VALLE 10TH ANNIVERSARY NEWSLETTER

In the beginning. . . Twelve years ago on a Saturday morning in the spring of 1983, two neighbors stood talking on a dirt road in a mountain village in Northern New Mexico. As they talked, they began to wonder if the sheep flocks in the valley might be a way to increase income and create new jobs in the area. They brought their ideas to another neighbor who had just decided to go full time into the sheep business.

Ten years later, these beginnings have yielded the revitalization of the ancient churro sheep breed and the strengthening of the Rio Grande Weaving Tradition. Four businesses: Tierra Wools, Pastores Lamb, Pastores Feed and General Store and Rio Arriba Wool Washing have combined annual sales nearly $500,000 and employ over 40 people. Over 150 families have experienced increased income through the organizations marketing of their arts, crafts and/or agricultural products.

10th Anniversary Celebration

July 24, 1993
Los Ojos, New Mexico
11:am to 11:pm

**Todos son envitados
All are Welcome**

Events:
Food Booths/Story Telling
Demonstrations/Arts & Crafts

Fig. 4.8. Ganados newsletter announcing the tenth-anniversary celebration

Ganados was not on the agenda. Varela requested the commission to hold an emergency session to consider a six-week pilot project. Maestas declined. At that point, Ganados informed the commission that it would occupy one of the WMAs until the NMDGF held hearings in the Chama Valley (NMDGF 1989b). They issued a press release announcing they would move two thousand sheep onto a WMA, "Our greatest desire is to be a partner with New Mexico Game and Fish. We have the same goals. Inappropriate land development both hurts our agricultural economy and hurts the wildlife. We stand prepared to work out an ecologically sound management plan which would improve wildlife habitat, improve the local economy, and hopefully limit the growth of land development" (Ganados del Valle 1989b).

This decision to trespass was not a means to access rangeland. It was intended to force the NMDGF into action by illustrating Ganados' desperation (Flores 1989b). This direct action strategy was similar to the tactics of environmental justice activists and other marginalized groups. They chose to use one of the few tools available to the subaltern — the withholding of cooperation.

As promised, Ganados' members committed an act of civil disobedience as they began moving their nineteen hundred sheep onto WMA land. The event, and the sight of large numbers of Hispanos on horseback trespassing with sheep, attracted widespread media coverage, and at least for a moment caused many to pause and consider the link between resource policy and marginalized communities. On August 21, NMDGF officers located the Ganados group by helicopter and issued a warning citation. The following day, NMDGF officers personally issued Ganados a trespass citation (*Rio Grande Sun* 1989). Clearly, a crisis situation had been reached in New Mexico, and it quickly became a spectacle (fig. 4.9).

The trespass, which lasted five days, had the desired effect of forcing both the NMDGF and the governor into action. On August 22, 1989, a meeting was held in Tierra Amarilla, during which two alternatives were identified (Schein 1989d, e). The state offered grazing near Lake Heron (a state park) at market rate, and local businessmen offered free grazing land on four hundred disputed acres (Schein 1989d). Ganados chose the former, mainly because the businessmen's offer, while greatly appreciated, was too close to town (Flores 1989a). On August 24,

Fig. 4.9. Resistance as spectacle. With members of Ganados del Valle beside him, Antonio Manzanares *(center)* conducts a news conference at the Humphries Wildlife Area west of Chama. *Photograph by Sidney Brink, courtesy of the* Albuquerque Journal.

Ganados gathered their flock and proceeded to Lake Heron, a thirty-two-mile drive that took five days (Flores 1989c). While the governor insisted that the law must be obeyed, he directed the NMDGF to work with livestock owners and be more flexible (Schein 1989d). The governor also announced the creation of a task force charged with the development of a research project to study how grazing might enhance the WMAS (Flores 1989c).

Having broken the law and pushed the conflict by using the threat of mass mobilization, Ganados was fairly certain that it was in a much stronger position to be considered a serious player in future resource policy. However, once the conflict shifted back to the world of research and policy, away from mass mobilization and the public spotlight, the entrenched and institutionalized power of hegemonic resource interests reasserted itself.

The Politics of Research

The task force was made up of representatives from the NMDGF, Ganados, environmental organizations, New Mexico State University (NMSU), hunters, and the community. The task force was ostensibly charged with developing a solid research plan that would meet the needs of the various parties and contribute to the scientific literature. In reality, however, the governor simply used the research effort as a tool to deflect conflict and tension.

At the first meeting, Drs. John Fowler and Phil Zwank, both of NMSU, were appointed to direct the research. "The Governor wants the research to embrace several areas of the state and all large game species. . . . To meet this objective the research will be very extensive and expensive to conduct" (Schickedanz 1989). The parameters were later broadened to encompass livestock versus wildlife, rather than just sheep and elk, with a research outline due October 14, 1989 (Schein 1989c). Not surprisingly, the points of difference around which the grazing conflict had revolved spilled over into the formulation of a research plan.

Strong differences emerged at the first meeting, and grew by the second. Those who felt the study must include the WMAs were opposed by those who felt they should be excluded. The WMAs became a microcosm of the larger philosophical differences between preservationists and sustainable environmentalists. While this was the most fundamental split, there also was opposition to Ganados itself. Some felt that Ganados had backed the NMDGF into a corner, and that the hunting and environmental communities had to close ranks. For example, hunters do not explicitly oppose grazing, but they joined forces with environmentalists and the NMDGF over this issue.

Most opposed structuring the research in order to meet Ganados' grazing needs, and the various constituencies drew upon policy, law, custom, and science to defend their position, illustrating the degree to which resource use has been fashioned with little thought given to subaltern populations. More importantly, it demonstrates the extent to which the rules of the game (whether the "game" is resource use, site location, or pesticide regulation) are established long before the subaltern ever become formally involved or recognized. Therefore, it is incumbent upon subordinated groups not only to break into the circle of participation, but to challenge established theory and practice that often assumes the mantle of natural, rational, fair, and value-free science. Accordingly, when we speak of environmental inequalities or environmental racism, much more is at issue than simply current policies and decisions. There is an entire history that has accumulated behind any given moment. To ignore this history, particularly how various groups have institutionalized their interests, is to offer only a limited snapshot of a much larger problem.

Hunters, for example, have mastered this process of defining a terrain, and then using custom and law to exclude others. They did this by arguing that the WMA lands were purchased with sportsmen's money through the PR program, and were not to be used by other groups (Weingarten 1990). Although large portions of the WMAs were bought with PR funds, it was not the only funding source. The Sargent WMA, for instance, was paid for with a combination of state general funds ($547,900), Colorado River Storage Act monies ($1,515,350), and Dingell-Johnson (DJ) funds ($1,430,000), with PR providing only $213,700 (NMDGF 1980). Regardless of diverse funding sources, other PR and DJ purchased lands do permit grazing. In fact, the Rio Chama WMA was grazed as recently as 1987, and the Marquez WMA in southern New Mexico was grazed until 1993 (Montoya 1990).

Although PR lands are partially paid for by sportsmen, that does not mean they own them. Nevertheless, sportsmen often have proprietary attitudes toward these lands. "Wildlife management areas are not public property. They are owned by a special interest group and financed out of dedicated funds donated by that group. They are private property open to public trespass" (Sherwood 1989, 15). One hunter wrote to the USFWS, "It is your responsibility to uphold the law and the rights of all sportsmen and not allow the sheep or any livestock to use WMA property" (Painter n.d.). Regardless of such sentiment, the lands are publicly owned.

More important for our analysis is the fact that hunters as a group have managed to have their interests carried out by the state through the use of DJ and PR funds. Building on this achievement, they were able to use WMA funding arguments to exclude other claims. The extent to which hunters are embedded in resource management at both the national and regional level allows them to discredit the claims of the less powerful, since they themselves have helped shape the prevailing discourse and practice (Balzar 1994).

The Nature Conservancy led the environmentalists' opposition to use of the WMAs by emphasizing the deed restrictions (Schein 1989c, footnote 27). Again, the existence and practice of an organization such as the Nature Conservancy is clearly within the province of the powerful and elite. Although environmentalists formally opposed Ganados, it was a textured opposition. The Sierra Club declined to take a formal position on the matter due to dissension within the ranks. Aware of the tensions between environmentalists and minorities, and of the charges of elitism, they did not want to exacerbate the situation. Some individual Sierra Club members, in contrast, favored the preservation of the WMAs and actively worked to protect them (and the elk) from Ganados.

Another reason some environmentalists felt compelled to oppose Ganados was their fear that failure to do so would jeopardize the credibility of wildlife preservation. Loss of credibility would hamper future efforts of a wildlife industry that had worked hard to earn the public's trust (Henderson 1990). This is an important point to appreciate when looking at how environmental concerns and practices developed apart from social justice concerns as well as how built-in inertia to change developed. Environmentalists had cultivated public support predicated on a specific environmental vision — would changing the vision constitute a betrayal or simply a potential loss of funding?

Still other environmentalists believed the situation was completely unfair. A number agreed that there was not enough land to go around in northern New Mexico. Others felt that while sheep in the past had caused tremendous damage, that did not necessarily mean that Hispanos had overgrazed; nor did it mean that a proper grazing program was unattainable, although perhaps expensive. Their ambivalence was heightened by their belief that most of the land had been stolen from the Hispanos (Freeman 1990; Cassutt 1990).

Other individuals, including members of Audubon and Sierra Club, were much harsher in their assessment. Some rejected the idea that Hispanos had any special claims to the land, as they had stolen it from the Indians, ". . . and the equity there, that's real hard to see" (Jervis 1990). In response to questions regarding the poverty of the area, one Audubon member thought if it was hard to make a living, then people should move. There were too many people in the north already, and the area would benefit from depopulation. To some, northern Hispanos were unrealistic whiners who needed to face the reality of urban wage-labor.

Regardless of such neo-Malthusian analyses, the reality of most environmentalists was worlds away from that of low-income rural Hispanos. They were relatively affluent (Cassutt 1990; Freeman 1990; Henderson 1990; Jervis 1990; Weingarten 1990; Waldman 1990), they had high educational levels (bachelor and graduate degrees), and secure, meaningful jobs that provided a measure of dignity and opportunity. Their lifestyle, in fact, entailed far greater consumption than the rural poor, and therefore consumed more resources and created greater environmental degradation. Although some empathized with what Ganados was trying to do, and one even described Ganados as "the best thing to ever happen to the North" (Henderson 1990), they still did not believe it was their responsibility to help Ganados succeed. Most environmentalists interviewed responded that taking into account social justice and the economic needs of local communities was important, but that it was the job of someone else. In effect, each organizational mission had already been set. One activist saw the situation as ". . . an environmental issue only because someone is trying to invade a wildlife area" (Jervis 1990). While the majority of activists recognized Ganados' project and efforts as environmental in scope, they were not adequately impressed to change the orientation of their organizations.

Although environmentalists were often at odds with the NMDGF and felt the agency did not operate in a sufficiently environmentally conscious manner, they supported the agency on this matter. Groups utilized their normal channels of dispersing information, initiated letter-writing campaigns, and pressured politicians. While New Mexican environmentalists did see the issue in diverse ways, they put aside their differences and united in opposition to Ganados.

Rallying for inclusion of the WMAs in the research proposal was a representative of the state land office, Ganados, the governor, Fowler and Zwank of NMSU, and a representative of the New Mexico Department of Agriculture. These are parties that are all committed to conservation, not preservation. Even though these actors fully supported Ganados in their efforts at community development, most regularly supported wise-use and multiple-use management anyway. Reflecting the attitude of several conservationists was Bill Humphries, then of the state land office. He said, "You can't take the people and the local economy out of the research. They are part of the environment" (Humphries in Schein 1989c). While Governor Carruthers was not adamant that the WMAs be included, he felt public lands were essential and that "some would end up being included" (Schein 1989c).

Given the broad research charge and lack of consensus, Zwank and Fowler devised a research plan that would take seven years and cost $1.97 million (Range Improvement Task Force and Cooperative Fish and Wildlife Unit 1989), and presented it to the governor. At that meeting, the entire process began to unravel. The governor, while encouraged, found the study unacceptable because of its prohibitive cost and its utilization of all three WMAs (Schein 1989d). The participants disagreed on many points that always led to the WMAs. Ganados, represented by Manzanares and Varela, not only felt that the cost was exorbitant, but that their concerns had been omitted. Therefore, they opposed the plan. The USFWS did not approve of the study because its representative did not recognize that any problem existed with WMA land in the first place. "We haven't seen anything so far to indicate there is a problem, so we see no need to investigate it" (Parsons in Schein 1989d).

Fowler devised a new proposal that was half as expensive and required use of the Humphries WMA only (Schein 1989a). He argued for the inclusion of the WMA because it was in the governor's mandate and was a necessary control. The commissioners discussed the issue and all opposed using WMAs in the research (NMDGF 1989a, 14–16). At the meeting's conclusion, Chairman Maestas proposed a formal policy prohibiting grazing on all WMAs, "namely the Humphries, Sargent, and Rio Chama areas." The motion was unanimously passed (NMDGF 1989a, 16) and essentially brought to a close the formal disagreement between the NMDGF and Ganados, as all policy openings were closed and all grazing prohibited. Because of this change in policy, there was no point in developing a research proposal. The issue had been decided by fiat. The struggle has continued, but not through established channels with the NMDGF. Instead, it has been contested through less formal wrangling between Ganados, environmentalists, and others.

What is important to appreciate at this point is how the weight and authority of science, and how research and resource policy, can work to the detriment of marginalized communities. This, of course, is not new. It has been well documented in antitoxics struggles, particularly the dismissal of local knowledge and observation. The case of Ganados is somewhat different in that it is not technical jargon and levels of statistical significance that are thwarting the efforts of a subaltern group. Instead, Ganados' efforts have been thwarted by the very ideas of science, resource management, and policy, and the processes instituted to handle issues in a fair and objective way.

Iris Young (1990) has written how our society has reached the point where formal equality, such as voting rights and antidiscrimination laws, has been extended to all. This does not, however, account for the unequal power that results from social difference. It is social difference that helps to explain how and why the policy and processes of the NMDGF worked against Ganados. As a predominantly Spanish-speaking population with low levels of formal education, Hispanos were not hired in large numbers by the NMDGF, and therefore had a minimal, if any, role in the development of policy. Interestingly, the earliest leaders of the NMDGF were Hispano, but this all changed as New Mexico became more Anglicized and wildlife management became both more scientifically oriented and institutionalized. Moreover, those Hispanos who might have been involved at the policy-setting level would have been hired based on their formal academic training in biology and related sciences, not because they come from an ethnic group with a long history of hunting, gathering, grazing, and horticulture. Thus, these individuals were hired precisely because they had internalized the dominant ideas of science and nature, and not because of their folk knowledge and practices. These processes of exclusion and transformation served to create a policy and process that did not necessarily reflect the needs and concerns of subaltern Hispanos, and that ultimately rendered them as outside the purview of resource management.

Equally as important as understanding the biased nature of research and resource policy is recognizing nature, resource management, environmentalism, and preservation as socially constructed. The polarization of wilderness and grazing patently reflects different values, positions, and political projects. Although they may appear to be irreconcilable, we must not overlook the extent to which these ideas are of our own making (Bennett and Chaloupka 1993). By deconstructing these categories, we can see that they entail their own values and biases, and that significant similarities exist between the two.

Given the history of European settlement and expansion in the western United States, it is readily understandable how environmentalists seek to segregate economic concerns from environmental ones, and why they promote wilderness. While wilderness is a vital tool in environmental management, it presents the danger of lulling us into a false sense of security. Knowing we have preserved such lands does not require us to alter an economy based on continual growth and expansion, change consumption patterns — how things are made, what is made, and how the benefits and costs of production are distributed — or change concomitant power relations.

Precisely because resource use has more often than not been highly destructive, and because of the historical roots of environmentalism, we can appreciate why the concepts of *wilderness, wild, natural,* and *preservation* have become the objectives of many environmentalists and of the public at large. As a society, we have rarely shown ourselves capable of using resources wisely, due to both the exigencies of our economy and our culture. The public, informed by mainstream environmentalism, is enthralled by national parks and cute fuzzy creatures. It strongly supports preservation and wilderness, without a full understanding of resource use and management. This attitude on the part of the public was epitomized in a letter opposing Ganados' initiative: "Keeping the area natural for elk and other animals is important!" (Wilkes n.d.). That a member of the public would consider WMA lands as natural shows the extent to which the attitudes and beliefs of mainstream environmentalism have become dominant and legitimized.

By unpacking these images and ideas, we can see that there is little that is *natural, pristine,* or *wild* in terms of the WMAs or elk. As previously mentioned, WMAs are *managed.* Each unit has a management plan that identifies problems which may include invader species, inadequate water supply for wildlife, or vegetative composition that does not support the greatest possible number of species. Once a problem has been identified, solutions are proposed. These may include mowing, burning, trimming trees, or grazing (NMDGF n.d., b, 5). Clearly the objective is not to let nature take its course, as Alston Chase (1987) has aptly demonstrated in his study of Yellowstone National Park. Rather, it is to promote the greatest number of the most desirable species — those that the wildlife industry, with the support of the public, has decided are charismatic mega-fauna (such as elk or bears). Other forms of wildlife, such as turkey, are secondary, and nongame species and plants rank even lower (NMDGF 1983, 3).

An illustration of this contradiction can be seen in attempts to reintroduce the gray wolf, a predator. The reintroduction of the wolf has been hotly debated. If we truly had an ecological point of view, its reintroduction would not be opposed since it is a natural part of an ecosystem.

Given the way elk have been institutionalized by state and federal agencies, as well as by hunting and environmental organizations, there are growing similarities between elk and domesticated animals. The entire framework surrounding elk is completely anthropocentric. In effect, they are allowed to flourish solely for human purposes: hunting, recreation, and viewing pleasure. They are a form of economic development, attracting hunters, environmentalists, and wildlife enthusiasts to the region to spend their tourist dollars. Elk, like other forms of wildlife, are what Hays (1987) has referred to as a "consumed" form of recreation, meaning that our enjoyment of wildlife is essentially an act of consumption. Evernden has gone to the roots of this anthropocentric viewpoint by noting that almost all of our approaches to nature are predicated on the assumption "that there is a thing called nature that needs our help. To 'husband' wild animals, or wilderness itself for that matter, is to treat them as domesticates" (1992, 101, 120). The very notions of nature and wildlife are defined in opposition to us; they are what humans are not. There is nothing inherently bad with this arrangement, but these ideas and activities are not a given or natural. Revealing these assumptions may not only help us to understand how the public may interpret the situation as one of elk being displaced when, in fact, elk were at record numbers; it may also lead us to consider other possibilities.

What is troubling is that when people believe we are actually putting nonhuman species first, we are not; or that pristine wilderness even exists, it does not (see Denevan 1992). Humans control almost every landscape. It is only a question of degree and orientation. Moreover, by shrouding what are really political issues in the language and imagery of nature and wilderness, we are relieved from confronting the social and economic consequences of traditional resource management that we ourselves have created.

The Struggle Continues

The lack of accessible grazing land and poverty are long-term structural problems confronting the region. Resolution cannot be achieved simply by altering policy, although that would help. More likely, it will come about through a shift of attitudes, an intense commitment to political change, a reorientation of the development trajectory, and a redistribution of the benefits of tourism and environmental protection.

The membership of Ganados believes that environmentalists are their potential allies because they both have a vested interest in directing and redirecting economic growth and development. While both eschew the unchecked proliferation of new development tracts, environmentalists prefer preservation while Ganados advocates environmentally and culturally appropriate economic development that will provide income to rural households. For the most part, environmentalists do not relish being viewed as the proverbial "bad guys," and Ganados does appreciate their influence and power. These factors led to the beginnings of mediation between the two groups, initiated by both Ganados and the Southwest Research and Information Center (SHRIC). Invitations were sent to selected environmentalists and to Indian and Hispano leaders from the region, particularly those involved in resource use and community development. At Ganados' request, NMDGF was not invited. There was too much history and animosity between NMDGF and the Hispano community, and it was felt that there was no benefit in rehashing old differences. Because of NMDGF's exclusion, Ganados could not discuss the WMAS. However, the discussion did include the exploration of possible solutions to Ganados' grazing problem (Varela 1991b, 2). The main focus of the meeting was on building a relationship between Ganados and environmentalists. Ganados believed that if they could build an alliance with environmentalists then perhaps they could serve as allies in the future.

In October 1990, the first meeting was spent uncovering the participants' differences. Ganados invited the group to Los Ojos where the environmentalists were able to get a clearer picture of rural Hispano life. By describing what Ganados meant to them, the weavers felt they had a real impact on the environmentalists. According to a member of Ganados (Salazar 1991), one environmentalist suggested that the WMAS never should have been placed in Tierra Amarilla given the history of the community and the dependence of the culture on the land.

For their part, Ganados learned a great deal about both the diversity and structure of environmental organizations, particularly how the leaders are beholden to their constituencies and are held accountable for their actions. In addition, Ganados realized that while the environmentalists needed to learn quite a bit more about economic development, they needed to learn more biology (Varela 1991a).

At November's meeting there was greater focus on alternative solutions to Ganados' grazing problem. Discussion turned to the possibility of environmentalists helping Ganados with fund raising in order to purchase land. A work group was established to develop possible solutions (Varela 1991a, b). At the April meeting, the work group presented a proposal suggesting that a consortium of environmental groups assist Ganados in devising a management plan that took into account the needs of both wildlife and livestock. Some environmentalists did not feel that they could help raise funds, but they could use their influence to encourage corporations to consider contributing towards a land purchase (Varela 1991b).

While mediation has not resulted in any specific solutions, the real result has been the increased understanding of one another. Though Ganados believes that some environmentalists had adopted a more open and willing attitude, this is tempered by the fact that a number of environmentalists have withdrawn from participation, largely due to directives from their organizations. Another stumbling block is the previously mentioned lawsuit against the Sierra Club for not carrying through its purchase of grazing land twenty years ago — a factor that may have increased tensions between the Sierra Club and Ganados (Griffin 1992, 17).

In the mid-1990s, as this is written, mediation has ceased and Ganados still does not have a permanent solution to its summer grazing problems. The last few years, they have been fortunate to secure a lease with Chama Land and Cattle Company, a large corporate ranch engaged in grazing and deluxe hunting opportunities. Nevertheless, they continue to explore ways to change policy and gather support, as they work to revitalize the economic, cultural, and ecological well-being of Los Ojos.

Ganados del Valle is an important example of the intersection between mainstream environmentalism and subordinate communities because it captures the complexity and ambiguity of the issues. It is not a cut and dry case. There are merits to WMAs and the elk habitat, as there are merits to Ganados' enterprise. The fact of Ganados' subalternity does not translate automatically or directly into sound ecological practices; the fact of oppression should not be worn as a badge of honor. While we may all celebrate in the triumphs of subaltern communities, I believe the pressing political and intellectual tasks are to identify the forces that oppress, as well as the means by which the resultant social relations can be changed. Ganados' struggle is one where a change on the part of mainstream environmentalists would have gone a long way toward assisting a subaltern group precisely because of environmentalists' organizational influence with the NMDGF and society as a whole. The fact that Ganados was not successful in implementing its plan illustrates the obstacles that relatively powerless groups face when they challenge dominant institutions and organizations.

We need to understand how subaltern environmental concerns vary from those of mainstream environmentalism. As should be clear, mainstream environmentalists have a specific vision, the meeting of which requires a different set of tools and strategies that are reflective of both their privileged economic position and their dominant Anglo culture. It is not unlikely that some of Ganados' claims about caring for the elk are exaggerated, but this must be understood as part of Ganados' vision of resource use, which entails its own strategies that are reflective of both their economic marginalization and social and political subordination. Because of their poverty and cultural history in the region, preservation is an option they cannot afford. This does not mean they do not act in an environmentally responsible manner or do not articulate their own forms of environmental consciousness. As one supportive environmentalist observed, "I think Ganados has a more sound environmental approach to their brand of agriculture than many others I've seen, so they are part of the environmental family by their choice" (Henderson 1990). While they may be part of the environmental family, Ganados has developed a very different relationship to the environment because of their subaltern status. Their practice of environmentalism, or the environmentalism of everyday life, can best be understood by examining it at the confluence of material needs, identity and meaning, and environmentalism.

Politics, Identity, and the Future of Environmentalism

The UFWOC's struggle against pesticides and Ganados' effort to graze offer a look at two similar instances of environmental activism. The context and issues differ, the specific goals vary, and the fact that they are both Chicano groups is not necessarily significant in and of itself. They are united, however, in that they are subaltern communities. Their economic and social marginality has situated them so that they encounter environmental issues within the context of domination simply because environmental issues and circumstances are structured along power relations. This structured inequality is evident not only in the immediate problem each group faced — pesticide exposure and a lack of grazing land — but also in the articulation and response to those problems. In both instances the needs of the communities in question were not reflected in either policy or regulation, nor was there a direct path to enable the groups to become part of the political process.

When they did insert themselves into the political and policy arena, their needs and concerns were not seriously entertained, their proposals were discredited, and they both faced strong opposition from various quarters. Because of the multifaceted nature of their subalternity, the extent to which these communities were subject to official erasure, and the structural and political forces arrayed against them, the resulting collective action was oppositional in nature. This last chapter will explore in greater detail not only the oppositional nature of these conflicts and how they were constituted, but also consider some of the political

implications presented by subaltern environmental movements for environmentalism, collective action, and the left as a whole.

The oppositional nature of subaltern struggles is the pivotal difference between mainstream environmentalism and the environmental
concerns of more peripheral groups. Although Robert Gottlieb in *Forcing the Spring* (1993) has argued that the history of U.S. environmentalism can be seen as an increasingly inclusive history — meaning that
environmental activists and actions may begin as outsiders but are
eventually incorporated into the mainstream — this should not be confused with subalternity. Though it is true that environmental ideas and
activism may be marginal at times, the voices carrying them are not.
Moreover, if they are, it is, perhaps, because they choose to be.[1] Neither
farmworkers nor members of Ganados could simply choose their social
status; it was far more inscribed by economic structures and forces,
racist institutions, ideologies, and customs.

Given this condition of subalternity, how do we go about understanding resistance and mobilization? Among social scientists, debate
exists as to what exactly constitutes resistance. Some have argued that
any effort to garner more dignity for oneself or to improve one's material and social lot, no matter how small, is an act of resistance (Scott
1985). In a similar vein, it has been suggested that the mere act of
survival on the part of the truly subaltern is an act of resistance, since
their very existence is despised.[2] Still, others have argued for the need to
distinguish any attempt to feel better on the part of the subaltern from
highly conscious and structured efforts to change local or regional
power relations. Although the merits and limits of each form of resistance should be readily apparent, and though overlap is bound to
exist, both the UFWOC and Ganados clearly engaged in highly conscious and orchestrated forms of struggle. The UFWOC and Ganados
could achieve some degree of autonomy, security, and dignity in their
lives only by gaining more power. Most groups, whether subaltern or
not, that wish to change the power relations in which they are embedded, must mobilize, engage in direct action, garner widespread public
support, and develop moral authority.

For this reason, subaltern environmental struggles are not strictly
environmental. Instead, they are about challenging the various lines of
domination that produce the environmental conflict or problem experi-

enced by the oppressed group in the first place. Since they must confront multiple sources of domination that include economic marginalization, patriarchy, nationalism, or racism, it is difficult to discern where the environmental part of a struggle begins and where it ends. Indeed, trying to do so may misrepresent the very nature of the struggle, as it suggests that environmental encounters are not colored by political economic structures. This tendency to disaggregate environmental concerns is a reflection of mainstream environmentalism's propensity to deny that its own environmental interactions are couched within a context of political economic privilege.

These particular case studies are especially illustrative because there is no consensus on what the environmentally correct position is. This ambiguity allows us to focus on the unifying themes of subaltern organizing rather than on the issue itself. While it is relatively easy to understand opposition to an incinerator, we must instead grapple with the underlying meanings and motivations of often contradictory mobilizations. This is not meant to discredit anti-incinerator efforts that have been quite significant in empowering people. Rather, there is little mystery as to why many communities reject such land use (Edelstein 1987). People are resisting the risks, pollution, anxiety, and uncertainty posed by such land uses along with the perceived political insult that such facilities represent to low-income and minority communities. These issues have served as a powerful force in mobilizing and empowering people. While they have sometimes led to continued activism and proactive development strategies (Bullard 1994), they do not necessarily change the material circumstances that create and sustain inequality.

The visions and goals of subaltern communities will vary in content and scope. In some cases it is unionization; in others, the prevention of wilderness sites, the cessation of "development" projects, or political and cultural autonomy. In all cases, it is an effort to change the prevailing power relations in order to create greater space for subaltern communities to pursue their goals of living with more dignity, meeting basic needs, and advancing political, economic, and cultural agendas. The case studies in this book present political projects centered on creating ecologically and culturally appropriate economic change, confronting a racist and exclusionary political and cultural system, and establishing an affirmative cultural and ethnic identity. That their environmental concerns were couched in the midst of these other powerful forces may be a defining feature of how subordinate groups intersect with environmental issues.

Because of their multidimensional character, these struggles feature elements of both old and new social movements and force us to question the validity of such a framework. Subaltern oppositional struggles are rooted in the old agenda of political economic change that focuses on improving material conditions and challenging the racist nature of economic activity. Although the Ganados project remained fairly localized, the UFWOC advocated a universal, coherent political agenda — the hallmark of modern movements. Their objective continues to be full unionization of all farmworkers, both in the United States and, eventually, in Mexico — hardly a local project.

Nevertheless, they also share with new social movements an emphasis on identity and quality-of-life issues. This seeming contradiction suggests that these movements and struggles cannot be reduced to either class struggle, civil rights, or identity politics. While these forces are mutually constituted, it is possible to discern the broad outlines of these various strands and how they interact. For example, anthropologist Frans Schryer has demonstrated in his investigation of Huasteca land takeovers in Mexico that though the land invasions were a form of class struggle, they were also a vehicle for expressing and contesting other values and issues, including politics, culture, and identity. The invasions essentially became the arena in which other tensions were played out, illustrating how forces such as economic organization, racism, and identity are intertwined.

> The complex relationship between relations of production and other aspects of society is also evident when one examines the process of class conflict. . . . Class conflicts by poor peasants who were part-time laborers involved more than just a fight for access to land. The men and women who undertook direct-action land invasions also fought over legal definitions, cultural values and control over village governments. Moreover, the struggle to change their society was expressed in different ways, depending on the nature of local level administrations, land tenure systems and ethnic regulations in each part of this diverse region. . . .
>
> Various aspects of its social organization and culture (including ethnicity) reinforce the class exploitation of poor peasants by capitalistic landowners.

Yet all of these aspects of society also became integral components of a class struggle that reached the level of a full-scale peasant revolt. (Schryer 1990, 318, 322)

Although Schryer's analysis focuses on conflict (not a small part of my case studies), many of his observations hold true in understanding the development and reproduction of domination and oppression. He points out that various forces may simultaneously constitute one another so that racism, for example, is complicit in the formation of a particular class structure, while class structure and exploitation reproduce racism. Because neither system is contained or static, they change in relation to one another. There is increasing awareness of how systems of racism, and the very practice of racism, have changed along with, and sometimes in ways seemingly counter to, the needs of capital (P. Cohen 1992; Montejano 1987). But these structured forces should not be seen in unidirectional terms, since collective agency, such as antiracist activism, can be sufficiently powerful to alter the racialized nature of class struggle.

When looking at the intersection of material relations and identity, several points of overlap can be identified. First, political economic constraints and problematic identities (such as denigrated ones, or those that are not widely shared) are formidable obstacles that activists have to confront and engage. These problems merge at a discursive level as activists articulate their situations and struggles. The issue of articulation is crucial, as social movement activists often do not see, or see but misread, the various forces oppressing them.

Without discrediting local knowledge or people's own understanding of their oppression, it is important to point out that any organizer can attest to the range of analyses that exist within dominated groups. The subaltern are not necessarily unified in terms of a single analysis and interpretation of a problem. They are individuals, and while they may experience similar structural conditions, the experience is processed both collectively and individually. In fact, discordant analysis is a problem that plagues social movements and may preclude participants from reaching a consensus on strategy. The fact that both the UFWOC and Ganados were able to articulate clear analyses and strategies that resonated with their respective communities was instrumental to their successful mobilization. Both drew a clear and well-understood connection between structural exploitation, oppression, and people's identities, thereby facilitating the development of cogent affirmative identities that enabled activists to engage in collective strategic resistance. This was illustrated in Ganados' efforts to present its members with the possibility of living out a desired identity and lifestyle. This contributed significantly to the success of the project.

While quality-of-life issues usually refer to the concerns and aspirations of people whose material needs have been met, the concerns of these groups force us to rethink this simplistic assumption. Without denying the centrality of class struggle or the oppressive economic structures being resisted, it should be patently clear that the communities in question are very much interested in the social and ecological consequences associated with their improved economic conditions. What sort of lifestyle can be expected? What kind of landscape will result? How will local resources be impacted? These were the sort of issues that were of great import to Ganados and the UFWOC, although each group weighted various concerns differently.

Quality-of-life issues, from a left perspective, are often seen as politically problematic. They are often construed to be apolitical, or worse, to serve only to obscure the blatant class interests of the privileged. This is often true. Ganados, for example, offers us another take, however, by illustrating how quality-of-life concerns may inform a political economic project, and in turn, be informed by it. We must never lose sight of large-scale structural patterns; neither can we assume to know the needs and concerns of the subaltern. The poor do care about more than just advancing their material position. Though it is clear that low-income and marginalized communities have not mobilized in large numbers around quality-of-life issues, we should bear in mind that questions of positionality define the issues.

Identity, Strategy, and Politics

Having presented a general overview of the connections between various social and economic forces in the creation of inequality and struggles, let us turn to more specific illustrations drawn from the previous chapters, focusing in particular on the roles and significance of strategy, identity, and politics. Strategy is especially relevant to those who wish to see theory and ideas translated into action. Such an examination offers a glimpse into the strengths and weaknesses of identity politics and other postmodern political projects, making clear the need for integrative forms of analysis and politics.

Both movements were similar in that each developed a strategy to change its situation. Both political projects required several steps: creating greater political consciousness among the potential participants, directly confronting entrenched economic and statist powers, presenting their cause to the larger public, cultivating support among various constituencies, and developing sufficient internal and external resources so that they could mobilize large numbers when necessary. In each of these steps, questions of identity, culture, ethnicity, and representation were interwoven through economic structures and racist formations and practices.

Identity politics, however, can be tricky. We cannot fall into the trap of ascribing a unitary resistance identity to oppositional subaltern groups, even though such groups may present themselves in a highly unified way. In reality, identities are rarely so cut-and-dried. Instead, they are marked by contradictions and continual change. More often, the identities of the subaltern are characterized by feelings of denigration, desire for the "other" (the dominant one), internalization of aspects of the dominant identity, and feelings of pride and resistance in terms of one's own oppressed group. Thus identities themselves are simultaneously sites of oppression and resistance. Furthermore, this mix and orientation of an identity can and does shift over time.

Both the UFWOC and Ganados had to build a positive collective identity among their constituencies in order to encourage them to act. Farmworkers, for example, had to be convinced that by uniting as a group of workers, their collective actions could challenge grower hegemony. Culture was fundamental to this process in various ways. Although the role of culture and identity both in Ganados' and the UFWOC's struggle is largely oppositional, it can be conceptualized in several discrete ways. First, activists consciously used culture as praxis in the course of organizing, that is, as the natural way of doing things (Bauman 1973). Second, they strategically used culture to foster in-group solidarity and ethnic identification, a strategy which draws upon "culture as difference." In this analysis I use culture very broadly to include economic forms of organization, power relations, gender dynamics, material artifacts, religion, and language.

Even though both mobilizations were the sites of identity formation and cultural processes, there were profound differences in how they were developed and expressed. For example, almost all forms of Chicano/Mexicano culture (with the notable exception of Hispano aesthetics) are considered inferior to Anglo-European culture by the majority society. However, because Mexicano culture is considered both undesirable and synonymous with poverty and backwardness, it was a source of oppression that contributed to farmworkers' subalternity. But its pejorative nature also enabled it to become a tool in building a positive and collective identity. It served as raw material in the creation of an enabling identity and fueled resistance. For the farmworkers, the fact that their culture was held in contempt meant that the development and usage of a consolidated and proud identity became a point of contention among potential supporters, as seen in ambivalence toward Catholicism and the tensions surrounding Chicano nationalism. In contrast, similar usages among Ganados served as a source of strength and support, rather than a liability.

In both cases, culture as praxis played a critical role in attracting people toward the project, not only by allowing them to feel comfortable, but by reinforcing a positive cultural identity. For instance, Ganados has drawn and organized members by striving to meet their needs in a culturally appropriate way, following local norms of everyday life and challenging household and community gendered divisions of labor only in nominal ways. The daily operation of the weaving workroom provides a case in point. Ganados is unusual compared to other work sites in that children are allowed in both the showroom and workroom, underscoring Rose's (1988) and Pardo's (1990) observations of how women combine work, family, and politics. Since almost all of the weavers are women, child care is a pressing issue (that providing child care is seen as the women's domain says a great deal about Hispano culture). Potential conflicts are averted by allowing the weavers to bring their children to work with them, or take a loom to their home, so one can weave and still tend children. Almost every woman interviewed felt that having her children nearby was one of the most important things about Ganados. Such flexibility was of great consequence because there would be significant domestic turmoil if the women were to abandon this responsibility. Women insisted that their husbands would be upset, placing a great strain on the family and perhaps jeopardizing their participation in Ganados.

The strategy of not forcing the weavers to choose between work and children also was important in that it allowed women to maintain their roles as homemakers and mothers, which in Hispano culture is a great source of individual identity that secures one's place in the community. None voiced the desire to surrender this central and meaningful part of their lives. Indeed, Ganados gave them the space to be homemakers in a highly desirable context. Having children accompany them while working at Tierra Wools was far more preferable to their other choices (such as working in a hotel or restaurant, or picking up trash for the United States Forest Service), all of which require outside child-care arrangements. Though this practice may be complicit with patriarchal family structure, the extent to which the women themselves are changing through Ganados should not be overlooked. Such developments will inevitably reshape the household and set the stage for a shift in household and community social relations.

Culture as praxis was key, then, to successfully organizing both movements. For the UFWOC, sending entire families on the boycott circuit fostered deep family support, which in turn, allowed the individual to fully commit to the project. For Ganados, the trick was flexibility in regard to work hours and child care.

Besides using culture as a form of organizational praxis, cultural symbolism was deliberately used to enhance a strong ethnic and group identity, that is, culture as difference. Among the internal organizing efforts of the UFWOC, material culture was carefully used in the development of a cohesive identity. The strategic use of symbols served to mobilize farmworkers and their supporters, by emphasizing the uniqueness, specific identity, and heritage of the UFWOC membership, both as a social class and as an ethnic group. This was evident in the UFWOC flag—a red banner with a boxy black eagle poised on it. Red was chosen because of its historic association with workers' rights; the boxy eagle was a militant appropriation of the dominant feature of the Mexican flag. The flag proclaimed, in no uncertain terms, exactly who they were: Mexican-origin workers who would no longer tolerate racist treatment or exploitation in the fields.

Initially, some feared the flag's militance would scare off supporters, but it was decided that the flag should embody their sentiments and aspirations. The flag eventually became an important symbol not only to farmworkers, but to all Chicano (and many Anglo) social justice activists. Although this was primarily geared to farmworkers, it had great success externally among potential allies and supporters. This particular representation inspired the desired feelings among several different populations: workers, supporters, and social justice activists of all types. The UFWOC did not hesitate to use and manipulate budding feelings of ethnic identification among Chicanos in order to garner external support. Though external support is always essential to an oppositional struggle, it was especially so for the UFWOC since their entire strategy was predicated on a large number of people being willing to boycott grapes, getting involved, and making sacrifices for the union. By framing the struggle as an ethnic one, that is, as a central issue that Chicanos should support, the UFWOC fostered an ethnic class consciousness that drew support from both Chicanos and elements of the larger Anglo society, all of which enhanced the union. Even though most Chicanos in the 1960s were urban workers rather than farm workers, they nevertheless experienced poverty and discrimination. The UFWOC's strategy was to tap into the growing ethnic awareness of Chicanos at the time, and farmworkers served as the ultimate symbol of oppression for an entire ethnic group.

The UFWOC's success in making their struggle central to the Chicano movement can be seen in a sample of Los Angeles publications.[3] Newspapers and magazines such as *La Raza*, *La Raza Magazine*, *Chicano Student News*, *La Causa*, and *Inside Eastside*, consistently reported on the UFWOC and the grape boycott, promoting UFWOC events. Chicano activists, particularly students, provided a ready pool of supporters. For example, the Brown Berets assisted the UFWOC in their boycott against Giumarra (*Chicano Student News* 1968, 6), the United Mexican American Students decided that *la huelga* would be a primary focus for the organization (*Chicano Student News* 1969, 3), and El Partido de la Raza Unida passed a resolution supporting the UFWOC through boycott participation, financial donations, and direct action when possible (Hernandez 1973). Ironically, while the support of the Chicano community was crucial, it was not always offered to the degree desired (*Inside Eastside* 1969, 2; *La Raza* 1969; Serda 1969). One Chicana union activist wrote in *El Malcriado*,

> Did you know that all summer volunteers that go to Delano and help the farmworkers, on their strike, are all Anglos? Why? Where is our Raza? Are we going to have to be under the White man all the time?
>
> Here in East Los Angeles every Chicano should make it a point to see to it that his grocery store isn't carrying scab grapes. If we can't count on our Raza to help us get rid of the grapes, there is no place left for us to go. Lets see more brown faces on the picket lines, even if its just for an hour. To get justice, we have to give a little. Viva la Causa! Viva la Raza! (Serda 1969, 11)

While it is obvious that the union felt entitled to Chicano support solely on the basis of ethnicity, it is important to appreciate the underlying assumptions of this ethnic identity. What is at work is a unitary Chicano identity. The assumption that all Chicanos should and do support the union ignores the possibility that the struggle may be contrary to some Chicanos' economic and political interests. In effect, the formation of a hegemonic or unified ethnic identity eliminates the possibility of including the diversity of voices that actually constitute any particular community. Despite such attempts at hegemonic representation, the contradictions were revealed through such things as uneven support.[4]

The problem of Mexicano culture itself — its supposedly degraded nature — presented both opportunities and disadvantages to the UFWOC, illustrating once again how culture can become not only the object of racism, but also the particular challenge that subaltern groups face when trying to organize. This is best seen by the UFWOC's use of Catholicism as an organizing tool, what Taylor (1975) has called the "cultural religious form" (p. 168). Here praxis and symbolism were successfully used internally, but were highly controversial when used externally. For instance, La Virgen de Guadalupe was carried on all marches (Taylor 1975, 168) and was present through the mass and in prayer (Day 1971, 47).[5] Here, religion was a form of praxis and reinforced culture as difference, but this tactic was derailed precisely because of Mexicanos' subalternity. The simple act of praying became not only a powerful act of resistance but also the subject of scorn. At one point a court injunction prohibited union members from picketing, but the injunction said nothing about praying or holding mass. Accordingly, members of the union parked a truck in front of a field, set up an altar and a shrine to La Virgen, and proceeded to hold continuous prayer vigils. The sight of elderly women praying on the ground in front of a field was not only jarring because of the mismatch of place and activity, but was symbolic of the economic and cultural injustice perpetrated against the UFWOC by both the growers and the state.

Thus, while such usages of religion were catalysts in the process of identity formation and mobilization, and were clearly forms of resistance, they were not without their problems. Catholicism is an essential part of a hegemonic Mexican and/or Chicano identity, and as such, Mexican Catholicism has been racialized and associated with the poor and the powerless other. Though many Anglo liberals actively supported the UFWOC and were intrigued with Chicano/Mexicano culture, Catholicism remained a point of contention. The images of Mexican Catholicism were so offensive to some Anglos that it infuriated them. One women wrote to the union, "I have sent food for 3 years. Now I shall try to dissuade anyone from supporting you. Take the Virgin of Guadalupe back to Mexico. You can't have her and the U.S. standard of living both, you selfish man [Chavez]" (Selzer n.d.). La Virgen is emblematic of all that is Indian, brown, and culturally backward, and as this woman was reminded of the cultural origins of the poor people she had once supported, she felt compelled to withdraw her support.

Likewise, many supporters opposed Chavez's legendary fasts, which became a highly contested point between Chavez and many liberal Anglo supporters (as well as some Chicanos). In general, the heavy role of religion, including the fast, was difficult for many to accept (Matthiessen 1969, 191; Levy 1975, 283). The left has traditionally been critical of religion as being an opiate of the masses, and of the Catholic Church for its supposed fatalistic and patriarchal characteristics. Certainly the Catholic Church has been responsible for vast human suffering, but this was one occasion when religion was liberating. Mexican Catholics used their religion, consciously and unconsciously, both as a source of inspiration and a strategic tool in their struggle for justice.

While the left and liberals alike wished to support oppressed workers, they wanted them to fit their notion of exploited brown workers.

They wanted to focus on the very real class struggle and the racist nature of agribusiness. Desirable cultural features might include songs, food, and the Spanish language, but many could not bring themselves to condone and support active religious participation.

This reveals yet another dimension of subalternity, that of a culture held in contempt even by supporters. The UFWOC's appropriation and strategic use of culture is important for defying the dominant society's disparagement of Mexicano/Chicano culture. By also resisting Anglo liberals' efforts to suppress their culture, activists demonstrated the extent to which they understood the nature of their oppression and how to overcome it. Mexican Catholicism was part of who farmworkers were; it was a large part of their identity that had to be affirmed in the course of empowerment. This is a striking example of the conflicts that can arise between would be supporters and subaltern groups, and is not unlike the contradictions which arise between environmentalists and marginalized communities. For example, environmentalists may support an indigenous group's subsistence use of resources, but controversy may arise when that same community wants to consider using more advanced forms of technology.

This particular cultural problem was not one that Ganados faced, since their culture was considered highly desirable and attractive by Anglos and others. Instead, it posed a different set of issues related to identity politics. The cultivation of an Hispano pastoral identity was pivotal in attracting local support, but was also consequential in how Ganados represented themselves to the larger outside community. In fact, by emphasizing different facets of their multiple identities to various publics, they were able to draw wide support from various groups.

One important identity which Ganados stressed was the fact that they were a nonwhite group. It was widely believed by Ganados' membership that environmentalists and resource managers were both elitist and racist, and did not wish to work with indigenous, low-income minority groups. This awareness allowed Ganados to use the current emphasis on environmental racism to their advantage, which has discursively been structured as one of nonwhites versus whites. By portraying themselves as an oppressed nonwhite group, Ganados aligned themselves with environmental justice groups, and managed to place the moral burden on white environmentalists. In this respect, Ganados' grazing problem came at an opportune time. Had the issue arisen twenty years earlier, few people would have recognized the larger context of these charges, the particular environmental model on trial, or the relevance of discriminatory natural resource policy.

> What is happening in northern New Mexico is a microcosm of what is happening around the world. Environmentalists and sporting interests find themselves at logger-heads with poor, mostly non-white communities over uses of sensitive environments and conservation of wildlife. Indigenous communities cannot be wished away nor can they be quashed. Successful conservation requires the innovative approach of treating animal, plant and human communities as interdependent, whole ecosystems.
>
> Conserving wildlife is not achieved by purchasing real estate and isolating adjacent communities from decision-making on the goals and management plans for these lands. (Varela 1989, A9)

Regardless of the fact that Ganados has skillfully used civil rights tactics and rhetoric, this has not been their primary tool or identity. Instead, they have emphasized that their culture is an endangered species, and that conservationists must learn to integrate the needs of poor and indigenous communities and cultures into their plans. They are able to do this because their culture is seen as desirable and worth saving (in stark contrast to that of the farmworkers).

Essentially, Ganados has managed to turn this enchantment with indigenous heritage (part of a larger fascination with the exotic) to their advantage. There are many forms of Hispano culture that are considered worthy. These include material, praxis, and symbolic aspects. Perhaps most well known are the material artifacts of the Southwest region associated with both the Indian and Hispano populations. As these objects have become intensely commodified (Works 1992; Mullins 1990; Rodriguez 1989), they have become symbolic of a place, a people (Indian and Hispano), and the vestiges of a way of life. Embedded within this last category are such desirable attributes as a rural lifestyle, an attachment to a pastoral economy (no matter how tenuous), and an intimate and authentic connection to the land (deBuys 1989) — or what Brown and Ingram (1987) have described in terms of water resource use as a community-based relationship.

Although never explicitly stated, the subtext of the fixation on material artifacts is that Hispano culture is in some ways superior to the dominant Anglo culture. In particular, Hispano culture is less environmentally destructive due both to its strong sense of place and its weak attachment to the market. This interpretation comes not only from Ganados' representation of itself as an endangered Hispano pastoral culture, but even more so from the larger society's fascination with indigenous culture, its sense of nostalgia (Lowenthal 1986), and its desire for meaning and community among the alienated. Ganados have capitalized on these trends and feelings to promote themselves. "Elk and deer are not endangered in northern New Mexico. But the survival of New Mexico's Hispanic pastoral culture is endangered. Ganados del Valle's proposal to graze the wildlife refuges is an opportunity to strengthen one of the United States' richest cultures, improve the wildlife habitat and raise the standard of living in one of the nation's poorest rural counties" (Ganados del Valle n.d.). Ganados has used such representations to develop tactical allies, particularly among arts and cultural groups. Organizations such as the Smithsonian have provided positive coverage, as has Cultural Survival, a group that promotes indigenous cultures. The truth is that it is far easier to garner support in today's society for cultural projects, especially a cultural tradition as attractive as that of Hispanos. The United States is tired of antipoverty programs, especially for the undeserving poor or the regular Mexicano masses, but Ganados is special. They are not just Mexicans. They are Hispanos, or Spanish Americans, and are, therefore, somewhat distanced from the less culturally desirable Mexican immigrant (see chapter 4, note 2).

Hispanos are considered more deserving for several reasons: the usurpation of their land base by Anglos, their historic connection to the land, and their attractive culture as epitomized in their beautiful artifacts. This observation is attested to by the degree to which the state has successfully sold the image of northern New Mexico by cultivating its sense of place. Culture (both Indian and Hispano) coupled with scenery are northern New Mexico's great selling points. Thus, supporters are not simply assisting an antipoverty program, they also are strengthening a romanticized and beautiful culture. This was not an option for the UFWOC since their culture was considered problematic and objectionable on several levels, rather than attractive or the object of desire.

There are, however, strategic difficulties that arise from presenting oneself in various ways, confirming that multiple identities do indeed pose political problems. Some Chicano activists would like to see Ganados assume a more militant position by raising the issue of Hispano land rights.[6] While it is often beneficial to unite with the land grant activists, Ganados wish to maintain their identity as a community development group. Manzanares described the conflicting pressures: "We're surrounded. We've got hardcore environmentalists, the Department of Game and Fish, the hunters, traditional Anglo ranchers, land-grant people and Hispanic rights groups on all sides — everyone has an agenda for us" (Manzanares in Jackson 1991, 45–46). Though this poses the possibility of broad support, it is also inevitable that Ganados will not be able to please each ally, presenting a new set of political problems. Because of different positions and conflicting political projects, the possibility did not exist of forming any type of united opposition. The most Ganados could do was try to seek common ground with each constituency in a strategic kind of way. Because of their subalternity and the multidimensional nature of their oppression, no one group shared their overall project. Indeed, had they perhaps been more narrowly defined, such as an Hispano rights group or as strict environmentalists, they might have been more successful. But the conditions of their marginality could not be neatly compartmentalized. Neither could their strategy to overcome it.

Even the UFWOC encountered a similar set of contradictions by cultivating various identities. For example, the UFWOC had to continually renegotiate their position vis-à-vis the larger Chicano movement. The UFWOC needed the support of the Chicano movement, but they risked becoming submerged within it, thereby losing their identity as a labor union (which in fact, did happen). Being part of the Chicano movement made it easy for antiunion forces to brand the UFWOC as communist and subversive (Committee Representing Our Pickers' Survival, n.d.; Ramirez 1968; Ramirez, Morales, and Mitchell, n.d.), which damaged their credibility. Similarly, while the UFWOC sought to build upon strong feelings of ethnicity, this same force became difficult to contain within the union and led to schisms and purges (although this has been denied [Chavez 1987]).

Clearly, understanding the role of identity in movements and struggles is imperative, but in the case of the subaltern, struggles cannot be reduced to identity conflicts. While the search and need for an enabling and appropriate identity is a subject unto itself, it is also intimately linked to larger issues of positionality, power, and struggles to overcome poverty. For this reason, and because of the multifarious ways in which social reality is constructed, it is impossible to categorize subaltern environmental movements as either old or new social movements. Indeed, the very effort to impose such a model on what is a far more complex reality testifies to the entrenched nature of modernity. Nevertheless, what is exciting about these movements, from a methodological perspective, is that they demonstrate the need to combine political economic perspectives with the tools provided by postmodernism. They also provide a model of how, at least in the case of the subaltern, these two aspects of life — materiality and identity — combine to create people's social reality. Any attempt to understand subaltern environmental movements must be placed at the nexus of social movements, identity politics, and the future of the left.

Toward a Postmodern Left

In this postmodern era, the left itself is struggling with its own identity. Some are trying to maintain a unified, "true" left but are finding that position threatened with irrelevancy as multiple forms of activism are springing up across the political landscape. In many regards, postmodernism has created valuable space to maneuver in reassessing the meaning and motives behind social movements. Simultaneously, postmodernism has also posed a serious challenge to understanding social movements because it denies any truth and has clear political consequences. Andrew Ross (1988) has aptly conveyed these in the phrase "universal abandon." Handler (1992) has challenged the hegemony of postmodernism by questioning what it does for poor and disenfranchised people. "The results of deconstruction politics are serious. Postmodernism celebrates its lack of global vision. The postmodernists defend their position with the claim, 'there *are* no grand narratives.' However, the opposition is not playing that game. It has belief systems, meta-narratives that allow theories of power, of action" (Handler 1992, 726).

While Handler does underscore the very real political problems posed by a highly relativistic viewpoint, we need not fall into the trap of choosing between despair or longing for the days of a well-defined economistic and hegemonic left. As Plotke (1990) has cogently argued, one reason NSMS appear to be so different is because they have been conceptualized in opposition to a hegemonic Marxism (whose existence in the United States was tenuous to say the least). Nevertheless, it is hard to deny that there is not something new about the social movements that have proliferated during the last several decades. The task becomes to contextualize the perceived split, to abandon the desire to impose totalizing frameworks on diverse realities, but *not* to abandon the desire for social and economic justice, human dignity, and efforts to promote ecological stewardship. Instead, it means that we must be open to various sorts of analyses in order to better understand and conceptualize subaltern struggles. Toward this end, political economy has many valuable tools to offer, but no single tool will consistently work in all cases.

Approaching social movements in this way enables us to see beyond the old and new dichotomy, facilitates a sharper understanding of present forms of collective action, and opens the door to new political opportunities and configurations. Entrenched concepts can, in fact, be barriers to effective action. By dropping the notion of old and new we can better assess who one's political allies and enemies are.

In the mid-1990s we face a situation where there is a presumed solidarity between a staggering number of causes and movements. Consequently, those involved in creating a more just global order often believe that highly disparate struggles are actually fighting the same or similar sets of power. For example, it is often assumed that those engaged in the struggle against racism share much in common with those involved in labor organizing, women's health, and the environment. This process of agglomeration is further intensified by the way the words "race," "class," and "gender" are routinely employed as a single term, in an inferred political agreement. It is assumed that the oppressed, and those committed to challenging various forms of domination, will identify and connect with those fighting on other fronts.

As we have seen in the case studies, however, that is not always so. Organized labor and environmentalists offered the UFWOC sparse support, and environmentalists actively opposed Ganados. Yet, within the larger society, such constituencies are routinely lumped together as some kind of left. Of course, there do exist good reasons why these assorted oppositional struggles are seen as similar. For one, as Aronowitz (1994) has pointed out, these struggles do exist in opposition to the dominant society's cultural values and politics. Moreover, among activists there are many instances of political unity. Nevertheless, anyone involved in coalition politics knows the difficulty of working with groups focused on different issues, and the even more difficult task of working with those who do not share the same politics — both representing realities of great import to environmentalism.

The idea that all those involved in oppositional politics can form a counterhegemonic plurality intent on creating radical change is highly doubtful and perhaps of limited efficacy. Even opening ourselves up to other ways of being, and becoming more aware of the oppression of others, does not guarantee that we will reach any level of political agreement. It is not inevitable that mainstream environmentalism will necessarily be supportive of subaltern struggles, and to presume that it will be entirely ignores the question of positionality. Given that there are a multitude of ways to "save" the environment, a desire for environmental quality may not be strong enough to unite, even temporarily, diverse groups. This is unfortunate for both the environment and for subaltern communities.

Furthermore, it does not appear that mainstream environmentalism will be moving in that direction. More conservative, market-oriented organizations, like the Environmental Defense Fund, are emerging as the new environmental leaders (Clifford 1994). The truth is that the two groups, subaltern and mainstream environmentalism, differ politically. There are times when mainstream groups will support such struggles, and times when they will not. We should appreciate that environmentalism is not an ideology unto itself. Rather, it is a set of interests expressed through various ideologies and political commitments. Nevertheless, the rise of oppositional environmental struggles is something that mainstream environmentalism will increasingly have to contend with, as subaltern movements will likely continue to grow in number and to attract increasing support. Because of the significance and size of these movements, it is imperative that we clearly understand what they

are about politically, as they are fundamentally challenging and changing both environmentalism and local social relations.

One problem that seems to exacerbate tensions and preclude full
partnership is the fact that while subaltern groups are contending with
very real environmental problems, such groups also know that environmentalism is an effective avenue in which to market themselves. The
world is excited about poor people jumping on the environmental
bandwagon, and marginal communities seek to obtain the maximum
mileage out of this connection. This should not diminish the legitimacy
of their concerns but emphasize their relative powerlessness as they
seek to secure societal approval and support for their mobilization
efforts. Because of the political shift to the right during the 1980s,
antipoverty efforts, let alone a progressive redistribution of wealth
and power, have not been politically viable ideas. Thus, activists have
sought to identify themselves with more politically palatable issues,
such as environmentalism.

By no longer conceiving of all environmental activities as part of
NSMs, mainstream and subaltern movements are decoupled. On the one
hand, such a move is emblematic of the uncertainty of the postmodern
era; on the other, new possibilities arise. Perhaps environmentalism will
rearrange itself so that those elements more willing to embrace an
oppositional point of view will organize themselves into a more coherent voice. Should this happen (and there are signs that it is), it will
allow the left to diversify itself by becoming involved in immediate and
relevant struggles while, hopefully, sharpening the collective analysis of
the problem (an historic strength of the left). If nothing else, the left
should take this opportunity to clarify and strengthen the linkages between identity politics, quality-of-life movements, and material struggles. Indeed, the way in which these struggles have been conceptualized
and articulated by the subjects themselves provides one model. This
will require, however, the left to begin to take identity politics very
seriously, and to develop more sophisticated and nuanced analyses of
environmental degradation, in which not everything is attributed to
capitalism.

Social injustice, growing inequality, and a looming environmental
crisis are the greatest threats facing the global community as we enter
the twenty-first century. We have little chance of seriously solving our

global environmental problems — such as the loss of biodiversity and the destruction of the rain forest — unless we also address global and local inequality. Ultimately, this will entail profound economic and cultural change, particularly for the privileged of the world. It will require a focus on meeting people's basic needs in the most ecologically sustainable way possible.

Subaltern environmental movements, while they may be criticized for being local, nonetheless offer us examples of how some communities have sought to change their social and ecological conditions. It is unreasonable to believe that somehow all subaltern groups will unite and challenge global capitalism and other institutionalized forms of power. That would be somewhat counter to their very purpose and nature. Conversely, these movements cannot be dismissed. They are an important and powerful feature of contemporary politics, and they have valuable lessons to teach us. They are a force to be reckoned with that will undoubtedly be a part of any solution or strategy for change. This does not mean that there is no role for traditional environmental regulations, policies, and technologies — quite the contrary. Hopefully, however, these will be harnessed to achieve a different set of goals. Just as surely as there is a need for forceful action at the grassroots level, there is a linked need for moral leadership in the policy, national, and global spheres. It is only by championing the universal goals of social and ecological justice that the left can learn to respond in various ways to the many challenges and realities that confront us on the road to social and environmental change.

Notes

Preface

1. The term "Chicano/Mexicano" refers simultaneously to persons born in the United States who are of Mexican ancestry (Chicanos) and to persons from Mexico. "Mexicano" is a Spanish language term that can also be used to describe something or someone as being closely related to Mexico and Mexican culture.

Because of significant migration to the United States from various countries in Latin America during the 1980s, political terminology and frameworks have shifted to include these diverse elements. Thus we often now speak of the Chicano/Latino population, which effectively includes people from Latin America as well as Chicanos. These case studies refer strictly to the Chicano/Mexicano population. Although the U.S. Latino population has since diversified, the population of Mexican origin still constitutes 62 percent of all Latinos (United States Bureau of the Census 1990d) and has one of the longest histories in this country.

Chapter 1: Subaltern Environmental Struggles

1. In this way it mimics the much larger pattern of diffusion in which knowledge, technology, and innovations flow outward from the "First World" to the "Third World" (see Blaut 1993). I use the terms "First World" and "Third World" fully conscious of the fact that they are social constructs. For a further discussion, see Said (1979); hereafter the quotation marks will be dropped.

2. Iain Chambers (1994) offers a different perspective by pointing out that in contemporary metropolitan areas the boundaries between the Third and First worlds are rapidly crumbling due to migrancy.

3. Within the United States most research on social movements has been

associated with the resource mobilization tradition. This tradition focuses on group dynamics, strategy, and resource access and use (Buechler 1993) and is thought to exist in contrast to the European and Latin American focus on identity formation (Cohen 1985).

4. Post-Fordism refers to the transition from highly structured and rigid forms of production to more flexible ones.

5. It should be pointed out that some Latin American scholars have rejected the theories and insights of Europeans as Eurocentric (Calderon, Piscitelli, and Reyna 1992).

6. I would not support casual accusations of racism. My concern here is that this discourse is limited to statistical proof while seemingly divorced from larger ideological issues.

7. I cite romanticism and conservation as antecedents because these two movements are commonly cited in most scholarly works. Although the urban-progressive movement was heavily involved in municipal housekeeping and addressed urban pollution (Melosi 1980), this segment of history is not included in any discussion of environmentalism's roots (see Gottlieb 1993). Ironically, the current grassroots urban-environmental movement closely parallels that of the urban progressives in several respects. First, the primary concern focuses on urban sanitation and is closely linked to public health issues. Second, women, then and now, are at the forefront of the movement (Hoy 1980). Third, both movements address issues of social justice and equity. In the 1920s occupational-health specialists, such as Alice Hamilton, were greatly concerned over the plight of the immigrant population and the impact of poverty on community health and well-being (Hamilton 1943; Slaight 1974). Because of such efforts, significant legislation, representing the United States' first efforts to clean up the urban environment, was passed during this time.

Although Hays (1987) has argued that conservation is actually quite removed from environmentalism, I still include conservation as an historical root for several reasons. While it is true, as Hays (1987, 13) argues, that conservation is concerned with efficient production, and environmentalism is more concerned with quality-of-life issues, the fact remains that conservation helped to define preservation by serving as its antimony. Moreover, both M. Cohen (1988) and Fox (1981) have demonstrated that the very first conservation efforts were one and the same with preservation activities. It wasn't until later, with professionalization, that differences arose that eventually led to two separate movements. Even more importantly, conservation and preservation present two different ways of thinking about nature, a dichotomous framework entrenched in our current way of thinking.

8. See also Nash (1982) for the same argument in terms of wilderness.

Chapter 2: Poverty, "Race," and Identity

1. Jackson's use of the term *black* reflects British racial categories in which all nonwhites are referred to as black. Of course, in the United States, black designates a very specific racial and ethnic group, African Americans.

2. For an exceptional discussion of hair as a racialized physical attribute, see Mercer 1990.

3. See Rodriguez (1991), Telles and Murguia (1990), and Bohara and Davila (1992) for research on the economic cost of being "fair" or "dark." The fact that the researchers chose to investigate this question underscores the importance of skin color, particularly in the consciousness of nonwhites. Additional insights can be garnered from the language nonwhites have developed to describe various shades of color, in which lighter skin is considered more desirable. A sampling of Spanish language terms include: *blanca* (white), *güera* (fair), and *morena* (dark). Recognition of the desirability of lighter skin is a response to racism, as it is thought better treatment is accorded to those with lighter skin. It is also an example of internalized racism.

4. See Cornel West's (1993) discussion of black nihilism, for example.

5. This observation is largely drawn from Gramsci's "War of Position," in which he recognizes that consciousness of one's oppressed state is the first step to revolution (Hoare and Smith 1971).

6. Of course, this can be taken to extremes in the form of ethnic nationalism and genocide. This still points, however, to the contingent nature of ethnicity.

7. Although there is a history of Chicano left activity, Mario Garcia (1984) has suggested that the radical tradition has been somewhat inflated, particularly in the 1960s and 1970s, when Chicano activists and scholars sought historical antecedents to the activism of the time. For examples of socialist and radical activity among Chicanos see Ruiz (1987); Rodriguez (1977); Nelson-Cisneros (1975); and Zamora (1975). Despite these examples, radicalism can hardly be said to be representative of the Mexican-American population, as most fall well within traditional liberal politics (Welch and Sigelman 1993). Indeed, there is a history of antileft activity on the part of some segments of the Chicano population (L. Chavez 1991; Ramirez 1968; and Ramirez, Morales, and Mitchell n.d.).

8. For excellent overviews of the Chicano Movement see Gomez Quinones (1990), Munoz (1989), and Hammerback et al. (1985). For detailed examinations of La Raza Unida Party, see Garcia 1989. In addition see Gomez Quinones (1978) on the Los Angeles student walk-outs; Lopez Tijerina (1978); Bell Blawis (1971); Gardner (1970); and Nabakov (1970) on La Alianza; and Jenkins

(1985); Kushner (1975); Day (1971); and Matthiessen (1969) on the farm-workers.

9. Even though most evidence suggests that Aztlan is probably near the present state of Nayarit in Mexico, Chicano activists and scholars have suggested it was in the Southwest (J. Chavez 1989). The development of the ancient concept of Aztlan as a modern part of an ethnic identity demonstrates how traditions are invented and the purposes they serve (Hobsbawm and Ranger 1983). For a variety of perspectives on Aztlan, see Anaya and Lomeli (1989).

10. The current thrust and language of cultural studies would note, and correctly so, that culture includes far more than these more traditional forms of expression. All the categories I have thus far considered, including economic forces and racism, belong to the realm of culture. Though fully cognizant of the fact that forms of economic organization and ethnicity are culturally produced, I have chosen to employ a more narrow set of cultural constructs in an effort to better understand the nature of subaltern environmental movements precisely because "culture as the ideational dimension of all human practices" (Leys and Mendell 1992, 8) is not sufficiently useful in trying to deconstruct the multi-faceted nature of social movements.

11. This usage of culture echoes Blaut's (1992) notion of cultural racism.

Chapter 3: The Pesticide Campaign

1. Lyrics to the song *El Picket Sign* as performed by Dr. Loco's Rockin' Jalapeno Band on the album *Movimiento Music* (adapted from Pinderhughes 1994, 36). Lyrics reprinted by permission from José Cuéllar.

2. During the period under consideration, the United Farm Workers was actually the United Farm Workers' Organizing Committee (UFWOC). UFWOC will be used when referring to the union in the 1960s and early 1970s. The name United Farm Workers was adopted in the mid-1970s and is used to denote the modern union.

3. The UFWOC was also active in the Salinas, Coachella, and Imperial Valleys, but most of the pesticide activities were located in the San Joaquin Valley.

4. The situation since then has changed somewhat. Mexicans and Mexican-origin people are still farmworkers, but there is also a significant Chicano and Latino middle class.

5. As recently as 1987, then California Congressman Pete Wilson urged the Immigration and Naturalization Service (INS) to "relax its enforcement of the new immigration law" so growers would not face worker shortages (C. Quintana 1987, 3 and 34).

6. Although growers wielded immense power through the 1970s, it appears that starting in the 1980s agriculture's influence began to ebb as the San Joaquin Valley became increasingly urbanized and experienced tremendous population growth. What is significant is that most of these newcomers are not connected to agriculture, "and at some point their sheer numbers will begin to tilt the politics of the Valley away from the farm/water/chemical axis" (R. Jones 1990, A3).

7. This attitude that has been found among slave owners (Woods 1993).

8. Ironically, growers' antiunion literature repeatedly stressed that if Chavez was truly concerned with helping the most needy, he would be organizing farmworkers in the south; not California grape workers (South Central Farmers Committee 1968; S. Gale 1969). But, as pointed out, it was precisely because of their more secure position that Delano grape workers were chosen.

9. Surprisingly, the University of California has still not found a way to mechanize table grape harvesting.

10. At one point during a UFWOC strike, a Kern County sheriff outlawed the use of the word *huelga,* meaning "strike," which was a favorite battle cry of the UFWOC (Taylor 1975, 142). On another occasion during the 1969 migrant farmworker hearings, a Kern County law enforcement agent testified that he had arrested protesters in order to prevent any disturbance. Senator Kennedy reminded the officer that he should review the U.S. constitution, which prohibits arresting people for what they might do.

11. For other examples of the lengths to which humans have gone to control nature, see McPhee (1989).

12. The director of the CDFA historically has been a grower (Paddock 1990).

13. Fortunately, this is no longer the case. The Environmental Protection Agency now oversees pesticides.

14. In 1992, pesticide regulation was finally transferred to a new statewide environmental agency, CAL-EPA (California Environmental Protection Agency 1992).

15. Dr. Lee Mizrahi conducted a study of the nutritional status of migrant children in Tulare County in 1969. As an afterthought, Mizrahi tested for pesticide residues. The results were shocking. Previous to the test, Mizrahi considered the pesticide issue to be "an emotional issue with little scientific basis, not to be taken very seriously." Of the fifty-nine children surveyed, twenty-seven had abnormally low cholinesterase levels (Mizrahi 1970, 1448). A depressed cholinesterase level indicates organophosphate poisoning (the most acutely toxic group of pesticides). Mizrahi felt the results could "only be classified as an epidemic" and sent the results and an accompanying letter to politicians, CRLA, UFWOC, the California DPH, and other interested medical

parties (Mizrahi 1969). What struck Mizrahi was that, with a few exceptions, the children did not work in the fields; they either simply lived near them or their parents worked in them. For this reason, pesticides should be considered a public health issue, and not be "limited to a concern between employer and employee" (Mizrahi 1969).

16. There is ample evidence of growers' opposition to the elimination of the short-handled hoe, their refusal to provide toilets and washing facilities, their longstanding opposition to the banning of DDT, and their resistance to placing signs stating which fields had been sprayed with which pesticides.

17. One example of the close relationship between the court system and growers was the famous Wheatland riot on the Durst ranch. When Durst summoned the law to break up the riot, he contacted the district attorney, who just happened to be his private lawyer.

Far more serious was the prosecution of Cannery and Agricultural Workers Industrialized Union (CAWIU) leaders, Pat Chambers and Caroline Decker. The Associated Farmers almost single-handedly led the prosecution effort. "From the moment the arrests were made, officials of the Associated Farmers worked in close cooperation with the Sacramento County district attorney to ensure that the cases were vigorously prosecuted." The Associated Farmers collected evidence, hired a district attorney, and used county secretarial resources (Daniel 1981, 252–53).

18. The UFWOC and CRLA played an important role in the national lawsuit, although this is rarely, if ever, mentioned in environmental history.

19. A 1950s survey of Kern-Kaweah chapter members reveals that their concept of "conservation" did not coincide with the concept as defined by Hays (1959, 1987). Instead, they saw conservation as pertaining to natural resources, including preservation.

20. David Averbuck, then UFWOC attorney, pointed out that it cost the union relatively little to file a lawsuit, but it cost the growers quite a bit. The UFWOC had only two full-time lawyers, Cohen and Averbuck, both of whom were paid below-market flat salaries. In contrast, the growers employed lawyers from across the state, all of whom charged by the hour. In this way, their lawsuits were a form of financial harassment (Averbuck 1991).

21. For example, in 1969 growers sued the UFWOC for $75 million (Alvarez 1973, 227).

22. This fear started with the cranberry scare of 1965, when a USDA official announced that cranberries were being sprayed with a carcinogen. Cranberry sales, subsequently, plunged for five years (Averbuck 1991).

23. See Harner (1969) for an overview of the early events of the case, and Ayala de Sifuentes (1972) for a legal analysis of the "trade secrets" argument.

24. Commissioner Howie and the sprayers filed an appeal with the Supreme Court that was denied.

25. The full impact of this decision is a bit cloudy. Both the court records and Judge Brown of Kern County confirm that the Riverside ruling prompted a policy reversal, but the CDFA has insisted that the records have always been public. The department's policy, established in 1960, gives quite a bit of latitude to county commissioners: "The Department typically has recommended that county agricultural commissioners, immediately upon receipt of a public information request, contact their County Counsel to review county procedures for responding to public information requests" (Okumura 1991). Further, CDFA administrators denied that any of the UFWOC access cases influenced access policy. This is confusing, however, because the closing documents of the court file state that "the Agricultural Commissioner of Kern County . . . has now been authorized by the state Department of Agriculture to disclose, and said Agricultural Commissioner in fact is complying with the state directive and affording access to the records heretofore closed by the effect of said preliminary injunction" (*Atwood Aviation v. Morley* 1971). The CDFA could not explain to me their role in the matter, and insisted that the documents have always been public (Okumura 1991).

26. "El Malcriado" roughly translates into "poorly raised," or "the bad seed."

27. Many conservatives in California were outraged by the CRLA. It was felt that they were using public monies to help the poor fight government agencies. "Now this sounds just fine. Legal help for the rural poor. But, in at least one case, the CRLA Office, using taxpayers' money is harassing a county welfare office to the point where the county Board of Supervisors has had to use the taxpayers money to hire a lawyer at $35 an hour to protect its county welfare director" (Reagan in Wrightson n.d., a). Both Murphy and Reagan threatened to cut off CRLA funding (Wrightson n.d., a and b; *Fresno Bee* 1968).

28. The other pesticides were aldrin, dieldrin, endrin, heptachlor, benzene hexachloride, lindane, parathion, phosdrin, Systox (demeton), and TEPP.

29. Whitaker and Baxter was a San Francisco law firm specializing in conservative and right-wing causes. "Farm organizations, in a rare display of solidarity, are backing the grape growers' hiring of the highly successful- and highly priced-public relations firm of Whitaker and Baxter" (Taylor 1969b, 1C).

30. See note 15.

31. This is not to deny the usefulness of lawsuits, but rather to bring attention to the differences of each strategy.

32. Pesticide enforcement is notoriously lax. Few violations are reported to

begin with, but the actual sanctions of individuals or firms is almost nonexistent (Paddock 1990, A19).

33. There is a long and violent history of the Teamsters trying to represent farmworkers. This was only the latest, and perhaps the most violent, episode (see Levy 1975; Taylor 1975).

34. This charge must be put into a political context. The fact is that there was little institutional and social support for farmworkers and their living and working conditions in the 1980s. According to Moses (1991), because the workers are poor, undocumented, and brown, no one gives a damn.

35. Fortunately, the latest generation of workers is beginning to organize, particularly at the local level. A conference held during the summer of 1991, formed Alianza Campesina. Participating groups included Union Campesina "Lazaro Cardenas," Organizacion del Pueblo Explotado y Oprimado, Congreso de Igualidad, Familias Campesinas Unidas, Associacion Civica "Benito Juarez," Comite de Campesinos de Gerawan Ranches, Comite del Tomato en el Valle de San Joaquin, Mixteca Campesina Activa, Western Farm Workers Association, and Union Local 78-B de la Fresh Fruit and Vegetable Workers (Zabin et al. 1993; *Semilla* 1989-1991; Villarejo 1991b).

36. The following is a comparison of the Teamsters and the UFWOC's health and safety clause from 1974 wine contracts.

UFWOC *and Almaden*	*Teamsters and Gallo*
1. Establishment of a health and safety committee and banning of dangerous chemicals.	1. Employer follows all laws and meets with union on alleged violations.
2. Employer provides safety gear.	2. Nothing.
3. Employer provides tools.	3. Worker pays for tools.
4. Health and Safety establishes reentry periods.	4. Nothing.
5. Employer provides adequate toilet facilities.	5. Nothing.
6. Employer provides adequate drinking water.	6. Nothing.
7. Workers guaranteed two fifteen-minute breaks per eight hours.	7. Worker guaranteed one ten-minute break per four hours.
8. Employer provides adequate first-aid supplies.	8. Nothing.
9. Worker has right to refuse dangerous work.	9. Nothing.

Source: *El Malcriado* 1974

Chapter 4: Ganados del Valle

1. "From the earth I was formed, the earth gives me food, the earth has sustained me, and in the end, to the earth I shall return."

2. The labeling of the Spanish-speaking people of this region has provoked great debate among academics and activists. Often, both local Anglos and Spanish-speakers themselves use the term "Spanish," emphasizing their Spanish roots. However, a look at both the customs and appearance of Hispanos suggests they are not solely of European heritage. "The racial characteristics of the people would indicate that a vast majority have varying percentages of Indian blood in them" (Weigle 1975, 33). With the first wave of settlers in the seventeenth century, Swadesh (1974, 12) observed, there were never more than three thousand people who were even culturally Spanish, and it is likely that the Indian servants and mestizos who accompanied them far outnumbered the Spanish. Swadesh's observation that ethnic identity is a function of the predominant relations rather than ancestry is entirely accurate (Swadesh 1974, 12, 45). Given both Spanish racism toward Indians and later Anglo prejudices toward both Indians and mestizos (Sunseri 1973), it is not surprising that many people choose to identify as Spanish.

During the course of my fieldwork (the summer of 1990, and part of summer of 1991), I found that young people would often identify as Spanish, Hispano, Hispanic, or less frequently, Chicano (spoken in English). The older people I encountered were far more likely to label themselves as *Mexicano* (in Spanish). José Rivera, a native of the area and the director of the Chicano studies center at the University of New Mexico, pointed out that during the 1940s, as Hispanos left their villages, they discovered that to the outside world they were simply another group of Mexican Americans. It was not difficult for Hispanos to realize the negative connotations of this identity, and they therefore took great pains to identify themselves as Spanish.

Scholars have readily picked up on this term and have gone to great lengths to distinguish this group of people from other Mexican-origin populations. Nostrand has hypothesized that the Spanish-speaking population of this region is culturally distinct from the rest of the Mexican-American population (1980). His article engendered a series of responses, primarily from Chicano scholars who disputed his finding that Hispanos were not related to the larger Chicano population (Blaut and Rios-Bustamante 1984; Rodriguez 1986). They argued instead that Hispanos are part of the larger Chicano population, and that their differences should be interpreted as regional variations. In response to the critique of Nostrand, a group of borderland scholars rose to his defense (Simmons 1984; Chavez 1984; Meinig 1984), charging that Blaut and Rios-

Bustamante, among others, were simply trying to advance their own ideological agenda.

I do not wish to join the debate as to the cultural uniqueness of New Mexicans, but I will use this opportunity to stress that ethnicity is neither essential nor static (see chapter 2). Instead, it is a continuously changing political construct. The fact that Hispanos may (or may not) share certain historical experiences with the larger Mexican-origin population is not as important as the fact that through the Chicano movement of the 1960s, Hispanos and other Mexican-origin peoples throughout the Southwest began to identify as a coherent community. This self-identification is the essence of ethnicity.

Major differences encountered between Hispanos and my own background (urban Mexican American) were, I believe, a function of their being rural and having a remnant land base. I acknowledge the difference in these historical experiences and call them "Hispanos."

3. See Griffin (1991) for a detailed description of the physical and human geography of the Upper Chama Valley.

4. See Wilson and Kammer (1989) for a cultural and architectural review of the valley and Swadesh (1965) for social settlement patterns.

5. The Tierra Amarilla Land Grant is famous for the fraudulent way in which it was acquired (Ebright 1989; 1987; 1985). The fact that WMA lands were once part of the grant adds a layer of tension to the conflict.

6. There is an extensive literature that documents the causes and consequences of the loss of grant lands (Carlson 1990; Ebright 1989, 1987; Gomez 1985; Gonzalez 1969; Knowlton 1973).

7. Regardless of whether it is true or not (Carlson 1990; Scott 1967), this is many locals' perception of the problem.

8. For more detailed information on both Lopez Tijerina and La Alianza, see Gardner 1970; Nabakov 1970; Bell Blawis 1971; and Lopez Tijerina 1978.

9. There are a litany of specific reasons why the region, particularly the Hispano and Indian populations, remains impoverished. These include lack of capital, lack of business management skills, discriminatory treatment from the state (in all its forms), corrupt and ineffective local political systems (largely controlled by Hispanos), loss of a land base, fragmentary landownership, an inability to adopt modern attitudes, and runaway real estate prices. For detailed discussions on the region's lack of economic development, see Eastman 1991, Peña 1991a, Weber 1991, Carlson 1990, de Buys 1989, Forrest 1989, Brown and Ingram 1987, Eastman, Carruthers, and Liefer 1971, and Knowlton 1964, 1962.

10. It is important to remember that Espanola, the largest city in the county, has 24 percent (7,900) of the county population. As a regional center, many of

these jobs are concentrated in Espanola, not in the more isolated rural villages. Though Espanola is part of Rio Arriba County, it is very different from the remainder of the county; it is a city, albeit a small one. The remaining 25,300 county residents live in small villages with populations ranging from less than 100 residents to Chama, which is the second largest center with a population of 1,100 (Bureau of Business and Economic Research 1989, 192).

11. It is less certain how women identify, because most studies have assumed the male perspective to be representative.

12. In 1990, lambs in New Mexico sold for $50.20 (per cwt), which has steadily been dropping from 1987 when the price was $83.30. Sheep sold for much less than lambs. In 1987 a cow brought in $57.20 (per cwt) and calves $84.50. In 1990 these prices had respectively risen to $68.00 and $96.80 (Sunwest Financial Services 1990, 33). Since the 1970s the cattle industry has dominated all of New Mexico agriculture in terms of value, but that trend appears to be changing. In 1970 livestock comprised 80 percent of all agricultural sales, while in 1989 that figure had dropped to 59 percent (Resta and Zink 1978, 1, 28; *New Mexico Stockman* 1989b).

13. In 1991 the Economic Development Department was separated from the Tourism Department for the first time in New Mexico history—a telling organizational structure.

14. See Weigle (1975, 1) for a description of early tourism efforts in New Mexico.

15. Alan Richardson, the New Mexico director of economic development stated that there has never been a systematic effort geared toward the economic development of northern New Mexico. There have been many small, private efforts, but the state itself does not engage in economic planning or development. His office existed only to provide assistance to private efforts. In July 1990 an organizational structure was approved to implement the state's long-range plan. The purpose of the organization was to facilitate cooperation among all parties involved in development, but regional development priorities and plans had not yet been established (Maes 1990, 1).

16. As an example of the region's inability to cope with rapid growth, during both 1990 and 1991 the water supply for Chama became so contaminated that citizens were advised to boil all water before cooking and drinking. In addition to water contamination, the Chama landfill was found to be in violation on several counts (*Rio Grande Sun* 1991b). In addition, the town has encountered water shortages that have hurt tourist-oriented businesses, particularly lodging establishments (Schein 1991). At one point, a campground just south of Chama supposedly had more than two thousand people in it, which is twice the population of Chama itself (Schein 1991).

17. A local joke suggests that only the very wealthy (who have the money) and the very poor (who supposedly have the time) can afford adobe homes.

18. New Mexico ranchers were the only western group to support the Taylor Grazing Act because they had illegally appropriated parts of the public domain and the act would legitimize their new holdings (Stout 1970, 318).

19. Despite such rhetoric, ranchers are not united in terms of a clear agenda, as seen in the limited success of the Sagebrush Rebellion (Coggins and Nagel 1990, 494).

20. More localized groups also exist, such as the Southwest Research and Information Center, the Water Information Network (WIN), the Wildlife Legislative Council, the New Mexico BLM Wilderness Coalition, and the Public Lands Action Network (PLAN). Environmental justice organizations can be found, such as the Southwest Organizing Project (SWOP), and the Tonantzin Institute. This discussion will limit itself to the mainstream groups, since they are dominant and were the primary ones involved in the grazing conflict.

21. These include Sierra Club, The Audubon Society, The Nature Conservancy, and National Wildlife Federation. Ironically, the organization reputed to be the most elitist, the Nature Conservancy, described their membership as a "real cross section" (Waldman 1990).

22. For an interesting exception, see Weisman 1993. The Grey Ranch in southern New Mexico is significant in terms of the relationship between public and private ownership and environmental quality. The Grey Ranch is considered one of the most ecologically diverse properties in North America, but has also been a privately-owned working ranch for years.

23. Pittman-Robertson and Dingell-Johnson refer respectively to federal excise taxes imposed on hunting and fishing equipment. Monies from the fund are used to acquire and maintain hunting and fishing habitat and are distributed to the state game and fish departments via the United States Fish and Wildlife Service.

24. Typically, new tracts of land are opened up to allow people to live close to nature. But of course their very actions spell disaster for wildlife.

25. Federal funds come primarily in the form of Federal Aid monies generated from the Pittman-Robertson and Dingall-Johnson excise taxes. See note 23 above.

26. The Little Chama Valley Ranch was renamed the Sargent.

27. NMDGF inquired with the following agencies and organizations: the state attorney general's office, The Nature Conservancy, the USFWS, and the General Services Department. The attorney general's office was consulted because of The Nature Conservancy's deed restriction, and it ultimately decided

that allowing Ganados to graze would be problematic. This opinion was based on the Binkley incident, which demonstrates a highly selective reading of history. Although the state's opinion recognized that grazing had occurred earlier, it did not address how this previous episode was not a basis for breaking the agreement. In fact, I found no evidence that the attorney general had been consulted the first time. Further, the state's opinion cited only the Binkley grazing incident as evidence of the detrimental impacts of grazing, with no mention of the fact that the grazing was terribly mismanaged. "As a result of this experiment, the U.S. Fish and Wildlife Service determined that livestock grazing conflicted with the original management intent" (Alley 1989, 4). The results did indicate a conflict, but the conflict cannot be attributed to grazing per se, since it was seriously mismanaged. Thus, based on this partial information, the attorney general's office advised the department against grazing on the Sargent WMA.

During the period when Binkley grazed and the management plan was written, the deed restriction was applicable but grazing was obviously allowed. The USFWS also knew the deed's contents (Stegman 1975), yet authorized grazing through a program amendment (NMDGF 1977a). Because the subsequent management plan did not prohibit grazing, there are only two possible explanations to explain the Binkley grazing. First, NMDGF flagrantly disregarded restrictive language, with minimal sanctions. Or, policy was such that management was left to NMDGF. Such a policy would be in keeping with earlier decision-making patterns. If NMDGF felt grazing could enhance the grasses, nobody questioned their decision. Nevertheless, in the case of Ganados, NMDGF felt it necessary to consult with The Nature Conservancy, who then insisted that the deed prohibited grazing:

> It is the Conservancy's position that the deed restriction prohibits any use of the Wildlife Area for grazing. The language of the deed is explicit—the property is to "be held solely as wildlife habitat." This clear limitation on use is subject to only three stated exceptions: a portion of the property may be used by snowmobiles; overnight camping is allowed in certain areas, and timber may be harvested to improve the wildlife habitat. Thus the parties considered alternative uses and determined to allow only these three. Grazing is not expressly allowed. Its omission could not have been an oversight, because the property was grazed at the time these matters were negotiated. The option between the Conservancy and the commission for the conveyance mentions that the grazing was to be terminated no later than October 31, 1975. Use of the property for grazing was thus contemplated by the parties and rejected. (Duprey 1989)

The Nature Conservancy felt morally obligated to fulfill the deed's intent, and should grazing occur they would take the "appropriate legal action" (Duprey 1989). Of course, grazing was not terminated in October 1975.

Federal aid was also used as an excuse. The USFWS does not prohibit grazing per se; in fact, at least nine wildlife refugees allow grazing (USFWS 1989), and WMAs in southern New Mexico have been grazed for years. It is always a question of management. In terms of grazing in general as well as land management research proposals, the central issue is, Will the activity in question lead to an enhanced wildlife habitat? Thus, according to USFWS criteria, there were two relevant questions raised by the Ganados case: Is the project substantial? Is grazing considered an accepted management tool (Raynor 1989)?

The assistant solicitor of the USFWS defined a substantial research project as meeting the purposes of PR if it had clear objectives, yielded benefits commensurate with its cost, and utilized accepted management principles (Raynor 1989, 1). Further, all property purchased with federal aid "must continue to serve the purpose for which acquired or constructed" (Alley 1989, 3–4). If such conditions are not met, the state risks having to reimburse all federal aid monies. Thus, the legal question becomes, Is grazing an accepted management method? It is a question obviously open to interpretation. The uncertainty of it all was underscored when the director of the NMDGF stated, "I would like to see some research that would tell us once and for all if livestock grazing is detrimental or beneficial" (Montoya in Schein 1989b).

The final legal issue centered on the competitive bidding process. NMDGF officials argued that grazing land is a public resource. Should it be opened up for grazing, allocation should be done through a competitive bidding process. Montoya saw no reason why Ganados, as an antipoverty group, should be favored, despite the fact that it was entirely the NMDGF's decision to make (Lithgow 1985).

28. Demonstrating the degree of uncertainty surrounding the efficacy of short-term grazing, an USFWS biologist wrote that a research project investigating the impacts of grazing could have three possible outcomes. First, the results could indicate that grazing is detrimental to wildlife. Second, it could show that grazing is neutral-to-beneficial to wildlife on previously grazed lands, but less so on ungrazed lands. And finally, the research could indicate that grazing actually improved the lands. He felt the second scenario most plausible, but illustrating the politically charged nature of the research, he hoped for the first so that professional resource managers could claim, "We told you so!" (Parsons 1989, 4).

Chapter 5: Politics, Identity, and the Future of Environmentalism

1. A good example of this is John Muir. He was a college-educated man who chose to live as a shepherd. Another example comes from the environmentalist motto, "chosen simplicity." Again, environmentalists emphasize reducing consumption and the simplification of lifestyles. Such simplicity, however, is not a choice for the subaltern.

2. While this may be true in some instances, it glosses over the fact that the subaltern may have an important economic function, or that they meet the needs of the privileged in other ways.

3. I am grateful to Ernie Chavez for sharing his collection of 1960s Chicano movement materials with me.

4. There was even a Chicano-led opposition to the UFWOC in both Los Angeles (Ramirez 1968; Ramirez, Morales, and Mitchell, n.d.) and among some workers in the valley (Committee Representing Our Pickers' Survival, n.d.).

5. La Virgen de Guadalupe is the patron saint of the Americas but most closely associated with Mexico because that is where she is said to have appeared in 1531.

6. There do exist land-grant activists who are waiting for the right opportunity to bring up their cases (Morales 1990), and there is the ongoing land-grant struggle of Amador Flores of Tierra Amarilla (Hales 1991; E. Martinez 1989; Wald 1989). Ganados recognizes the kind of fear that this type of activity can strike in Anglo hearts. They have been careful to separate themselves from land-grant activists and have explicitly stated that they are not interested in *regaining* grant lands, but rather in *using* the land. Nevertheless, some Anglos see all Hispanos as the same. "What Ganados is after is the entire 500,000 acres of the [Tierra Amarilla] land grant" (Jim Mundy in J. Baker, *Newsweek*, Sept. 18, 1989, 39).

Bibliography

The following list refers to the archives, libraries, special collections, and personal files from which the data were collected. Each collection is identified and abbreviated for convenience in the bibliography.

BANCROFT   Bancroft Library, University of California, Berkeley, California.

BEALE   Local History Room, Kern County Beale Memorial Library, Bakersfield, California.

CORONADO   Coronado Room, Zimmerman Library, University of New Mexico, Albuquerque, New Mexico.

DATA   Bureau of Business and Economic Research Data Bank, University of New Mexico, Albuquerque, New Mexico.

EL MAL   *El Malcriado* Collection, Archives of Labor and Urban Affairs, Wayne State University, Detroit, Michigan.

FEDREC   *Ponce v. Fielder et al.,* United States District Court, Central District of California, Ninth Circuit, Case CV69–700 WPG, Federal Records Center-Los Angeles, Laguna Niguel, California.

FOWLER   Personal File, Professor John Fowler, New Mexico State University, Las Cruces, New Mexico.

FRESNO   *Solis and Torres v. Fielder,* Case 145434, Superior Court of California, Fresno County.

GDV   Grazing File, Ganados del Valle, Los Ojos, New Mexico.

KERNA   *Atwood Aviation, Inc. v. Seldon C. Morley,* Case 103595, Superior Court of California, Kern County, California.

KERNC   *Cohen v. the Superior Court of the State of California for the County of Kern,* Case 1043, Court of Appeal of the State of California, Fifth Appellate District.

MILLER   Personal Files, Anita Miller, Esq., Potter and Kelly, Albuquerque, New Mexico.

MM   Marion Moses Collection, Archives of Labor and Urban Affairs, Wayne State University, Detroit, Michigan.

NCAD   National Campaign for Agricultural Democracy (1967–70), Archives of Labor and Urban Affairs, Wayne State University, Detroit, Michigan.

NMDGF   Ganados Files, New Mexico Department of Game and Fish, Santa Fe, New Mexico.

OFFP   United Farm Workers Office of the President (1962–71), Archives of Labor and Urban Affairs, Wayne State University, Detroit, Michigan.

SAC   *Ponce v. Fielder et al.,* Case 191712, Superior Court of California, Sacramento, California.

SANTILLAN   Richard and Gloria Santillan Collection, Chicano Studies Library, University of California, Berkeley, California.

SC   Sierra Club, Rio Grande Chapter, Albuquerque Group, Albuquerque, New Mexico.

STATE   Southwest Room, New Mexico State Library, Santa Fe, New Mexico.

SWOP   Southwest Organizing Project, Albuquerque, New Mexico.

UFWOC   United Farm Workers Organizing Committee (1962–66), Archives of Labor and Urban Affairs, Wayne State University, Detroit, Michigan.

USFWS   Ganados Files, United States Fish and Wildlife Service, Region Two, Albuquerque, New Mexico.

ZWANK   Personal File, Professor Phil Zwank, New Mexico State University, Las Cruces, New Mexico.

Abascal, R. 1991. California Rural Legal Assistance. Interview with Author. Berkeley, California, April 11.

Acuna, R. 1989. *Occupied America*. 3d ed. New York: Harper & Row.

Adams, J., L. Dunlap, J. Hair, F. Krupp, J. Lorenz, M. McCloskey, R. Peterson, P. Pritchard, W. Turnage, and K. Wendelowski. 1986. Background and Synopsis of the Issues. In *An Environmental Agenda for the Future*. Ed. R. Cahn. Washington, D.C.: Island Press, pp. 1–23.

Aguilar, G. 1991. Ganados del Valle. Interview with Author. Plaza Blanca, New Mexico, August 13.

Alexander, D. 1990. Bioregionalism: Science or Sensibility? *Environmental Ethics* 12:161–73.

Allen, T. 1994. *The Invention of the White Race*. New York: Verso.

Alley, S. 1989. Letter to William Montoya. August 17. NMDGF.

Almaguer, T. 1980. Keeping the 'House of Labor' Divided: The Attitude of Organized Labor toward the Japanese-Mexican Labor Association in 1903. In *Work, Family, Sex Roles, and Language*. Ed. M. Barrera, A. Camarillo, and F. Hernandez. The National Association for Chicano Studies, 1979. Berkeley: Tonatiuh-Quinto Sol International, pp. 9–32.

Alston, D., ed. 1990. *We Speak for Ourselves: Social Justice, Race, and Environment*. Washington, D.C.: Panos Institute.

Alvarez, S. 1973. The Legal and Legislative Struggle of the Farmworkers. In *Voices: Readings from El Grito*. Ed. O. Romano. Berkeley: Quinto Sol Publications, pp. 219–361.

Anaya, R., and F. Lomeli, eds. 1989. *Aztlan: Essays on the Chicano Homeland*. Albuquerque: Academia/El Norte Publications.

Anderson, T. L., and D. R. Leal. 1991. *Free Market Environmentalism*. Boulder: Westview Press.

Anderton, D., A. Anderson, J. Oakes, and M. Fraser. 1994. Environmental Equity: The Demographics of Dumping. *Demography* 31:229–48.

Andres, L., E. Oatman, and R. Simpson. 1979. Re-Examination of Pest Control Practices. In *Biological Control and Insect Pest Management*. Davis: Agriculture Experiment Station, University of California, Division of Agriculture and Natural Resources Bulletin 1911:1–10.

Anthias, F. 1990. Race and Class Revisited: Conceptualizing Race and Racisms. *Sociological Review* 38:19–42.

Anzaldua, G., ed. 1990. *Making Face, Making Soul: Haciendo Caras*. San Francisco: Aunt Lute Books.

Arax, M. 1994. Union's Focus on Fields Starts to Bear Fruit. *Los Angeles Times*, July 18, A3, A16.

Aronowitz, S. 1994. The Situation of the Left in the United States. *Socialist Review* 23:5–79.

Atwood Aviation, Inc. v. Seldon C. Morley. 1968. *Memorandum of Points and*

*Authorities in Support of Temporary Restraining Order and Prelimi-
nary Injunction.* Case 103595. August 22. KERNA.

———. 1969a. *Amended Complaint to Enjoin Disclosure of Reports.* January
28. KERNA.

———. 1969b. *Memorandum of Points and Authorities on Date of Order to
Show Cause of Hearing.* January 26. KERNA.

———. 1969c. *Order on Order to Show Cause and Decision Granting Preliminary Injunction.* March 27. KERNA.

———. 1971. *Remittitur.* December 10. KERNA.

Austin, R., and M. Schill. 1991. Black, Brown, Poor and Poisoned: Minority
Grassroots Environmentalism and the Quest for Eco-Justice. *Kansas
Journal of Law and Public Policy* 1:69–82.

Averbuck, D. 1991. Phone Conversation with Author, August 27.

Ayala de Sifuentes, L. 1972. Trade Secret Protection of Pesticide Reports. *Atz-
lan* 3:283–306.

Balzar, J. 1994. A Surprise Bounty for Hunters. *Los Angeles Times,* March 16,
A1, A13.

Baron, H. 1985. Racism Transformed: The Implications of the 1960s. *Review
of Radical Political Economics* 17:10–33.

Barrera, M. 1979. *Race and Class in the Southwest: A Theory of Racial Inequality.* Notre Dame: University of Notre Dame Press.

Bauman, Z. 1973. *Culture as Praxis.* London: Routledge and Kegan Paul.

Baxter, J. 1987. *Las Carneradas: Sheep Trade in New Mexico, 1700–1860.*
Albuquerque: University of New Mexico Press.

Bebbington, A. 1993. Modernization from Below: An Alternative Indigenous
Development? *Economic Geography* 69:274–92.

Bebbington A., H. Carrasco, L. Peralbo, G. Ramon, J. Trujillo, and V. Torres.
1993. Fragile Lands, Fragile Organizations: Indian Organizations and
the Politics of Sustainability in Ecuador. *Transactions of the Institute of
British Geographers* 18:179–96.

Bell Blawis, P. 1971. *Tijerina and the Land Grants.* New York: International
Publishers.

Bennett, J., and W. Chaloupka, eds. 1993. *In The Nature of Things: Language,
Politics and the Environment.* Minneapolis: University of Minnesota
Press.

Berman Santana, D. 1993. Kicking Off the Bootstraps: Environment, Development and Community Power in Puerto Rico. Ph.D. diss., University of
California, Berkeley.

Berry, W. 1986. *The Unsettling of America: Culture and Agriculture.* 2d ed. San
Francisco: Sierra Club Books.

Bishop, G., D. David, and T. Watson. 1979. Cultural Practices in Pest Management. In *Biological Control and Insect Pest Management*. Davis: Agriculture Experiment Station, University of California, Division of Agriculture and Natural Resources Bulletin 1911:61–71.

Blauner, B. 1992. Talking Past Each Other: Black and White Languages of Race. *American Prospect* 10:54–64.

Blaut, J. 1992. Cultural Racism. *Antipode* 24:289–99.

———. 1993. *The Geographer's Model of the World*. New York: Routledge.

Blaut, J., and A. Rios-Bustamante. 1984. Commentary on Nostrand's 'Hispanos' and their 'Homeland'. *Annals of the Association of American Geographers* 74:157–64.

Board Members. 1969. Board Meeting Agenda. May 26. Box 1, Folder 8. MM.

Boggs, C. 1986. *Social Movements and Political Power*. Philadelphia: Temple University Press.

Bohara, A., and A. Davila. 1992. A Reassessment of the Phenotypic Discrimination and Income Differences among Mexican Americans. *Social Science Quarterly* 73:114–19.

Borrelli, P. 1988. Environmentalism at a Crossroads. In *Crossroads: Environmental Priorities for the Future*. Ed. P. Borrelli. Washington, D.C.: Island Press, pp. 3–25.

Boston, T. 1987. *Race, Class and Conservatism*. Boston: Unwin Hyman.

Bramwell, A. 1989. *Ecology in the 20th Century, a History*. New Haven: Yale University Press.

Broad, R., and J. Cavanagh. 1993. *Paradise Plundered*. Berkeley: University of California.

Brown, J. 1969. Memo to Boycotters. July 19. Box 25, Folder 15. NCAD.

———. n.d. Memo to Boycotters re Pesticide Information Campaign. Box 9, Folder 29. UFWOC.

Brown, L., and H. Ingram. 1987. *Water and Poverty in the Southwest*. Tucson: University of Arizona Press.

Brown, P., and S. Masterson-Allen. 1994. The Toxic Waste Movement: A New Type of Activism. *Society and Natural Resources* 7:269–87.

Brown Welsh, J. 1988. Environmental Protection: Luxury of the Rich or Requirement of the Poor? In *Crossroads: Environmental Priorities for the Future*. Ed. P. Borrelli. Washington, D.C.: Island Press, pp. 287–94.

Bryant, B., and P. Mohai. 1992. Introduction to *Race and the Incidence of Environmental Hazards*. Ed. B. Bryant and P. Mohai. Boulder: Westview Press, pp. 1–9.

Buechler, S. 1993. Beyond Resource Mobilization: Emerging Trends in Social Movement Theory. *Sociological Quarterly* 34:217–35.

Bullard, R. 1990. *Dumping in Dixie: Race, Class, and Environmental Quality.* Boulder: Westview Press.

——, ed. 1993a. *Confronting Environmental Racism: Voices from the Grass-roots.* Boston: South End Press.

——, ed. 1993b. Unequal Environmental Protection: Incorporating Environmental Justice in Decision Making. Unpublished manuscript. Sociology Department, University of California, Riverside.

——. 1994. *Unequal Protection: Environmental Justice and Communities of Color.* San Francisco: Sierra Club Books.

Bureau of Business and Economic Research. 1989. *New Mexico Statistical Abstract.* Albuquerque: The University of New Mexico.

Bureau of Economic Analysis. Regional Economic Information System. 1991. Full-Time and Part-Time Employees by Major Industry, Rio Arriba County, 1969–89. DATA.

Burgess, T. 1990. Wilderness — The Issue. *New Mexico Stockman* 56:32. CORONADO.

Burke, L. 1993. Environmental Inequities in Los Angeles. Master's thesis, University of California, Santa Barbara.

Burma, J., and D. Williams. 1960. *An Economic, Social and Educational Survey of Rio Arriba and Taos Counties.* Prepared for Northern New Mexico College. CORONADO.

Buttel, F. 1992. Environmentalization: Origins, Processes, and Implications for Rural Social Change. *Rural Sociology* 57:1–27.

Buttel, F., and W. Flinn. 1977. Conceptions of Rural Life and Environmental Concern. *Rural Sociology* 42:544–55.

Cable, S., and M. Benson. 1993. Acting Locally: Environmental Injustice and the Emergence of Grass-Roots Environmental Organizations. *Social Problems* 40:464–77.

Cahn, R., ed. 1986. *An Environmental Agenda for the Future.* Washington, D.C.: Island Press.

Calderon, F., A. Piscitelli, and J. L. Reyna. 1992. Social Movements: Actors, Theories, and Expectations. In *The Making of Social Movements in Latin America.* Ed. A. Escobar and S. Alvarez. Boulder: Westview Press, pp. 19–36.

California Department of Public Health. 1958. Reports of Occupational Disease Attributed to Pesticides and Agricultural Chemicals. Berkeley: Bureau of Adult Health.

——. 1967. Occupational Disease in California Attributed to Pesticides and Other Agricultural Chemicals. Bureau of Occupational Health and Environmental Epidemiology. In *Occupational Safety and Health Act of*

1969: Hearings before the Select Subcommittee on Labor of the Committee on Education and Labor. 91st Cong.

California Environmental Protection Agency. 1992. *CAL/EPA the First Six Months: A New Force for Environmental Improvement.* Sacramento: California Environmental Protection Agency.

Calkin, B. 1990. Memo to Rose Strickland re Sierra Club Range Policy. February 21. SC.

Campbell, G. 1990. Grape Boycott Has an Impact, Chavez Claims. *Bakersfield Californian,* September 3, A15–16. UFW 1990s Vertical File. BEALE.

Capek, S. 1993. The Environmental Justice Frame: A Conceptual Discussion and an Application. *Social Problems* 40:5–24.

Carlson, A. 1990. *The Spanish-American Homeland: Four Centuries in New Mexico's Rio Arriba.* Baltimore: The Johns Hopkins Press.

Carpenter, R., and J. Dixon. 1985. Ecology Meets Economics: A Guide to Sustainable Development. *Environment* 27:6–11, 30–32.

Cassutt, K. 1990. Santa Fe Activist. Interview with Author. Santa Fe, New Mexico, July 24.

Cater, J., and T. Jones. 1987. Asian Ethnicity, Home Ownership and Social Reproduction. In *Race and Racism.* Ed. P. Jackson. London: Allen and Unwin, pp. 191–211.

Chacon, R. 1980. The 1933 San Joaquin Valley Cotton Strike: Strike Breaking Activity in California Agriculture. In *Work, Family, Sex Roles, and Language.* Ed. M. Barrera, A. Camarillo, and F. Hernandez. The National Association for Chicano Studies, 1979. Berkeley: Tonatiuh-Quinto Sol International, pp. 33–69.

Chambers, I. 1994. *Migrancy, Culture, Identity.* New York: Routledge.

Charland, B. 1989. Economic Development Isn't Just Numbers, It's Ideas. *Rocky Mountain News,* July 24, 44. GDV.

Chase, A. 1987. *Playing God in Yellowstone.* New York: Harcourt Brace Jovanovich.

Chavez, C. 1969a. Letter to Martin Zaninovich. January 14. Box 46, Folder 6. OFFP.

———. 1969b. Letter to Quentin Reynolds. June 2. Box 9, Folder 29. UFWOC.

———. 1987. Group Interview with Chicano Graduate Student Association. University of Wisconsin, Madison, April.

———. 1989a. My Anger and Sadness Over Pesticides. *Sacramento Bee,* April 16, 1, 6. Pesticides Vertical File. BEALE.

———. 1989b. UFW Death Reports Premature. *Bakersfield Californian,* October 22. UFW 1980s Vertical File. BEALE.

———. 1991. Effective Protest Doesn't Require a Majority. *Los Angeles Times,*
    January 11, B10.

Chavez, C., and L. Steinberg. 1970. *Collective Bargaining Agreement between
    the United Farm Workers Organizing Committee and Wonder Palms
    Ranch, a Partnership by David Freedman and Company, Inc., Lionel
    Steinberg, Partner.* March 31. BANCROFT.

Chavez, F. A. 1984. Rejoinders. *Annals of the Association of American Geog-
    raphers* 74:171.

Chavez, J. 1989. *The Lost Land: The Chicano Image of the Southwest.* Albu-
    querque: University of New Mexico.

Chavez, L. 1991. *Out of the Barrio.* New York: Basic Books.

Chicago Daily News. 1969. Walking Death, Chavez Tells [of] DDT Peril.
    Newsclipping with Comments. October 18. Box 25, Folder 31. NCAD.

Chicano Student News. 1968. Who Are the Brown Berets? March 15, 6. SAN-
    TILLAN.

———. 1969. UMAS Conference, vol. 1, p. 3. SANTILLAN.

Christensen, J. 1988. A Different Kind of Bean Field. *High Country News.*
    October 24, 26–27. GDV.

Citizens for a Better Environment (CBE). 1989. *Richmond at Risk: Community
    Demographics and Toxic Hazards from Industrial Polluters.* San Fran-
    cisco.

Clement, R. 1972. The Pesticides Controversy. *Environmental Affairs* 2:445–
    68.

Clifford, F. 1994. Environmental Movement Struggling as Clout Fades. *Los
    Angeles Times,* September 21, A1, A22–24.

Coggins, G. C., and D. K. Nagel. 1990. 'Nothing Beside Remains': The Legacy
    of James G. Watt's Tenure as Secretary of the Interior on Federal Land
    Law and Policy. *Boston Environmental Affairs Law Review* 17:473–
    550.

Cohen, Jean. 1985. Strategy or Identity: New Theoretical Paradigms and Con-
    temporary Social Movements. *Social Research* 52:663–716.

Cohen, Jerry. 1969a. Letter to Stephen Wall. January 7. KERNA.

———. 1969b. Meeting of May 23, 1969. Box 46, Folder 6. OFFP.

———. 1969c. Statement of Jerome Cohen. August 1. *Hearings before the Sub-
    committee on Migratory Labor of the Committee on Labor and Public
    Welfare,* 3008–31.

———. 1969d. Statement of Jerry Cohen. November 21. *Occupational Safety
    and Health Act of 1969: Hearings before the Select Subcommittee on
    Labor of the Committee on Education and Labor,* 1347–55.

———. 1991. Interview with Author. Carmel Valley, California, April 8.

Cohen, M. 1988. *The History of the Sierra Club, 1892–1970*. San Francisco: Sierra Club Books.

Cohen, P. 1992. It's Racism What Dunnit: Hidden Narratives in Theories of Racism. In *'Race', Culture, and Difference*. Ed. J. Donald and A. Rattansi. Newbury Park, Calif.: Sage Publications, pp. 62–103.

Cohen v. Superior Court. n.d. *Commissioner Morley's Return to (Amended) Petition for Writs of Mandate, and to Real Parties in Interest's Opposition to Said (Amended) Petition*. KERNC.

Cole, L. 1992. Empowerment as the Key to Environmental Protection: The Need for Environmental Poverty Law. *Ecology Law Quarterly* 19:619–83.

Colopy, J. 1994. The Road Less Traveled: Pursuing Environmental Justice through Title VI of the Civil Rights Act of 1964. *Stanford Environmental Law Journal* 13:125–89.

Colquette, K. M., and E. Henry Roberston. 1991. Environmental Racism: The Causes, Consequences, and Commendations. *Tulane Environmental Law Journal* 5:153–207.

Committee Representing Our Pickers' Survival. n.d. Representation with Marxism: An Open Letter to One Cesar Chavez. Box 47, Folder 5. OFFP.

Commoner, B. 1990. *Making Peace with the Planet*. New York: Pantheon Books.

Connell, S. 1984. Grape Boycott Reinstated. *Bakersfield Californian*, July 12, A1, A4.

———. 1987. Cancer Victims Drawn into Union Dispute. *Bakersfield Californian*, November 8, B1–2.

Consumers' Rights Committee. 1969. Violence at the Supermarket . . . Why the Grape Boycott *Must* Be Ended! UFW 1960s Vertical File. BEALE.

Corwin, M. 1989. Growers Reap Benefits of Switch to Organic Farming. *Los Angeles Times*, Section A, July 23, 1, 31, 32.

Cotgrove, S., and A. Duff. 1980. Environmentalism, Middle-Class Radicalism and Politics. *Sociological Review* 28:333–51.

Cruse, H. 1987. *Plural but Equal: A Critical Study of Blacks and Minorities and America's Plural Society*. New York: William Morrow and Company.

Cutter, S. 1995. Race, Class and Environmental Justice. *Progress in Human Geography* 19(1): 107–18.

Dalton, R., and M. Kuechler, eds. 1990. *Challenging the Political Order: New Social and Political Movements in Western Democracies*. New York: Oxford University Press.

Dalton, R., M. Kuechler, and W. Bürklin. 1990. The Challenge of New Movements. In *Challenging the Political Order: New Social and Political Movements in Western Democracies*. Ed. R. Dalton and M. Kuechler. New York: Oxford University Press, pp. 3–20.

Dalzell, T., and H. Teller. 1973. USDA Destroys Poisoned Scab-Safeway Lettuce. February 23, *El Malcriado* 6(4): 3. Box 1965–76. EL MAL.

Daniel, C. 1981. *Bitter Harvest: A History of California Farmworkers, 1870–1941*. Berkeley: University of California Press.

Daniels, D. 1969. Presiding Representative. *Occupational Safety and Health Act of 1969: Hearings before the Select Subcommittee on Labor of the Committee on Education and Labor*.

Darnovsky, M. 1992. Stories Less Told: Histories of U.S. Environmentalism. *Socialist Review* 22:11–54.

Davis, D., and J. McMurtry. 1979. Introduction to *Biological Control and Insect Pest Management*. Davis: Agriculture Experiment Station, University of California, Division of Agriculture and Natural Resources Bulletin 1911:i–ii.

Day, M. 1971. *Forty Acres: Cesar Chavez and the Farm Workers*. New York: Praeger Publishers.

deBuys, W. 1981. Fractions of Justice: A Legal and Social History of the Las Trampas Grant, New Mexico. *New Mexico Historical Review* 56:71–97.

———. 1989. *Enchantment and Exploitation*. Albuquerque: University of New Mexico Press.

Denevan, W. 1992. The Pristine Myth: The Landscape of the Americas in 1492. *Annals of the Association of American Geographers* 80:369–85.

Deutsch, S. 1987. *No Separate Refuge: Culture, Class and Gender on an Anglo-Hispanic Frontier in the American Southwest, 1880–1940*. New York: Oxford Univeristy Press.

Devall, B., and G. Sessions. 1985. *Deep Ecology: Living as if Nature Mattered*. Salt Lake City: Gibbs M. Smith, Inc.

DeVoss, D. 1987. How the Bugs Finally Won. *Los Angeles Times Magazine*, September 20, 18–22, 34.

Diamond, I., and G. Feman Orenstein, eds. 1990. *Reweaving the World: The Emergence of Ecofeminism*. San Francisco: Sierra Club Books.

Dobson, A. 1990. *Green Political Thought*. New York: Routledge.

Dominick, R. 1988. The Roots of the Green Movement. *Environmental Review* 12:1–30.

Donald, J., and A. Rattansi. 1992. Introduction to *'Race', Culture, and Difference*. Newbury Park, Calif.: Sage Publications, pp. 1–8.

Dunbar Ortiz, R. 1980. *Roots of Resistance: Land Tenure in New Mexico, 1680–1980.* Los Angeles: University of California, Los Angeles, Chicano Studies and American Indian Centers Publication.

Dunlap, R. 1987. Polls, Pollution and Politics Revisited: Public Opinion on the Environment in the Reagan Era. *Environment* 29:7–11, 32–37.

———. 1989. Public Opinion and Environmental Policy. In *Environmental Politics and Policy.* Ed. J. Lester. Durham: Duke University Press, pp. 87–134.

Dunlap, R., G. Gallup, and A. Gallup. 1993. Of Global Concern: Results of the Health of the Planet Survey. *Environment* 35:6–15, 33–39.

Dunlap, R., and A. Mertig. 1992. The Evolution of the U.S. Environmental Movement from 1970–1990: An Overview. In *American Environmentalism: The U.S. Enviromental Movement 1970–1990.* Ed. R. Dunlap and A. Mertig. Philadelphia: Taylor and Francis, pp. 11–26.

Dunlap, T. 1981. *DDT: Scientists, Citizens and Public Policy.* Princeton: Princeton University Press.

Duprey, D. 1989. Letter to Bill Montoya. July 12. NMDGF.

Eastman, C. 1991. Community Land Grants: The Legacy. *Social Science Journal* 28:101–17.

Eastman, C., G. Carruthers, and J. Liefer. 1971. Contrasting Attitudes toward Land in New Mexico. *New Mexico Business Review* 24:3–20.

Eastman, C., and J. Gray. 1987. *Community Grazing: Practice and Potential in New Mexico.* Albuquerque: University of New Mexico Press.

Ebright, M., ed. 1985. *The Tierra Amarilla Grant: A History of Chicanery.* Santa Fe: Center for Land Grant Studies.

———. 1987. New Mexican Land Grants: The Legal Background. In *Land, Water and Culture: New Perspectives on Hispanic Land Grants.* Ed. C. Briggs and J.Van Ness. Albuquerque: University of New Mexico Press, pp. 15–64.

———. 1989. *Spanish and Mexican Land Grants and the Law.* Manhattan: Sunflower University Press.

Edelstein, M. 1987. *Contaminated Communities: The Social and Psychological Impacts of Residential Toxic Exposure.* Boulder: Westview Press.

Ekins, P. 1992. *A New World Order: Grassroots Movements for Global Change.* New York: Routledge.

Elenes, V. 1991. Farmworker Pesticide Exposure: Interplay of Science and Politics in the History of Regulations, 1947–1988. Master's thesis, University of Wisconsin, Madison.

Eller, J., and R. Coughlan. 1993. The Poverty of Primordialism: The Demystification of Ethnic Attachments. *Ethnic and Racial Studies* 16:183–202.

El Malcriado. 1969a. Health and Safety . . . The Most Important Issue. September 15–October 1, 3(12): 3, 6. Box 1965–76. EL MAL.

———. 1969b. Negotiations: Why They Failed . . . How They Could Succeed. September 15–October 1, 3(12): 4. Box 1965–76. EL MAL.

———. 1969c. New Attempt to See Poison Records. August 15–September 15, 3(11): 7, 15. Box 1965–76. EL MAL.

———. 1969d. Reflections on the Poisoning of Food and Man. October 15–31, 3(4): 4. Box 1965–76. EL MAL.

———. 1974. Contracts Compared: UFW-Alamden vs. Teamster-Gallo. May 29, 7(5): 7. Box 1965–76. EL MAL.

Emel, J., and R. Peet. 1989. Resource Management and Natural Hazards. In *New Models in Geography.* Ed. R. Peet and N. Thrift. London: Unwin Hyman, pp. 49–76.

Eppers, B. 1990. President's Message. *New Mexico Stockman* 56:6. CORONADO.

Erickson, B. 1990. Forward on All Fronts. In *Call to Action: Handbook for Ecology, Peace, and Justice.* Ed. B. Erickson. San Francisco: Sierra Club Books, pp. 1–7.

Escobar, A. 1992a. Culture, Economics, and Politics in Latin American Social Movements, Theory, and Research. In *The Making of Social Movements in Latin America.* Boulder: Westview Press, pp. 62–85.

———. 1992b. Imagining a Post-Development Era? Critical Thought, Development and Social Movements. *Social Text* 10:20–56.

Escobar, A., and S. Alvarez, eds. 1992. *The Making of Social Movements in Latin America.* Boulder: Westview Press.

Evans, W. 1990a. Interview with Author. New Mexico Department of Game and Fish, Santa Fe, July 20.

———. 1990b. New Mexico Department of Game and Fish. Interview with Author. Santa Fe, New Mexico, July 18.

Evernden, N. 1992. *The Social Creation of Nature.* Baltimore, Md.: Johns Hopkins University Press.

Farm Workers Action Committee. n.d. Housewives and Mothers, Protect Your Family and Grapeworkers from Lethal Pesticides. Box 25, Folder 22. NCAD.

Farnsworth, C. 1971. Memo to the Boycott Department. March 25. Box 48, Folder 2. OFFP.

Ferguson, D., and N. Ferguson. 1983. *Sacred Cows at the Public Trough.* Bend: Maverick Publications.

Fielder, J. 1970. Statement of Jerry W. Fielder, Department of Agriculture, State of California. *Occupational Safety and Health Act of 1969: Hearings before the Select Subcommittee on Labor of the Committee on Education and Labor,* 1337–47.

Fish, J., ed. 1987. *Wildlands: New Mexico* BLM *Wilderness Coalition Statewide Proposal.* New Mexico BLM Wilderness Coalition. SC.

Fisher, H. 1964. Statement of Hugo Fisher. *California Assembly Interim General Research Committee Subcommittee on Pesticides.*

Fisher, L. 1952. *The Harvest Labor Market in California.* Institute of Industrial Relations. Berkeley: University of California.

FitzSimmons, M. 1989. The Matter of Nature. *Antipode* 21:106–20.

FitzSimmons, M., and R. Gottlieb. 1988. A New Environmental Politics. In *Reshaping the U.S. Left: Popular Struggles in the 1980s.* Ed. M. Davis and M. Sprinkler. London: Verso, pp. 114–30.

Fjetland, C. 1983. Letter to Harold Olson. November 14. Sargent File. USFWS.

Fleming, B. 1933. The Problem of Soil Erosion in New Mexico. *New Mexico Business Review* 2:90–94.

Flint, S. 1990. Making Things Happen. *Rio Grande Sierran,* April/May. STATE.

Flores, C. 1989a. Carruthers Outlines Plan to End Illegal Grazing. *Albuquerque Journal,* August 23, A1, A3.

——. 1989b. Committee Backs Sheep-Grazing Protest. *Albuquerque Journal,* August 20, A3.

——. 1989c. Sheep To Be Moved from Wildlife Area. *Albuquerque Journal,* August 24, A1, A3.

Foreman, I. 1986. Acres of Trouble. *Albuquerque Journal,* November 16, C1, C4.

Forrest, S. 1989. *The Preservation of the Village.* Albuquerque: University of New Mexico Press.

Forter, S. 1989. UFW Grape Boycott Fails to Gain Support. *Bakersfield Californian,* April 8, A1–2. UFW 1980s Vertical File. BEALE.

Fortmann, L., and J. Kusel. 1990. New Voices, Old Beliefs: Forest Environmentalism among New and Long-Standing Rural Residents. *Rural Sociology* 55:214–32.

Fowler, J., and J. Gray. 1980. *Market Values of Federal Grazing Permits in New Mexico.* Las Cruces: New Mexico State University, Cooperative Extension Service, Range Improvement Task Force.

Fox, S. 1981. *John Muir and His Legacy: The American Conservation Movement.* Boston: Little, Brown and Company.

Freeman, R. 1990. Santa Fe Activist. Interview with Author. Santa Fe, New Mexico, July 19.

Fresno Bee. 1968. MAPA Assails Reagan Stand on Legal Grant. January 9, 8A. NCAD.

———. 1969a. Chavez Charges Pesticide Health Hazards: Call [for] Statewide Parley. January 22. Box 25, Folder 15. NCAD.

———. 1969b. Tulare Children Show Pesticide Poison Signs. Newsclipping with Comments. November 24. Box 25, Folder 16. NCAD.

Freudenberg, N. 1984. *NOT In Our Backyards!* New York: Monthly Review Press.

Freudenburg, W. 1991. Rural-Urban Differences in Environmental Concern: A Closer Look. *Sociological Inquiry* 61:167–98.

Friedmann, J., and H. Rangan, eds. 1993a. *In Defense of Livelihood.* West Hartford: Kumarian Press.

———. 1993b. Introduction to *In Defense of Livelihood.* West Hartford: Kumarian Press, pp.1–21.

Fuss, D. 1989. *Essentially Speaking.* New York: Routledge.

Galarza, E. 1964. *Merchants of Labor: The Mexican Bracero Story.* Santa Barbara: McNally and Loftin Publishers.

———. 1977. *Farm Workers and Agribusiness in California 1947–1960.* Notre Dame: University of Notre Dame Press.

Gale, R. 1972. From Sit-In to Hike-In: A Comparison of the Civil Rights and Environmental Movements. In *Social Behavior, Natural Resources, and the Environment.* Ed. W. Burch, N. Sheek, and L. Taylor. New York: Harper and Row, pp. 280–305.

Gale, S. 1969. Delano Exhibit at New College. *Delano Record,* March 4. UFW 1960s Vertical File. BEALE.

Ganados del Valle. 1984. A Proposal to Cooperatively Graze the Humphries and Sargent Game Lands. May 30. GDV.

———. 1989a. A Proposal to Improve Wildlife Habitat on the Rio Chama, Humphries, and Sargent Wildlife Areas. August. GDV.

———. 1989b. Press Release. August 18. GDV.

———. 1993. Ganados del Valle 10th Anniversary Newsletter. Summer. GDV.

———. n.d. The Grazing Proposal and the Issues. GDV.

Garcia, I. M. 1989. *United We Win: The Rise and Fall of La Raza Unida.* Tucson: Mexican American Studies Research Center, University of Arizona.

Garcia, Maria. 1990. United States Forest Service. Interview with Author. El Rito, New Mexico, August 1.

Garcia, Mario. 1984. Mexican American Labor and the Left: The Asociacion Nacional Mexico-Americana, 1949–1954. In *The Chicano Struggle: Analyses of Past and Present Efforts.* National Association for Chicano Studies. Binghamton: Bilingual Press, pp. 65–86.

Gardner, R. 1970. *Grito! Reies Tijerina and the New Mexico Land Grant War of 1967.* Indianapolis: Bobbs-Merrill.

Gedicks, A. 1993. *The New Resource Wars.* Boston: South End Press.

Getze, G. 1969. Suits Ask Ban on DDT in California: Crop Confiscation. *Los Angeles Times,* Section A, April 15, 3, 31. Box 25, Folder 9. NCAD.

Gibson, K., and J. Graham. 1992. Rethinking Class in Industrial Geography: Creating a Space for an Alternative Politics of Class. *Economic Geography* 68:109–27.

Gillam, J. 1969. State to Ban Use of DDT on Grapes Effective March 1. *Los Angeles Times,* December 16. Box 49, Folder 12. OFFP.

Gilroy, P. 1991. *There Ain't No Black in the Union Jack: The Cultural Politics of Race and Nation.* Chicago: The University of Chicago Press.

———. 1992. The End of Antiracism. In *'Race,' Culture, and Difference.* Ed. J. Donald and A. Rattansi. Newbury Park, Calif.: Sage Publications, pp. 49–61.

———. 1993. It Ain't Where You're From, It's Where You're At. In *Small Acts.* London: Serpent's Tail, pp. 120–45.

Girard, G. 1970. UFWOC, 26 Growers Sign Pact. *Bakersfield Californian,* July 30. Box 25, Folder 15. NCAD.

Giroux, H. 1993. Living Dangerously: Identity, Politics and the New Cultural Racism: Towards a Critical Pedagogy of Representation. *Cultural Studies* 7:1–27.

Giumarra, J. 1970. Statement of John Giumarra Jr., General Counsel, Giumarra Vineyards Corporation, Edison, California. In *Migrant Seasonal Farmworkers Powerlessness: Hearings before the Subcommittee on Labor and Public Welfare.* U.S. Senate. 91st Cong., September 30, 1969, pt. 6-C:3760–75.

Goldberg, D. 1993. *Racist Culture.* Cambridge: Blackwell Publishers.

Goldman, B. 1994. *Not Just Prosperity: Achieving Sustainability with Environmental Justice.* National Wildlife Federation.

Goldschmidt, W. 1947. *As You Sow.* New York: Harcourt, Brace and Company.

Gomez, P. 1985. The History and Adjudication of the Common Lands of Spanish and Mexican Land Grants. *Natural Resources Journal* 25:1039–80.

Gomez Quinones, J. 1978. *Mexican Students por La Raza.* Santa Barbara: Editorial la Causa.

———. 1990. *Chicano Politics: Reality and Promise, 1940–1990.* Albuquerque: University of New Mexico.

Gonzales, S. 1987. Elk Projects Date from 1910–1911. *New Mexico Wildlife* 32:6–34. STATE.

Gonzalez, N. 1969. *The Spanish Americans of New Mexico.* Albuquerque: University of New Mexico Press.

Gottlieb, R. 1993. *Forcing the Spring: The Transformation of the American Environmental Movement.* Washington, D.C.: Island Press.

Gottlieb, R., and H. Ingram. 1988. Which Way Environmentalism? Toward a New Movement. In *Winning America.* Ed. C. Hartman and M. Raskin. Boston: South End Press, 114–30.

Graham, F. 1990. *The Audubon Ark: A History of the Audubon Society.* New York: Alfred Knopf.

Grauberger, J. 1989. Ganados del Valle . . . Regional Marketing at Its Best. *National Wool Grower* (December): 24–25. GDV.

Green, M. 1969. DDT Petition Brews Political Poison for Finch. Newsclipping with Comments. *Fresno Bee,* October 26, 6A. Box 25, Folder 15. NCAD.

Greenberg, M. 1993. Proving Environmental Inequity in Siting Locally Unwanted Land Uses. *Risk: Issues in Health and Safety* (summer): 234–52.

Gregory, S. 1993. Race, Rubbish, and Resistance: Empowering Difference in Community Politics. *Cultural Anthropology* 8:24–48.

Griffin, D. 1991. Human Impacts on Vegetation in the Upper Chama Valley, New Mexico. Unpublished manuscript. Geography Department, University of Wisconsin, Madison.

———. 1992. Land Use Conflict, Landscape Change, and Sustainability in the American West: A Case Study from the Chama Valley of New Mexico. Master's thesis, University of Wisconsin, Madison.

Griffith, C. 1990. Scientific Wildlife Management at Risk. *New Mexico Outdoor Reporter* 57:11. STATE.

Growers. 1969. Growers' Proposed Health and Safety Clause in July 1969 Negotiations. Box 25, Folder 9. NCAD.

Guha, Ramachandra. 1989. Radical American Environmentalism and Wilderness Preservation: A Third World Critique. *Environmental Ethics* 11: 71–83.

———. 1990. *The Unquiet Woods: Ecological Change and Peasant Resistance in the Himalaya.* Berkeley: University of California Press.

Guha, Ranajit. 1988a. Preface to *Selected Subaltern Studies.* Ed. R. Guha and G. Chakravorty Spivak. New York: Oxford University Press, pp. 35–36.

———. 1988b. The Prose of Counter Insurgency. In *Selected Subaltern Studies.* New York: Oxford University Press, pp. 45–86.

Gullett, S. 1988. Robert Redford's New Mexico Love Affair. *New Mexico Monthly* 1: 12–16. GDV.

Gutierrez, R. 1986. Unraveling America's Hispanic Past: Internal Stratification and Class Boundaries. *Aztlan* 17:79–101.

Hales, C. 1991. *Tierra o Muerte: Land or Death*. Video Produced by KBDI-TV, Denver, Colo.

Hall, S. 1991. Brave New World. *Socialist Review* 51:57–64.

———. 1992. New Ethnicities. In *'Race', Culture, and Difference*. Ed. J. Donald and A. Rattansi. Newbury Park, Calif.: Sage Publications, pp. 252–59.

Hamilton, Alice. 1943. *Exploring the Dangerous Trades: The Autobiography of Alice Hamilton, M.D.* Boston: Northeastern University Press.

Hamilton, C. 1989. Apartheid in an American City. Los Angeles: Labor/Community Strategy Center. Reprint. *Los Angeles Weekly*, December/January.

Hammerback J., R. Jensen, and J. A. Gutierrez. 1985. *A War of Words: Chicano Protest in the 1960s and 1970s*. Westport, Conn.: Greenwood Press.

Handler, J. 1992. Postmodernism, Protest, and the New Social Movements. *Law and Society Review* 26:697–731.

Hannah, M. 1992. Foucault Deinstitutionalized: Spatial Prerequisites for Modern Social Control. Ph.D. diss., Pennsylvania State University.

Hanson, A. 1989. The Making of the Maori: Culture Invention and Its Logic. *American Anthropologist* 91:890–902.

Harner, R. 1969. Poisons, Profits, and Politics. *Nation*, August 25, 134–37. UFW 1960s Vertical File. BEALE.

Harper, A., A. Cordova, and K. Oberg. 1943. *Man and Resources in the Middle Rio Grande Valley*. Albuquerque: University of New Mexico Press. CORONADO.

Harris, G. 1990. Chama Land and Cattle Company. Interview with Author. Chama, New Mexico, August 6.

Harrison, B., and B. Bluestone. 1988. *The Great U-Turn: Corporate Restructuring and the Polarization of America*. New York: Basic Books.

Hartmire, W. 1969. Some Comments on the Grape Negotiations. August 4. Box 61, Folder 3. OFFP.

Harvey, D. 1974. Population Resources and the Ideology of Science. *Economic Geography* 50:256–77.

———. 1991. Flexibility: Threat or Opportunity? *Socialist Review* 91:65–78.

———. 1993. Class Relations, Social Justice and the Politics of Difference. In *Place and the Politics of Identity*. Ed. M. Keith and S. Pile. New York: Routledge, pp. 41–66.

Hays, S. 1959. *Conservation and the Gospel of Efficiency: The Progressive Conservation Movement, 1890–1920.* Cambridge: Harvard University Press.

——. 1987. *Beauty, Health, and Permanence.* Cambridge: Cambridge University Press.

Heberlein, T. 1987. Stalking the Predator. *Environment* 29:6–11, 30–33.

Heiman, M. 1990. From Not In My Backyard! to Not In Anybody's Backyard! Grassroots Challenge to Hazardous Waste Facility Siting. *Journal of the American Planning Association* 56:359–62.

Henderson, D. 1990. Santa Fe Activist. Interview with Author. Santa Fe, New Mexico, July 24.

Hernandez, E. 1973. El Partido de la Raza Unida: Fresno Convention. *La Raza* 1(12).

Hershcopf, M. 1988. Letter to Daniel Sutcliffe. June 3. USFWS.

Heskin, A. 1991. *The Struggle for Community.* Boulder: Westview Press.

Hightower, J. 1976. Hard Tomatoes, Hard Times: The Failure of the Land Grant College Complex. In *Radical Agriculture.* Ed. R. Merrill. San Francisco: Harper and Row, pp. 87–110.

Hill Collins, P. 1991. *Black Feminist Thought.* New York: Routledge.

Hoare, Q., and G. N. Smith, eds. 1971. *Selections from the Prison Notebooks of Antonio Gramsci.* New York: International Publishers.

Hobsbawm, E., and T. Ranger, eds. 1983. *The Invention of Tradition.* Cambridge: Cambridge University Press.

Hofrichter, R., ed. 1993. *Toxic Struggles.* Philadelphia: New Society Publishers

hooks, b., and C. West. 1991. *Breaking Bread.* Boston: South End Press.

Horst, S. 1990. A Gentler Grip on the Earth. *Christian Science Monitor,* March 27. GDV.

House of Representatives. 1969. *Occupational Safety and Health Act of 1969: Hearings before the Select Subcommittee on Labor of the Committee on Education and Labor.* San Francisco: November 21–22.

Hoy, S. 1980. Municipal Housekeeping: The Role of Women in Improving Urban Sanitation Practices, 1880–1912. In *Pollution and Reform in American Cities, 1870–1930.* Ed. M. Melosi. Austin: University of Texas Press, 171–98.

Huerta, D. 1985. Discussion. In *California Farm Labor Relations and Law.* Ed. W. Fogel. Los Angeles: Institute of Industrial Relations, University of California, Los Angeles, pp. 127–37.

——. 1991. United Farm Workers. Interview with Author. Valencia, California, May 10.

Humphries, B. 1990. New Mexico State Land Office. Interview with Author. Santa Fe, New Mexico, August 7.

Inglehart, R. 1990. *Culture Shift in Advanced Industrial Societies*. Princeton: Princeton University Press.

Ingram, H., and D. Mann. 1989. Interest Group and Environmental Policy. In *Environmental Politics and Policy*. Ed. J. Lester. Durham: Duke University, pp. 135–57.

Inside Eastside. 1969. UFWOC Needs Your Help. 2(8): 2.

Jackson, D. 1991. Around Los Ojos, Sheep and Land Are Fighting Words. *Smithsonian* 22:37–47.

Jackson, P. 1987. *Race and Racism: Essays in Social Geography*. London: Allen and Unwin.

———. 1989. *Maps of Meaning*. London: Unwin Hyman.

Jackson, P., and J. Penrose, eds. 1994. *Constructions of Race, Place and Nation*. Minneapolis: University of Minnesota.

James, A. 1990. United States Forest Service. Interview with Author. El Rito, New Mexico, August 2.

Jelinek, L. 1976. *The California Farm Bureau Federation, 1919–1964*. Ph.D. diss. University of California, Los Angeles.

Jenkins, C. 1985. *The Politics of Insurgency: The Farm Worker Movement in the 1960s*. New York: Columbia University Press.

Jervis, T. 1990. Los Alamos Activist. Interview with Author. Los Alamos, New Mexico, July 19.

Johnston, B. R., ed. 1994. *Who Pays the Price? The Sociocultural Context of Environmental Crisis*. Washington, D. C.: Island Press.

Jones, L. 1970. Labor and Management in California Agriculture, 1864–1964. *Labor History* 11:23–40.

Jones, R. 1990. A New Face for Empire of San Joaquin. *Los Angeles Times*, May 29, A3.

Jordan, C., and D. Snow. 1992. Diversification, Minorities and the Mainstream Environmental Movement. In *Voices from the Environmental Movement: Perspectives for a New Era*. Ed. D. Snow. Washington, D.C.: Island Press, pp. 71–109.

Jukes, T. 1971. DDT, Human Health and the Environment. *Environmental Affairs* 1: 534–64.

Kaemper, M. 1990. Small Landowners Still Dislike Elk Permit Plan. *Rio Grande Sun*, October 11, B8.

Kaplan, D., and A. Pease, eds. 1993. *Cultures of United States Imperialism*. Durham: Duke University Press.

Kellert, S. 1978. Attitudes and Characteristics of Hunters and Anti-Hunters. *Proceedings of Forty-third North American Wildlife Conference*, 412–23.

Keppel, B. 1987. Castle and Cooke to Buy Tenneco's Farm Operation. *Los Angeles Times*, September 24, 1–2.

Kernberger, K. 1990. *The Quiet Ones*. Video produced by KNME-TV, Albuquerque, New Mexico.

Kerr, M., and C. Lee. 1993. From Conquistadores to Coalitions. *Southern Exposure* 21:8–19.

Kimball, R. 1991. Environmentalists Gaining Strength in West, Author Says. *Albuquerque Journal*, April 26, B2.

Knowlton, C. 1962. Area Development in New Mexico: Implications for Dependency and for Economic and Social Growth. Proceedings of the New Mexico Conference of Social Welfare, 1961–1962. CORONADO.

———. 1964. One Approach to the Economic and Social Problems of Northern New Mexico. *New Mexico Business*, September.

———. 1973. Causes of Land Loss among the Spanish Americans in Northern New Mexico. In *The Chicanos*. Ed. G. Lopez y Rivas. New York: Monthly Review Press, pp. 111–21.

Kobayashi, A., and L. Peake. 1994. Unnatural Discourse: 'Race' and Gender in Geography. *Gender, Place and Culture* 1:225–44.

Koppes, C. 1983. Environmental Policy and American Liberalism: The Department of the Interior, 1933–1953. *Environmental Review* 7:17–41.

———. 1987. Efficiency/Equity/Esthetics: Towards a Reinterpretation of American Conservation. *Environmental Review* 11:127–46.

Krueger, W. 1988. Nature, History and Ownership. In *Rangelands*. Ed. B. Buchanan. Albuquerque: University of New Mexico, pp. 1–7.

Krupp, F. 1986. New Environmentalism Factors in Economic Needs. *Wall Street Journal*, November 20.

Kushner, S. 1975. *Long Road to Delano*. New York: International Publisher.

Kutsche, P., and J. Van Ness. 1981. *Cañones: Values, Crisis and Survival in a Northern New Mexico Village*. Albuquerque: University of New Mexico Press.

Lacey, M., ed. 1991. *Government and Environmental Politics*. Baltimore: Johns Hopkins University Press.

Laclau, E. 1985. New Social Movements and the Plurality of the Social. In *New Social Movements and the State in Latin America*. Amsterdam: CEDLA (Centre for Latin American Research and Documentation), pp. 27–42.

LaGanga, M. 1989. Bug Busters. *Los Angeles Times*, October 1, 1, 5.

La Raza. 1969. Estimado Amigo Angelino. 2:4. SANTILLAN.

Legal Department. 1968. Memo to Boycott Staff. September 3. Box 25, Folder 10. NCAD.

Legal Office. 1969. Important Pesticide Information, September 1. Box 25, Folder 21. NCAD.

Lester, J., ed. 1989. *Environmental Politics and Policy.* Durham: Duke University Press.

Lester, J., D. Allen, and D. Milburn-Lauer. 1994. Race, Class, and Environmental Quality: An Examination of Environmental Racism in the American States. Paper presented at the Annual Meeting of the Western Political Science Association, Albuquerque, New Mexico, March.

Levy, J. 1975. *Cesar Chavez: Autobiography of La Causa.* New York: W.W. Norton and Company.

Lewis, M. 1992. *Green Delusions: An Environmentalist Critique of Radical Environmentalism.* Durham: Duke University Press.

Leys, C., and M. Mendell. 1992. Capitalism, Socialism, Culture and Social Movements. In *Culture and Social Change.* Ed. C. Leys and M. Mendell. Montreal: Black Rose Books, pp. 1–18.

Liebman, E. 1983. *California Farmland: A History of Agricultural Land Holdings.* Totowa: Rowman and Allanheld.

Limerick, P. 1988. *The Legacy of Conquest.* New York: W.W. Norton and Company.

Lithgow, C. 1985. Letter to Harold Olson. July 10. NMDGF.

Logsdon, P. n.d. In Rio Arriba County, New Mexico. *sheep! magazine,* pp. 11–15. GDV.

Lopez, D., and Y. Espiritu. 1990. Panethnicity in the United States: A Theoretical Framework. *Ethnic and Racial Studies* 13:198–224.

Lopez, I., E. Garduno, K. Radke, M. Vittor, L. Roycroft, J. Zamora, and the Environmental Defense Fund, Inc., Petitioners. 1969a. *Memorandum of Points and Authorities in Support of a Petition for the Issuance of a Proposed Regulation Repealing the Tolerance for DDT on Raw Agricultural Commodities.* October 7. Petitions Control Branch, Food and Drug Administration. NCAD.

———. 1969b. *Request for the Immediate Repeal of All Tolerances for DDT on Raw Agricultural Commodities.* October 31. NCAD.

Lopez Tijerina, R. 1978. *Mi Lucha por la Tierra.* Mexico: Fondo de Cultura Economica.

Los Angeles Times. 1969. House Group Charges Pesticides Go Unpoliced. News clipping with Comments. November 17. Box 25, Folder 31. NCAD

Lowe, G., T. Pinhey, and M. Grimes. 1980. Public Support for Environmental Protection. *Pacific Sociological Review* 23:423–45.

Lowenthal, D. 1986. *The Past Is a Foreign Country.* Cambridge: Cambridge University Press.

Lyons, J., and F. Zalon, eds. 1990. Progress Report: Vice President's Task Force on Pest Control Alternatives. *California Agriculture* 44:11–22.

Maes, J. 1990. Coordination: The Key to Implementing the State's Long-Range Economic Development Plan. *Developing New Mexico* 2:1.

Maestas, A. 1991. Ganados del Valle. Interview with Author. Los Ojos, New Mexico, August 9.

Maestas, G. 1990. Sheep Grazing Has No Place in New Mexico's Wildlife Areas. *Albuquerque Journal,* January 12, A7. GDV.

Majka, L., and T. Majka. 1982. *Farm Workers, Agribusiness and the State.* Philadelphia: Temple University Press.

Manes, C. 1990. *Green Rage: Radical Environmentalism and the Unmaking of Civilization.* Boston: Little, Brown and Company.

Mann, E. 1991. *LA 's Lethal Air.* Los Angeles: Labor/Community Strategy Center.

Manzanares, A. 1990. Ganados del Valle. Interview with Author. Los Ojos, New Mexico, August 18.

Marston, E. 1992. An Alternative to the Bumper-Sticker Approach to Grazing. *High Country News,* March 23, pp. 6–27.

Martin, P., S. Vaupel, and D. Egan. 1986. Farmworker Unions: Status and Wage Impacts. *California Agriculture* 40:11–13.

Martinez, E. 1989. Return to New Mexico: The Dispossessed Keep Pushing. *Z Magazine* 2:25–30.

Martinez, L. 1993. Interview with Author. Tijuana, Mexico. August 21.

Martinez, S. 1991. Ganados del Valle. Interview with Author. Los Ojos, New Mexico, August 9.

Massey, D. 1984. *Spatial Divisions of Labour: Social Structures and the Geography of Production.* Basingstoke, U.K.: Macmillan.

———. 1994. *Space, Place, and Gender.* Minneapolis: University of Minnesota Press.

Matthiessen, P. 1969. *Sal Si Puedes: Cesar Chavez and the New American Revolution.* New York: Random House.

McCaull, J. 1976. Discriminatory Air Pollution. *Environment* 18:26–31.

McPhee, J. 1989. *The Control of Nature.* London: Hutchinson Radius.

McWilliams, C. 1939. *Factories in the Fields.* Boston: Little, Brown, and Company.

Medina, A. 1991. Interview with Author. Los Angeles, California, March 1.

Medina, E. 1991. Interview with Author. San Diego, California, May 14.

Meinig, D. 1984. Rejoinders. *Annals of the Association of American Geographers* 74: 171.

Melone, M. 1993. The Struggle of the Seringueiros: Environmental Action in the Amazon. In *In Defense of Livelihood*. Ed. J. Friedmann and H. Rangan. West Hartford: Kumarian Press, pp. 106–26.

Melosi, M., ed. 1980. *Pollution and Reform in American Cities, 1870–1930*. Austin: University of Texas Press.

Melucci, A. 1988. Social Movement and the Democratization of Everyday Life. In *Civil Society and the State: New European Perspectives*. Ed. J. Keane. London: Verso, pp. 245–60.

Menchaca, M. 1993. Chicano Indianism: A Historical Account of Racial Repression in the United States. *American Ethnologist* 20:583–603.

Mercer, K. 1990. Black Hair/Style Politics. In *Out There: Marginalization and Contemporary Cultures*. Ed. R. Ferguson, M. Gever, T. Minh-ha, and C. West. New York: The New Museum of Contemporary Arts, pp. 247–64.

Merchant, C. 1989. *Ecological Revolutions: Nature, Gender, and Science in New England*. Chapel Hill: University of North Carolina Press.

———. 1992. *Radical Ecology*. New York: Routledge.

Milby, T. 1970. Statement of Thomas H. Milby, M.D., Chief, Bureau of Occupational Health and Environmental Epidemiology, California Department of Public Health. In *Occupational Safety and Health Act of 1969: Hearings before the Select Subcommittee on Labor of the Committee on Education and Labor* (San Francisco), 1385–411.

Miles, R. 1989. *Racism*. London: Routledge.

Miliband, R. 1988. Class Analysis. In *Social Theory Today*. Ed. A. Giddens and J. Turner. Stanford: Stanford University Press, pp. 325–46.

Miller, A., and E. Potter. 1986. *Land Use in Rio Arriba County: Problems and Opportunities*. Santa Fe: Potter and Kelly Law Firm.

Miller, J. 1987. Introduction to *Valuing Wildlife*. Ed. D. Deck and G. Goff. Boulder: Westview Press, pp. 5–11.

Mines, R., and P. Martin. 1986. *A Profile of California Farm Workers*. Berkeley: Giannini Information Series, no. 86–2, University of California.

Mitchell, R., A. Mertig, and R. Dunlap. 1992. Twenty Years of Environmental Mobilization: Trends among National Environmental Organizations. In *American Environmentalism: The U.S. Environmental Movement 1970–1990*. Ed. R. Dunlap and A. Mertig. Philadelphia: Taylor and Francis, pp. 11–26.

Mitchell, R. C. 1979. Silent Spring/Silent Majorities. *Public Opinion* 2:16–20.

Mizrahi, L. 1969. Letter to Lowell Chamberlain. September 24. Box 25, Folder 19. NCAD.

———. 1970. Statement of Dr. Lee Mizrahi. *Occupational Safety and Health Act of 1969: Hearings before the Select Subcommittee on Labor of the Committee on Education and Labor* (San Francisco), 1448–65.

Mocho, P. 1987. A Letter from Pete. *New Mexico Stockman* 53:6. CORONADO.

Moffatt, K. 1990. No Middle Ground in Grazing Debate. *Albuquerque Journal,* April 22, 7.

Moghadam, V. 1994. Women and Identity Politics in Theoretical Comparative Perspective. Introduction to *Identity Politics and Women.* Ed. V. Moghadam. Boulder: Westview, pp. 3–26.

Mohai, P. 1985. Public Concern and Elite Involvement in Environmental-Conservation Issues. *Social Science Quarterly* 66:820–38.

———. 1990. Black Environmentalism. *Social Science Quarterly* 71:744–65.

Mohai, P., and B. Bryant. 1992. Environmental Justice: Weighing Race and Class as Factors in the Distribution of Environmental Hazards. *University of Colorado Law Review* 63:921–32.

Montejano, D. 1987. *Anglos and Mexicans in the Making of Texas, 1836–1986.* Austin: University of Texas Press.

Montoya, B. 1990. New Mexico Department of Game and Fish. Interview with Author. Santa Fe, New Mexico, August 7.

Morales, M. 1990. Canjilon Resident. Interview with Author. Canjilon, New Mexico, August 16.

Moses, M. 1968a. Letter to Cesar Chavez. July 14. Box 2, Folder 3. MM.

———. 1968b. Letter to Charles Wurster. July 15. Box 2, Folder 3. MM.

———. 1968c. Letter to Ralph Nader. July 8. Box 2, Folder 3. MM.

———. 1991. Pesticide Education Center. Interview with Author. San Francisco, California, February 21.

———. 1993. Farmworkers and Pesticides. In *Confronting Environmental Racism: Voices from the Grassroots.* Ed. R. Bullard. Boston: South End Press, pp. 161–78.

Moses, M., and G. Padilla. 1966. Letter to Anastacio Medina. December 3. Letter Courtesy of A. Medina.

Mouffe, C., and E. Laclau. 1985. *Hegemony and Socialist Strategy: Towards a Radical Democratic Politics.* Trans. W. Moore and P. Cammack. London: Verso.

Muir, D. 1993. Race: The Mythic Root of Racism. *Sociological Inquiry* 63: 339–50.

Mullins, M. 1990. Policies of Patronage: A Study of Indian Arts and Rural

Development in the American Southwest. Paper presented at Woodrow Wilson Rural Policy Colloquium, October 19, Oakland California.

Munoz, C. 1989. *Youth, Identity, and Power*. New York: Verso.

Nabakov, P. 1970. *Tijerina and the Courthouse Raid*. 2d ed. Albuquerque: University of New Mexico Press.

Nagel, J. 1982. The Political Mobilization of Native Americans. *Social Science Quarterly* 19:37–45.

———. 1986. The Political Construction of Ethnicity. In *Competitive Ethnic Relations*. Ed. S. Olzak and J. Nagel. Orlando: Academic Press, pp. 93–112.

Nagel, J., and S. Olzak. 1982. Ethnic Mobilization in New and Old States: An Extension of the Competition Model. *Social Problems* 30:127–43.

Nagel, J., and C. M. Snipe. 1993. Ethnic Reorganization: American Indian Social, Economic, Political, and Cultural Strategies for Survival. *Ethnic and Racial Relations* 16:203–35.

Nagengast, C., and M. Kearney. 1990. Mixtec Ethnicity: Social Identity, Political Consciousness and Political Activism. *Latin American Research Review* 25:61–92.

Nash, J. 1992. Interpreting Social Movements: Bolivian Resistance to Economic Conditions Imposed by the International Monetary Fund. *American Ethnologist* 19:275–93.

Nash, M. 1989. *The Cauldron of Ethnicity in the Modern World*. Chicago: University of Chicago Press.

Nash, R. 1982. *Wilderness and the American Mind*. 3d ed. New Haven: Yale University Press.

Nature Conservancy. 1975. *Warranty Deed*. September 8. NMDGF.

Nelson-Cisneros, V. 1975. La Clase Trabajadora en Tejas, 1920–1940. *Aztlan* 6:239–65.

New Mexican. 1989. Promotional Tourism Must Involve State Planning. August 7, A8.

New Mexico Department of Game and Fish. 1912–1989. Annual Reports. NMDGF.

———. 1964. Airway Lease between State Game Commission, State of New Mexico, and State Park and Recreation Commission, State of New Mexico. Rio Chama File. USFWS.

———. 1977a. Program Narrative. Amendment no. 3: Livestock Grazing. Minutes of March 3 meeting. Sargent File. USFWS.

———. 1977b. Program Narrative. W.A. "Bill" Humphries Wildlife Area Addition. February 23. NMDGF.

———. 1978–81. Short Form Application for Grazing Permit. Applicant, Mrs. Virginia Binkley. Acquired from NMDGF under Freedom of Information Act, 1989. GDV.

———. 1980. The Edward Sargent Fish and Wildlife Area Management Plan. Sargent File. USFWS.

———. 1983. The Edward Sargent Fish and Wildlife Area Mangement Plan. June. NMDGF.

———. 1984. Bill Humphries Wildlife Area Management Plan. January 27. NMDGF.

———. 1985. Commission Action Narrative. Agenda no. 10: Grazing Plan. Presentation by Antonio Manzanares. Minutes, July 25, pp. 12–13. NMDGF.

———. 1989a. Commission Action Narrative. Agenda no. 7: Sheep Grazing on Wildlife Areas. Presentation by Dr. John Fowler. Minutes, December 15, pp. 13–16. NMDGF.

———. 1989b. Minutes, August 18, p. 4. NMDGF.

———. n.d., a. Little Chama Valley Ranch Acquisition. Sargent File. USFWS.

———. n.d., b. *Management Plan for Humphries Wildlife Area*. Humphries File. USFWS.

New Mexico Department of Labor. 1991. *New Mexico Labor Market Review* 20 (June 28).

New Mexico Department of Tourism. 1991. *Tourism and Travel News*. Travel and Marketing Division.

New Mexico Economic Development and Tourism Department. 1988. *Developing New Mexico*.

———. 1990a. *Developing New Mexico* 2(5).

———. 1990b. *Developing New Mexico* 2(6).

New Mexico People and Energy. 1980. BLM: Its Policies and Programs. Albuquerque: New Mexico People and Energy Power Structure Report. CORONADO.

New Mexico Stockman. 1988. 54(3). CORONADO.

———. 1989a. *Livestock Industry Objects to National Forest Planning Proposal* 55:32. CORONADO.

———. 1989b. 55(8). CORONADO.

New Mexico Wildlife. 1989a. 34(1). STATE.

———. 1989b. 34(4). STATE.

Nicholson, M. 1987. *The New Environmental Age*. Cambridge: Cambridge University Press.

North Central New Mexico Economic Development District. 1973–74. Planning Activities for the NAPO Area.

———. 1975. Overall Economic Development Program, Sections 1 and 2.

———. 1977. Regional Development Plan.

Nostrand, R. 1980. The Hispanic Homeland in 1900. *Annals of the Association of American Geographers* 70:382–96.

———. 1984. Hispano Cultural Distinctiveness: A Reply. *Annals of the Association of American Geographers* 74:164–67.

Okumura, D. 1991. California Department of Food and Agriculture. Letter to Author. June 19.

Olson, H. 1983. Letter to Michael Spear. November 7. Sargent File. USFWS.

———. 1988. Letter to Maria Varela. May 10. NMDGF.

Omi, M. 1992. Shifting the Blame: Racial Ideology and Politics in the Post-Civil Rights Era. *Critical Sociology* 18:77–98.

Omi, M., and H. Winant. 1987. *Racial Formation in the United States: From the 1960s to the 1980s.* New York: Routledge and Kegan Paul.

Ong, P., and E. Blumenberg. 1993. An Unnatural Trade-Off: Latinos and Environmental Justice. In *Latinos in a Changing U.S. Economy.* Ed. R. Morales and F. Padilla. Beverly Hills: Sage Publications, pp. 207–25.

Ortiz, I. 1991. Latino Organizational Leadership Strategies in the Era of Reaganomics. In *Latinos and Political Coalitions.* Ed. R. Villareal and N. Hernandez. New York: Greenwood Press, pp. 81–98.

Otten, M. 1989a. Safeway Refuses to Pull Grapes: Chavez Declares Boycott of 1200 Stores. *Bakersfield Californian,* September 21, B4. UFW 1980s Vertical File. BEALE.

———. 1989b. Two Hundred UFW Supporters Rally against Pesticides. *Bakersfield Californian,* December 19. UFW 1980s Vertical File. BEALE.

Paarlberg, R. 1994. The Politics of Agricultural Resource Use. *Environment* 36:6–20, 28–32.

Pacific Business. 1971. Rendering unto Cesar. March–April. UFW 1970s Vertical File. BEALE.

Packer. 1969. UFWOC Claims Chemical Pesticides. February 8, 22B. Box 25, Folder 15. NCAD.

Paddock, R. 1990. Conflicting Goals Cloud State's Pesticide Policy. *Los Angeles Times,* September 17, A1, A18–A19.

Paddock, R., and D. Jehl. 1989. Preschoolers Face 'Intolerable Risk' from Pesticides, Group Says. *Los Angeles Times,* Section A, February 1, 3, 23.

Padilla, F. 1985. *Latino Ethnic Consciousness.* Notre Dame: University of Notre Dame Press.

Paehlke, R. 1989. *Environmentalism and the Future of Progressive Politics.* New Haven: Yale University Press.

Painter, L. n.d. Letter to Secretary of Interior Lujan. USFWS.

Pandol, J. 1989. Chavez Offers No Incentive to Growers. *Bakersfield Californian,* November 15, B8. UFW 1980s Vertical File. BEALE.

Pardo, M. 1990. Identity and Resistance: Mexican American Women and Grassroots Activism in Two Los Angeles Communities. Ph.D. diss., University of California, Los Angeles.

Parsons, D. 1989. Memo to Phil Zwank. November 30. ZWANK.

———. 1990. United States Fish and Wildlife Service. Interview with Author. Albuquerque, New Mexico, July 30.

Pasternak, J. 1991. Pollution Is Choking Farm Belt. *Los Angeles Times,* April 22, A1, A3.

Pease, W., R. Morello-Frosch, D. Albright, A. Kyle, and J. Robinson. 1993. *An Environmental Health Policy Report.* Center for Occupational and Environmental Health, School of Public Health, University of California, Berkeley.

Peet, R. 1985. The Social Origins of Environmental Determinism. *Annals of the Association of American Geographers* 75:309–23.

Peet, R., and M. Watts. 1993. Introduction: Development Theory and Environment in an Age of Market Triumphalism. *Economic Geography* 69: 227–53.

Peluso, N. 1992. *Rich Forests, Poor People: Resource Control and Resistance in Java.* Berkeley: University of California.

Peña, D. 1991a. An American Wilderness in a Mexican Homeland. Paper presented at Western Social Science Association Annual Conference, April 24–28, at Reno, Nevada.

———. 1991b. San Luis Vega and Garrett Hardin: The Commons in Cross-Cultural Perspective. Paper presented at Western Social Science Association, April 24–28, at Reno, Nevada.

Penrose, J., and P. Jackson. 1994. Conclusion: Identity and the Politics of Difference. In *Constructions of 'Race,' Place and Nation.* Ed. P. Jackson and J. Penrose. Minneapolis: University of Minnesota Press, pp. 202–9.

Pepper, D. 1993. *Eco-Socialism: From Deep Ecology to Social Justice.* New York: Routledge.

Perfecto, I. 1992. Pesticide Exposure of Farm Workers and the International Connection. In *Race and the Incidence of Environmental Hazards.* Ed. B. Bryant and P. Mohai. Boulder: Westview Press, pp. 177–203.

Petulla, J. 1977. *American Environmental History.* San Francisco: Boyd and Fraser Publishing.

———. 1980. *American Environmentalism: Values, Tactics, Priorities.* College Station: Texas A&M University Press.

Pezzoli, K. 1993. Sustainable Livelihood in the Urban Milieu: A Case Study from Mexico City. In *In Defense of Livelihood*. Ed. J. Friedmann and H. Rangan. West Hartford: Kumarian Press, pp. 127–55.

Pierce, J., N. Lovrich, T. Tsurutani, and T. Abe. 1989. *Public Knowledge and Environmental Politics in Japan and the United States*. Boulder: Westview Press.

Pinderhughes, R. 1994. Dr. Loco and His Rockin' Jalapeno Band: Confronting Environmental Racism through Music. *Race, Poverty, and the Environment* 4:35–36.

Piven, F. F., and R. Cloward. 1978. *Poor People's Movements: Why They Succeed, How They Fail*. New York: Vintage Books.

Plotke, D. 1990. What's So New about New Social Movements? *Socialist Review* 20:81–102.

Polenz, A. 1988. Letter to Daniel Sutcliffe. June 24. NMDGF.

Ponce, V. v. J. Fielder. 1969a. *Complaint*. SAC.

——. 1969b. *Complaint for Injunctive and Declaratory Relief*. April 14. FEDREC.

Price, G. 1990. The Truth about Environmentalists. *New Mexico Stockman* 56:34. CORONADO.

Proffitt, S. 1993. Arturo Rodriguez. *Los Angeles Times*, September 26, M3.

Puleston Fleming, J. 1985. Ganados del Valle: A Venture in Self-Sufficiency. *New Mexico Magazine*, September, 39–42. GDV.

Pulido, L. 1994a. People of Color, Identity Politics, and the Environmental Justice Movement. Unpublished manuscript. Geography Department, University of Southern California.

——. 1994b. Restructuring and the Contraction and Expansion of Environmental Rights in the United States. *Environment and Planning* A26, pp. 915–36.

——. 1996. Romancing the Land: Oppositional Resource Struggles. *Capitalism, Nature and Socialism* 7:4.

Quintana, C. 1987. Wilson Urges INS to Ease Up Enforcement to Aid Growers. *Los Angeles Times*, June 19, 3, 34.

Quintana, P. 1989. Letter to Bill Montoya. August 15. GDV.

——. 1990. Ganados del Valle. Interview with Author. Los Ojos, New Mexico, August 15.

——. n.d. Agricultural Economic and Market Potential for the Chama Valley. GDV.

Ramirez, A. 1968. News Release: Spanish Surname Citizens for Wallace. February 22. Box 47, Folder 7. OFFP.

Ramirez, A., J. Morales, and V. Mitchell. n.d. 'The M.A.F.I.A.' The Mexican-American Fraud in America. Box 47, Folder 5. OFFP.

Rangan, H. 1993. Romancing the Environment: Popular Environmental Action in the Himalayas. In *In Defense of Livelihood*. Ed. J. Friedmann and H. Rangan. West Hartford: Kumarian Press, pp. 155–81.

Range Improvement Task Force and Cooperative Fish and Wildlife Research Unit. 1989. *Wildlife Habitat Enhancement through Controlled Livestock Grazing*. College of Agriculture and Home Economics, New Mexico State University. October 19. FOWLER.

Raynor, P. 1989. Memo to Max Best. October 5. ZWANK.

Razee, D. 1966. Strike that Isn't a Strike Has Delano Growers Puzzled. *California Farmer*, March 19, 7, 20. BEALE.

Redclift, M. 1987. *Sustainable Development: Explaining the Contradictions*. London: Methuen.

Rees, W. 1990. The Ecology of Sustainable Development. *Ecologist* 20:12–16.

Reich, P. 1992. Greening the Ghetto: A Theory of Environmental Race Discrimination. *University of Kansas Law Review* 41:271–314.

Reiger, J. 1986. *American Sportsmen and the Origins of Conservation*. Rev. ed. Norman: University of Oklahoma.

Reinecker, T. 1988. Letter to Daniel Sutcliffe. June 8. NMDGF.

Resta, M., and L. Zink. 1978. The Agricultural Sector. In *The New Mexico Economy: Change in the 1970s*. Governor's Council of Economic Advisors. Albuquerque: State of New Mexico. DATA.

Richardson, A. 1990. State of New Mexico Economic Development and Tourism Department. Interview with Author. Santa Fe, New Mexico, July 25.

Rio Arriba County Policies Planning Task Force. 1987. *Rio Arriba County Policies Plan and Implementation Strategies*. Santa Fe: Potter and Kelly Law Firm.

Rio Grande Sun. 1989. Sheep Growers Face Summer of Frustration. August 24, A3. GDV.

———. 1991a. 1990 Land Sales in County Topped $11 Million Mark. February 21, 36.

———. 1991b. State Issues Boil Over. April 11, B1.

———. 1991c. Tourism Here Growing Steadily. January 24, B1.

Rivera, J. 1990. University of New Mexico. Interview with Author. Albuquerque, New Mexico, July 27.

Roderick, K. 1989. Cancer Cluster Claimed in Farm Town of Earlimart. *Los Angeles Times,* September 15, 30.

Rodriguez, C. 1991. The Effects of Race on Puerto Rican Wages. In *Hispanics in the Labor Force*. Ed. E. Melendez, C. Rodriguez, and J. Barry Figueroa. New York: Plenum Press, pp. 77–98.

———. 1992. Race, Culture, and Latino 'Otherness' in the 1980 Census. *Social Sciences Quarterly* 73:930–37.

Rodriguez, C., and H. Cordero-Guzman. 1992. Placing Race in Context. *Ethnic and Racial Studies* 15:523–42.

Rodriguez, O. 1977. *The Politics of Chicano Liberation*. New York: Pathfinder Press.

Rodriguez, S. 1986. *The Hispano Homeland Debate*. Palo Alto: Stanford Center for Chicano Research. Working Paper Series no. 7.

———. 1989. Art, Tourism, and Race Relations in Taos: Toward a Sociology of the Art Colony. *Journal of Anthropological Research* 45:77–99.

Rogers, M. L. 1990. *Acorn Days: The Environmental Defense Fund and How It Grew*. New York: Environmental Defense Fund.

Roosens, E. 1989. *Creating Ethnicity: The Process of Ethnogenesis*. Newbury Park, Calif.: Sage.

Rose, M. 1988. *Women in the United Farm Workers: A Study of Chicana and Mexicana Participation in a Labor Union, 1950–1980*. Ph.D diss., University of California, Los Angeles.

Roseberry, W. 1989. *Anthropologies and Histories: Essays in Culture, History, and Political Economy*. New Brunswick: Rutgers University Press.

Rosenbaum, R. 1986. *Mexicano Resistance in the Southwest*. Austin: University of Texas Press.

Ross, A., ed. 1988. *Universal Abandon? The Politics of Postmodernism*. Minneapolis: University of Minnesota Press.

Ruffins, P. 1989. Blacks' Health Suffer Yet Remain Inactive on Environment. *Los Angeles Times*, August 27, 3, 6.

Ruiz, V. 1987. *Cannery Women, Cannery Lives*. Albuquerque: University of New Mexico.

Runsten, D. 1991. California Institute of Rural Studies. Interview with Author. Berkeley, California, February 20.

Russell, D. 1990. The Rise of the Grass-Roots Toxics Movement. *Amicus Journal* 12:18–21.

Rutherford, J. 1990. A Place Called Home: Identity and the Cultural Politics of Difference. In *Identity, Community, Culture and Difference*. Ed. J. Rutherford. London: Lawrence and Wishart, pp. 9–27.

Sacks, K. 1989. Toward a Unified Theory of Class, Race, and Gender. *American Ethnologist* 16:534–50.

Said, E. 1979. *Orientalism*. New York: Vintage Books.

Salazar, G. 1989. Testimony before U.S. House Interior Oversight Subcommittee. Taos, New Mexico, July 29. GDV.

———. 1991. Ganados del Valle. Interview with Author. Chama, New Mexico, August 12.

Salazar, J. 1991. Tierra Amarilla Resident. Interview with Author. Tierra Amarilla, New Mexico, August 13.

Sale, K. 1993. *The Green Revolution*. New York: Hill and Wang.

Sanchez, C. 1982. Letter to Harold Olson. August 26. Sargent File. USFWS.

Sandoval, L. 1990. Soil Conservation Service. Interview with Author. Chama, New Mexico, August 15.

Saragoza, A. 1990. Recent Chicano Historiography: An Interpretive Essay. *Aztlan* 19:1–77.

Sayer, A. 1992. Radical Geography and Marxist Political Economy: Towards a Re-Evaluation. *Progress in Human Geography* 16:343–60.

Sayer, A., and R. Walker. 1992. *The New Social Economy: Reworking the Division of Labor*. Cambridge: Blackwell.

Scheffer, V. 1991. *The Shaping of Environmentalism in America*. Seattle: University of Washington Press.

Schein, M. 1985. Sheep Grazing Proposal Nixed. *Rio Grande Sun*, September 12. GDV.

———. 1989a. Grazing Issue on Agenda for Commission Meeting. *Rio Grande Sun*, December 14, B1–2.

———. 1989b. Grazing Study Would Carry $2 Million Price Tag. *Rio Grande Sun*, October 19, A1–2.

———. 1989c. Ranchers Get Study, Coyotes Get Sheep. *Rio Grande Sun*, September 7, A1–2.

———. 1989d. Sheep Ranchers Consider Private Grazing Options. *Rio Grande Sun*, August 24, A1–2.

———. 1989e. Some Say Land Grants Are Real Issue. *Rio Grande Sun*, August 24, A3.

———. 1991. Lodgers Say Water Shortage Hurt Weekend Business. *Rio Grande Sun*, July 11, B1–2. GDV.

Scherle, Mr. 1970. Member of the Select Subcommittee on Labor. *Occupational Safety and Health Act of 1969: Hearings before the Select Subcommittee on Labor of the Committee on Education and Labor. House of Representatives*. San Francisco: November 21–22.

Schickedanz, J. 1989. Memo to Dean John Owens. September 15. ZWANK.

Schryer, F. 1990. *Ethnicity and Class Conflict in Rural Mexico*. Princeton: Princeton University Press.

Scott, A. 1990. *Ideology and the New Social Movements*. London: Unwin Hyman.

Scott, James. 1985. *Weapons of the Weak*. New Haven: Yale University Press.

———. 1990. *Domination and the Arts of Resistance: Hidden Transcripts*. New Haven: Yale University Press.

Scott, Janny. 1988. Child Cancer Cluster Poses Puzzle. *Los Angeles Times*, September 21, 1, 3.

Scott, W. 1967. Spanish Land Grant Problems Were Here before the Anglos. *New Mexico Business* 20:1–9. CORONADO.

Seager, J. 1993. *Earth Follies: Coming to Feminist Terms with the Global Environmental Crisis*. New York: Routledge.

Sector, B. 1990. Harvesting Limits on Chemicals. *Los Angeles Times*, May 23, A1, A22.

Segur, H. 1991. Phone Conversation with Author. March 2.

Selcraig, B. 1993. Culture Clash, Santa Fe Style. *Los Angeles Times Magazine*, September 5, 20–24.

Selzer, M. n.d. Letter to Cesar Chavez. Box 47, Folder 5. OFFP.

Semilla. 1989–91. Un periodico de Proyecto Laboral Agricola. Davis, California.

Serda, H. 1969. The Picket Needs Help. *Chicano Student Movement* 1:11.

Serrano, A. 1990. Ganados del Valle. Interview with Author. Los Ojos, New Mexico, August 17.

Serrano, R., Sr. 1990a. Los Ojos Resident. Interview with Author. Los Ojos, New Mexico, August 10.

———. 1990b. Los Ojos Resident. Interview with Author. Nutrias, New Mexico, August 18.

Shabecoff, P. 1993. *A Fierce Green Fire: The American Environmental Movement*. New York: Hill and Wang.

Sherwood, B. 1989. Letter to the Editor. *High Country News*, December 18, 15.

Shiva, V. 1989. *Staying Alive: Women, Ecology, and Development*. London: Zed Books.

Sierra Club, Delta Chapter. 1970. Aerial Spraying of MIREX: A Giant Step Backward. BANCROFT.

Sierra Club, Kern-Kaweah Chapter. 1952–79. *Road Runner*. BANCROFT.

———. 1957. Membership Survey. *Road Runner* 6(3). BANCROFT.

———. 1961. *Road Runner* 8(3). BANCROFT.

———. 1969. Water Pollution. *Road Runner* 16(5). BANCROFT.

———. 1970. *Road Runner* 17(8): 6. BANCROFT.

Simmons, M. 1984. Rejoinders. *Annals of the Association of American Geographers* 74:170–71.

Siri, W. 1979. *Reflections on the Sierra Club, the Environment, and Moun-
taineering, 1950s–1970s.* Interview Conducted by Ann Lage. Regional
Oral History Office, The Bancroft Library. Sierra Club History Series.

Slaight, W. R. 1974. Alice Hamilton: First Lady of Industrial Medicine. Ph.D.
diss., Case Western Reserve University.

Slater, D., ed. 1985. *New Social Movements and the State in Latin America.*
Amsterdam: CEDLA (Centre for Latin American Research and Documentation).

Smith, J. 1988. Letter to Sutcliffe. June 1. NMDGF.

Smith, J. N., ed. 1974a. The Coming of Age of Environmentalism in American
Society. In *Environmental Quality and Social Justice in Urban America.*
Ed. J. N. Smith. Washington, D.C.: The Conservation Foundation.

———. 1974b. *Environmental Quality and Social Justice in Urban America.*
Washington, D.C.: The Conservation Foundation.

Smith, S. 1994. Immigration and Nation-Building in Canada and the United
Kingdom. In *Constructions of Race, Place and Nation.* Ed. P. Jackson
and J. Penrose. Minneapolis: University of Minnesota, pp. 50–77.

Soja, E., and B. Hooper. 1993. The Spaces that Difference Make. In *Place and
the Politics of Identity.* Ed. M. Keith and S. Pile. New York: Routledge,
pp. 183–205.

Solis, R., and L. Torres v. J. Fielder. 1970a. *Alternative Writ of Mandate.* June
12. FRESNO.

———. 1970b. *Petition For Writ of Mandate.* June 12. FRESNO.

Someshwar, S. 1993. People versus the State? Social Forestry in Kolar, India. In
In Defense of Livelihood. Ed. J. Friedmann and H. Rangan. West Hartford: Kumarian Press, pp. 182–208.

South Central Farmers Committee. 1968. The Delano Grape Story . . . from the
Growers' View. UFW 1960s Vertical File. BEALE.

Spear, M. 1985. Letter to the Honorable Manuel Lujan. January 28. USFWS.

Spivak, G. 1988. Can the Subaltern Speak? In *Marxism and the Interpretation
of Culture.* Ed. C. Nelson and L. Grossberg. Urbana: University of Il-
linois, pp.271–313.

State of New Mexico Taxation and Revenue Department. 1991. Taxation and
Revenue System Analysis of Gross Receipts Tax by Standard Industrial
Classification, Rio Arriba County: 1981, 1983, 1984, 1985, 1986,
1987, 1988, 1989, 1990. Report no. 080. DATA.

Stavins, R. 1989. Harnessing Market Forces to Protect the Environment. *Environment* 31:5–7, 28–35.

Stegman, J. 1975. Letter to Ladd S. Gordon. February 21. Sargent File. USFWS.

Stout, J. 1970. Cattlemen, Conservationists, and the Taylor Grazing Act. *New Mexico Historical Review* 45:311–32.

Sunseri, A. 1973. Anglo Attitudes toward Hispanos, 1846–1961. *Journal of Mexican American History* 3:76–88.

Sunwest Financial Services, Inc. 1990. *New Mexico Progress Economic Review of 1990*. Albuquerque. DATA.

Suro, R. 1992. Twenty-Year-Old Gift Leads to Dispute with Sierra Club. *New York Times,* May 13, A16.

Swadesh, F. L. 1965. Property and Kinship in Northern New Mexico. *Rocky Mountain Social Science Journal* 2:209–14.

———. 1974. *Los Primeros Pobladores: Hispanic Americans of the Ute Frontier.* Notre Dame: University of Notre Dame Press.

Swift, J. 1970. Letter in Occupational Safety and Health Act of 1969. *Hearings before the Select Subcommittee on Labor of the Committee on Education and Labor.* House of Representatives. San Francisco: November 21–22, 1544–47.

Szasz, A. 1994. *Ecopopulism: Toxic Waste and the Movement for Environmental Justice.* Minneapolis: University of Minnesota.

Tapia, J., and G. Silvers. 1990. *Impacts of Sheep Grazing on Three Wildlife Areas in Rio Arriba County, New Mexico.* Student Project, City and Regional Planning, University of New Mexico. GDV.

Tatarian, R. 1989. UFW's Logic Wanting. *Bakersfield Californian,* November 3, B5. UFW 1980s Vertical File. BEALE.

Taylor, B., H. Hadsell, L. Lorentzen, and R. Scarce. 1993. Grass-Roots Resistance: The Emergence of Popular Environmental Movements in Less Affluent Countries. In *Environmental Politics in the International Arena.* Ed. S. Kamieniecki. Albany: State University of New York, pp. 69–90.

Taylor, D. 1992. Can the Environmental Movement Attract and Maintain the Support of Minorities and the Poor? In *Race and the Incidence of Environmental Hazards.* Ed. B. Bryant and P. Mohai. Boulder: Westview Press, pp. 28–54.

Taylor, L. 1988. The Importance of Cross-Cultural Communication between Environmentalists and Land-Based People. *Workbook* 13:90–100.

Taylor, R. 1969a. Workers' Health Chief Raps Pesticide Secrets. Newsclipping with Comments. *Fresno Bee,* November 22, 5B. Box 25, Folder 31. NCAD.

———. 1969b. Public Relations: Key Weapon in Grape Battle. *Fresno Bee,* November 9, C1–2. Box 19, Folder 17. NCAD.

———. 1975. *Chavez and the Farm Workers*. Boston: Beacon Press.

———. 1987. Cancer Cluster Probe Focuses on Dozen Pesticides. *Los Angeles Times*, December 31, 3, 20.

———. 1991. *Los Angeles Times*. Phone Conversation with Author. July 3.

Telles, E., and E. Murguia. 1990. Phenotypic Discrimination and Income Differences among Mexican Americans. *Social Science Quarterly* 71:682–96.

Temple-Trujillo, R. 1974. Conceptions of the Chicano Family. *Smith College Studies in Social Work* 45:1–20.

Thrupp, L. 1992. Politics of the Sustainable Development Crusade: From Elite Protection to Social Justice in Third World Resource Issues. *Environment, Technology and Society* 58:1–7.

Tienda, M., and V. Ortiz. 1986. Hispanicity and the 1980 Census. *Social Science Quarterly* 67:3–20.

Tober, J. 1989. *Wildlife and the Public Interest: Nonprofit Organizations and Federal Wildlife Policy*. New York: Praeger.

Torell, A., and J. Doll. 1990. *The Market Value of New Mexico Ranches, 1980–1988*. Las Cruces: Agricultural Experiment Station Bulletin no. 718, New Mexico State University.

Torrell, A., S. Ghosh, and J. Fowler. 1988. *Economic Considerations for Setting Grazing Fees on New Mexico State Trust Lands*. Agricultural Experiment Station, College of Agriculture and Home Economics, Special Report no. 81. Las Cruces: New Mexico State University.

Torres, P. 1990. Rio Arriba County Extension. Interview with Author. Espanola, New Mexico, August 13.

Trevor-Roper, Hugh. 1983. The Invention of Tradition: The Highland Tradition of Scotland. In *The Invention of Tradition*. Ed. E. Hobsbawm and T. Ranger. Cambridge: Cambridge University Press, pp. 15–41.

Tsukamoto, G. 1988. Letter to Daniel Sutcliffe. June 7. NMDGF.

United Church of Christ Commission for Racial Justice. 1987. *Toxic Wastes and Race in the United States*. New York: United Church of Christ.

United Farm Workers. 1995. Collective Bargaining Agreement Between Bear Creek and United Farm Workers of America, AFL-CIO, March 17.

United Farm Workers Organizing Committee. 1969a. Flyer. Its a Matter of Good Health for You to Support the Grape Boycott. Box 9, Folder 29. UFWOC.

———. 1969b. Memo. Pesticides and You. September 30. Box 25, Folder 20. NCAD.

———. 1969c. Negotiation Notes. July 3. Box 46, Folder 6. OFFP.

———. 1969d. Press Release. January 21. Box 29, Folder 19. NCAD.

———. 1969e. Press Release. Chavez Challenges Fielder on DDT. December 17. Box 49, Folder 12. OFFP.

———. 1969f. *Proposed Agreement between* UFWOC, *Thomas Griffin, Atwood Aviation Company, C. Seldon Morley, and Table Grape Growers in Kern County.* KERNA.

———. n.d., a. Flyer. California Grape Workers Are Killed and Maimed Every Year by the Pesticides You Are Eating. Box 1, Folder 5. MM.

———. n.d., b. Press Briefing. Box 25, Folder 20. NCAD.

———. n.d., c. Questions and Answers on UFWOC and Pesticides. Box 9, Folder Box 1, Folder 5. MM.

———. n.d., d. Why Boycott Grapes? Deadly Dangerous Pesticides Used on GRAPES! Box 25, Folder 22. NCAD.

United States Census Bureau. 1990a. Income in 1989 of Households, Families, and Persons by Race and Hispanic Origin, New Mexico. Summary of Social, Economic and Housing Characteristics.

———. 1990b. Income and Poverty Status in 1989, New Mexico. Summary of Social, Economic and Housing Characteristics.

———. 1990c. Hispanic Origin, Rio Arriba County, New Mexico. Summary of Census of Population and Housing, Tape File 3C.

———. 1990d. Hispanic Origin, United States. Summary of 1990 Census of Population and Housing. Tape File 3C.

United States Census of Agriculture. 1987. Selected Characteristics of Farms Operated by Females, Persons of Spanish Origin, and Specified Racial Groups: 1987 and 1982. State Data, California Census, p. 21.

United States Congress. 1970. *Migrant and Seasonal Farmworker Powerlessness: Hearings before the Subcommittee on Migratory Labor of the Committee on Labor and Public Welfare United States Senate.* 91st Cong., 1st and 2d sess. on Pesticides and the Farmworker. August 1, 1969, part 6–A; September 29, 1969, part 6–B; September 30, 1969, part 6–C. Washington, D.C.: U.S. Government Printing Office.

United States Fish and Wildlife Service, Region 2. 1989. Letter to Karl Hess. September 1. USFWS.

United States Forest Service. 1990. *A Strategic Plan for the 90s: Working Together for Rural America.* Washington, D.C.

United States General Accounting Office. 1983. *Siting of Hazardous Waste Landfills and their Correlation with Racial and Economic Status of Surrounding Communities.* Washington, D.C.: United States General Accounting Office.

University of California. 1982. *Agricultural Resources of California Counties.* Division of Agricultural Sciences. Davis: University of California.

Uribe v. Howie. 1971. 19 C.A. 3d 194; 96 *Cal. Rptr.* 493.

User Surveys of Land Development Regulations and Review Process. n.d. MILLER.

Valdez Martinez, V. 1990. Tierra Amarilla Resident. Interview with Author. Tierra Amarilla, New Mexico, August 16.

Valle, G. 1986. United Health Centers of the San Joaquin Valley. Interview with Author. Earlimart, California, June.

van den Berghe, Pierre. 1967. *Race and Racism: A Comparative Perspective.* New York: John Wiley and Sons.

Van den Berghe, Pierre. 1994. *The Quest for the Other: Ethnic Tourism in San Cristóbal, Mexico.* Seattle: University of Washington.

Van den Bosch, R. 1978. *The Pesticide Conspiracy.* Berkeley: University of California Press.

Vanneman, R., and L. W. Cannon. 1987. *The American Perception of Class.* Philadelphia: Temple University Press.

Varela, Maria. 1987. Letter to Honorable Garrey Carruthers. April 15. GDV.

———. 1988. Letter to Senator Pete Dominici. February 12. GDV.

———. 1989. Grazing Is Legitimate Method for Improving Wildlife Habitat. *Albuquerque Journal,* December 28, A9. GDV.

———. 1990a. Developing Selective Tourism Strategies for the Chama Valley. *New Mexico Progress.* Albuquerque: Sunwest Financial Services, Inc., 1–5. GDV.

———. 1990b. Ganados de Valle. Interview with Author. Tierra Amarilla, New Mexico, August 3.

———. 1991a. Ganados del Valle. Interview with Author. Los Angeles, California, June 3.

———. 1991b. Interim Report to the Needmore Fund. May 16. GDV.

———. 1994. Economic 'Growth' vs. 'Development' of Rural Communities — It Means the Difference between Local and Outside Control. *Workbook* 19:58–59.

Vigil, G. 1990. United States Forest Service. Interview with Author. Santa Fe, New Mexico, August 7.

Vigil, M. 1990. The Ethnic Organization as an Instrument of Political and Social Change: MALDEF, A Case Study. *Journal of Ethnic Studies* 18: 15–31.

Villarejo, D. 1991a. California Institute of Rural Studies. Interview with Author. Sacramento, California, February 2.

———. 1991b. California Institute of Rural Studies. Phone Conversation with Author. July 22.

———. 1994. Agricultural Pesticide Use in California Climbs Sharply, Shows No Sign of Abating. *Rural California Report* 6:4–5.

Vogeler, I. 1981. *The Myth of the Family Farm: Agribusiness Dominance of U.S. Agriculture.* Boulder: Westview Press.

Wagon Mound Redevelopment Agency. 1964. An Overall Economic Development Program. OEDP Provisions Plan. Redevelopment Area Designated (RAD). CORONADO.

Wald, A. 1989. Land and Freedom or Death. *Against the Current* 4:3–6.

Waldman, B. 1990. Santa Fe Activist. Interview with Author. Santa Fe, New Mexico, July 24.

———. 1991. Letter to Author. October 31.

Walker, R. 1985. Class, Division of Labor and Employment in Space. In *Social Relations and Spatial Structures.* Ed. D. Gregory and J. Urry. New York: St. Martin's Press, pp. 164–89.

Wall, S. 1969. Letter to Jerome Cohen. January 8. KERNA.

Warren, K. 1990. The Power and the Promise of Ecological Feminism. *Environmental Ethics* 12:125–46.

Watts, M. 1983. *Silent Violence.* Berkeley: University of California Press.

———. 1991. Mapping Meaning, Denoting Differences, Imagining Identity: Dialectical Images and Postmodern Geographies. *Geografiska Annaler* 73B:7–16.

———. 1993. Development I: Power, Knowledge, Discursive Practice. *Progress in Human Geography* 17:257–72.

Weber, K. 1991. Necessary but Insufficient: Land, Water, and Economic Development in Hispanic Southern Colorado. *Journal of Ethnic Studies* 19: 127–42.

Webster, Y. 1992. *The Racialization of America.* New York: St. Martin's Press.

Weigle, M., ed. 1975. *Hispanic Villages of Northern New Mexico: A Reprint of Volume II of the 1935 Tewa Basin Study with Supplementary Materials.* Santa Fe: Lightening Tree.

Weingarten, D. 1990. Albuquerque Activist. Interview with Author. Albuquerque, New Mexico, July 27.

Weisman, A. 1993. Paradise Ranch. *Los Angeles Times Magazine,* March 21, 24–28, 46–48.

Welch, S., and L. Sigelman. 1993. The Politics of Hispanic Americans: Insights from a National Survey, 1980–1988. *Social Science Quarterly* 74:76–94.

Welsome, E. 1990. Wildlife Grazing Angers Ranchers. *Albuquerque Tribune,* February 27, 3.

Wernette, D., and L. Nieves. 1992. Breathing Polluted Air. *EPA Journal* 18:16–17.

West, C. 1993. *Race Matters.* Boston: Beacon Press.

West, I. 1964. Occupational Disease of Farm Workers. *Archives of Environmental Health* 9:92–98.

———. 1969. *Affidavit of Irma West, M.D.* January 24. KERNA.

Westphall, V. 1983. *Mercedes Reales: Hispanic Land Grants of the Upper Rio Grande Region.* Albuquerque: University of New Mexico Press.

Wilkes, D. n.d. Letter to Manuel Lujan. USFWS.

Wilkinson, C. 1992. *Crossing the Next Meridian.* Washington, D.C.: Island Press.

Wilmsen, C. 1994. The Vallecitos Federal Sustained Yield Unit: A Case Study of Forest Management and Rural Poverty in Northern New Mexico. Paper presented at the Annual Meetings of the Association of American Geographers, April, San Francisco, California.

Wilson, C., and D. Kammer. 1989. *Community and Continuity: The History, Architecture and Cultural Landscape of Tierra Amarilla.* Santa Fe: New Mexico Historic Preservation Division.

Wilson, J. W. 1980. *The Declining Significance of Race.* 2d ed. Chicago: The University of Chicago Press.

Winant, H. 1994. *Racial Conditions: Politics, Theory and Comparisons.* Minneapolis: University of Minnesota.

Wisner, B. 1995. Luta, Livelihood, and Lifeworld in Contemporary Africa. In *Ecological Resistance Movements: The Global Emergence of Radical and Popular Environmentalism.* Ed. B. Taylor. Albany: State University New York.

Woods, C. 1993. Development Arrested: The Delta Blues, the Delta Council, and the Lower Mississippi Delta Development Commission. Ph. D. Diss., University of California, Los Angeles.

Works, M. 1992. A Place for Things: Material Culture and Socio-Spatial Processes in Northern New Mexico. Paper presented at the Annual Meetings of the Association of American Geographers, April, San Diego, California.

World Commission on Environment and Development. 1987. *Our Common Future.* Oxford: Oxford University Press.

Worster, D. 1985. *Rivers of Empire.* New York: Pantheon Books.

Wright, A. 1992. *The Death of Ramon Gonzalez.* Austin: University of Texas.

Wrightson, J. n.d., a. OEO Reagan Proposal 'Breach of Trust to Poor'. Box 18, Folder 10. NCAD.

———. n.d., b. Reagan Takes Aim at Poverty War Project. Box 18, Folder 10. NCAD.

Wurster, C. 1991. State University of New York, Stony Brook. Letter to Author. April 4.

Yapa, L. 1993a. Theorizing Social Movements of the Poor. Unpublished manuscript. Geography Department, Pennsylvania State University.

———. 1993b. What Are Improved Seeds? An Epistemology of the Green Revolution. *Economic Geography* 69:254–73.

Young, I. 1990. *Justice and the Politics of Difference.* Princeton: Princeton University Press.

Zabin, C., M. Kearney, A. Garcia, D. Runsten, and C. Nagengast. 1993. *Mixtec Migrants in California Agriculture.* Davis, Calif.: California Institute for Rural Studies.

Zamora, E. 1975. Chicano Socialist Labor Activity in Texas, 1900–1920. *Aztlan* 6:221–38.

Zimmerer, K. 1993. Soil Erosion and Social (Dis)courses in Cochabamba, Bolivia: Perceiving the Nature of Environmental Degradation. *Economic Geography* 69:312–27.

Zimmerman, M. 1987. Feminism, Deep Ecology, and Environmental Ethics. *Environmental Ethics* 9:21–44.

Index

Abascal, Ralph, 86, 99
Abiquiu Corporation, 144
AFL-CIO, 71
African Americans, 19, 45, 215n. 1
agribusiness, 59, 67, 95, 122
    challenges to, 100, 101, 104
    legislation and, 65–66
    and pesticides, 73–74, 81–83, 89
Agricultural Workers Organizing
    Committee (AWOC), 70
agriculture
    ecology and, 163–64, 190
    in northern New Mexico, 133,
        137, 223n. 12
    racialized structure of, 62–63
aldrin, 120
Alianza, La, 50, 133, 144
American Federation of Labor, 65
American Friends Service Commit-
    tee, 133
Anglo Americans, 49, 65, 67, 68
    in northern New Mexico, 127,
        130, 132, 144
    racialization of, 134–35

antipoverty movement, 132–33
application records, 91, 93–97
Associated Farmers, 67
Audubon (magazine), 87
Audubon Society, 23, 86, 87, 150,
    181, 224n. 21
Averbuck, David, 100–101, 102,
    218n. 20
Aztlan, 50, 216n. 9

Bakersfield, 62
Big Three, 60, 81
Binkley, Virginia, 168, 173
booklets on pesticide use, 76–77
Boone and Crockett Club, 154
boycotts, 55, 71, 90, 95, 105–9, 112,
    114, 200
Bracero program, 68, 69
Brower, David, 22
Brown, Rachel, 164
Brown Berets, 200
Bullard, Robert, 19
Bureau of Business and Economic
    Research (N.M.), 141

Bureau of Land Management (BLM), 148, 150
Bureau of Occupational Disease, 95–96

CAL-EPA, 121, 217n. 14
California, xiv, 36, 50, 59, 61(fig.), 68
    pesticide regulation in, 81–83
    pesticides in, 75–81
    Spanish language issues in, 44–45
California Agricultural Code, 104
California Agricultural Relations Board, 122
California Aqueduct, 68
California Department of Food and Agriculture (CDFA), 75, 76, 102, 104, 113, 219n. 25
California Department of Public Health (DPH), 75–76, 77
California Farm Bureau, 66
California Farm Bureau Federation, 111
California Rural Legal Assistance (CRLA), 85–86, 99, 100, 218n. 18, 219n. 27
cancer clusters, 122
capital, 35–36, 37, 65
carcinogens, 99–100
Carruthers, Garrey, 183
Carson, Rachel, 22, 99, 103
Castle and Cook, 66
Catholicism, 54, 201–2
Causa, La, 200
CDFA. See California Department of Food and Agriculture
Central Americans, 51, 122
Central Valley, 60, 63
Central Valley Project, 68

Chama, 142, 223n. 16
Chama Land and Cattle Company, 158, 189
Chama Valley, 126(fig.), 130, 131(fig.), 134, 177
Chama Valley Chamber of Commerce, 141
Chase, Alston, 186
Chavez, Cesar, 122
    efforts of, 59, 69, 113, 202
    and growers, 109, 111–12, 217n. 8
    union organizing by, 70, 91
Chevron Oil Company, 66
Chicano movement, 49–50, 51, 200–201
Chicanos, Chicanas, 32, 34, 59, 198, 213n. 1
    antipoverty movement, 132–33
    class and, 50–51, 72, 216n. 4
    identity, xviii–xix, 49, 51–52, 200
Chicano Student News, 200
Chinese, 62
Chipko, 27
Churro Breeding program, 165
civil rights, 18, 19, 23, 28, 51, 59, 101, 108
class, 38–39, 45–46, 50–51
class structure, 32, 60
class struggle, 39–40, 58–59, 71, 203
class theory, 37–38
Clean Water Act, 23
Clinica, La, 144
Coachella Valley, 108, 116
Cohen, Jerry, 90, 91, 93–94, 113
colonialism, 36, 130, 132
Colorado River Storage Act, 180
Commoner, Barry, 103, 105

communities, 39, 144–45, 146, 193–
94. *See also* rural communities
Community Service Organization
(CSO), 70
conservation, 22, 149, 214n. 7
contracts, union, 84, 90, 113, 114–
20
Cooperativa, La, 144
corporations, 24, 66. *See also* agribusiness; growers
cotton production, 81
Cotton Strike of 1933, 65
CRLA. *See* California Rural Legal
Assistance
Crusade for Justice, 50
CSO, 70
cultural domination, 20
cultural production, 16
Cultural Survival, 205
culture, 32, 193, 198, 209
and development, 145, 151
differential, 52–53
and grazing rights, 174–75
material, 53–54
Mexicano, 201–2
as praxis, 54–55, 198–99
symbolism in, 199–200
and tourism, 205–6
use of, 203–5
cyclamates, 99–100

DDD, 120
DDT, 72, 88, 103, 108
banning, 99, 100–102, 103
litigation and, 86–87
workers and, 113, 120
debt-for-nature swaps, 25–26
Defenders of Wildlife, 23
Delano, 70

Department of Health, Education,
and Welfare (HEW), 99
Desert Grape League, 66
development. *See* economic development
dieldrin, 120
Dingell-Johnson Act, 155, 180,
224nn. 23, 25
disinvestment, 35, 36
division of labor, 36–37, 40

Earth First!, 150
economic development, xvi, 14, 27,
40, 54, 68, 223n. 15
community, 125, 127, 144–45
and ethnic identity, 16, 128
by Ganados del Valle, 164–67,
187–90
and habitat loss, 143–44
and investment, 35–36
and sheep industry, 137–38
Economic Development and Tourism
Department (N.M.), 141
economic growth, 14–15
economics, 27, 29, 35, 38, 185
and racism, 32, 194–95
rural, 161, 162
economy, 15–16, 38–39, 129, 133–
35
Ecuador, 16
EDF. *See* Environmental Defense
Fund
Elenes, Victoria, 74
elitism, 26, 170–71, 224n. 21
elk, 28, 127, 157–58, 159, 185, 186–
87, 189
employment, 135–39, 142–43, 167,
222–23n. 10
empowerment, 105
endrin, 120

environment, xxii, 14, 15, 163–64,
    190
Environmental Defense Fund (EDF),
    23, 27, 86, 87, 99, 105, 209
environmentalism, xiii, xvii–xviii, 7,
    128, 179, 185, 188, 204, 214n. 7
    and grazing rights, 127, 181
    mainstream, 20–24
    participation in, 26–27, 208–9
    pesticides and, 86–90
    ranching and, 146–53
    and resource management, 162–
        63
    subalterns and, 3–4, 5–6, 14–16,
        25, 27–30, 192–93, 210, 211
environmental movements, 12–13
Environmental Policy Institute, 23
EPA, 100
Escobar, Arturo, 13, 29
ethnicity, 16, 60, 67, 204, 215n. 6
    and farmworkers, 62–63
    of Hispanics, 48–56
    and identity, 33–34, 47–48, 193,
        200–201, 216n. 9, 221–22n. 2

farmers, small, 66, 139–40
farmworkers, xviii–xix, 50, 64, 100,
    114, 218n. 16, 220n. 34, 227n. 4
    collective identity of, 197–98
    conditions of, 69–70
    contracts for, 115–20
    health and safety of, 94–96, 99
    organization of, 67–68, 71–72,
        121–23, 220n. 35
    and pesticide use, 76–78, 81,
        83–86, 90–91, 101, 103–4,
        123–24
    racialization of, 62–63
    racism and, 19–20, 32, 37
    unionization of, 59–60, 217n. 8

FDA, 99
federal government, 68, 74–75, 113,
    133, 139, 224nn. 23, 25. See also
    various agencies; bureaus
Federal Insecticide Act, 75
Federal Insecticide Fungicide Roden-
    ticide Act (FIFRA), 75
Federal Land Management and Plan-
    ning Act, 148
Federal Mediation Service, 112
Fielder, Jerry, 81, 101, 104
FIFRA, 75
Filipinos, 63, 70
Finch, Director, 99, 100
First World, 6, 12, 13, 16–20, 213nn.
    1, 2
fish and game codes, 75
food, pesticide residues on, 105, 107,
    108
Food and Drug Administration
    (FDA), 99
Forcing the Spring (Gottlieb), 192
Ford Foundation, 133
Fowler, John, 179, 183
Freedman, David, 116–17
Freshpict, 115
Fresno, 62, 104, 117
Fresno County, 60, 81
fruit crops, 81. See also grape pro-
    duction

Ganados del Valle
    collective identity of, 197–98
    culture and, 54, 198–99, 205
    defined, xiv, 125, 127
    economy of, 38, 129, 137, 139,
        144–45, 162, 187–90
    elk and, xix, 27–28
    history of, 130

identity issues of, 28, 32, 49, 53,
128, 203–4, 206
*Proposal to Improve Wildlife
Habitat...* , 171–72
research and, 179–87
resistance by, 40, 191, 192–93,
195–96, 209
resource management and, 165–
79
sheep industry of, 163–65, 225–
26n. 27
vision of, 39
Gardner, Judge, 96
gender, 16, 33, 67, 145
Getty Oil, 66
G.I. Forum, 49
Gilroy, Paul, 170
Giroux, Henry, 44
Giumarra, John, 78, 200
Goldman, Ben, 6
Gonzalez, Corky, 50
Gottlieb, Robert, 192
Grape and Fruit Tree League, 66
grape production, 70, 71, 107, 108,
111–12, 217nn. 8, 9
grazing, 140, 224–26n. 27
and Ganados project, 127, 167–
79, 187–90, 205
and poverty, 163–64, 187
research on, 179–87, 226n. 28
and wildlife, 146–63
Great Depression, 65, 132
Group of Ten, 23–24
growers
contracts with, 115–20
and farmworkers, 20, 62, 63,
67–68, 84, 218n. 16
lawsuits against, 101–5, 218n.
20

and pesticide use, 76–77, 78–79,
81–83, 91, 93
power of, 65–66, 218n. 17
and UFWOC, 109–14, 217n. 8
Guha, Ramchandra, 5–6
Guha, Ranajit, 4–5
Gutierrez, José Angel, 50

habitats, xiii, 143–44
Hall, Stuart, 127, 175
Hardrock Mining Law, 146
Harvey, David, 46
health, 89–90
UFWOC demands and, 115, 117–
19, 220n. 36
of workers, 94–96, 99, 109, 111,
116, 119–20, 217–18n. 15
Health and Safety Committee, 85
heptachlor, 87
Heron, Lake, 177, 178
HEW, 99
Hispanics, 45, 48–56
Hispanos, 28, 132, 153, 182, 185
culture of, 198–99, 204–5
identity of, 49, 53, 174–75, 221–
22n. 2
income of, 135–36
landownership by, 139–40, 144
poverty of, 35, 127, 130
racialization of, 134–35
and sheep industry, 137, 139
Howie, Robert, 95, 101, 219n. 24
Huastecas, 194
Huerta, Dolores, 69, 70, 113
Humphries, Bill, 183
Humphries Wildlife Management
Area, 159, 160, 169, 171, 172,
183

hunting, 127, 157
    elk, 159–60
    and grazing research, 179–80
    and grazing rights, 153–56

identity, 193, 194
    Chicano, xviii–xix, 200–201
    and development, 16, 128
    and environmental movements,
        13, 29
    and ethnicity, 47–56, 216n. 9,
        221–22n. 2
    group, 33–34, 39
    Hispano, 28, 128
    issues of, 46–47, 174–75, 194–
        95
    and marginalization, 32–33
    politics of, 7, 9, 197–98
    racism and, 31–32, 42
    use of, 203–4, 206–7
ideology, 45–46
*Ideology and the New Social Move-
    ments* (Scott), 10–11
immigration, 36, 49, 216n. 5
Imperial Valley, 89
income, 135–36, 140(fig.)
inequality, xx, xxii, 5, 34, 191
Injury Control Project, 76
Inside Eastside, 200
integrated pest management (IPM),
    89
investment, 35–36
IPM, 89
Itliong, Larry, 70
Izaak Walton League, 23, 154

Jackson, Peter, 41
Jicarilla Apache, 139, 174
Jukes, Thomas, 88

justice
    environmental, xx, 6, 13, 16–20,
        224n. 20
    social, 28, 153

Kern County, 60, 67, 84, 217n. 10
    lawsuits in, 95, 96–97, 219n. 25
    pesticide use in, 76, 77, 81, 91–
        92
Kern-Kaweah chapter (Sierra Club),
    87, 88, 218n. 19
Kings County, 60
Koch, James, 169

labor, 35, 69, 122, 132
    organization of, 64–65, 67, 71,
        91, 208–9, 220n. 35
    in sheep industry, 137–38
Laclau, Ernesto, 161
land, 129, 144, 187, 194
    ownership of, 132, 139–40
    public use of, 145–63, 179–87,
        193
land acts, 62
land grants, 62, 130, 133, 227n. 6
Latin America, xiii, 12, 13, 51
Latinos, 52, 213n. 1, 216n. 4
lawsuits
    to ban pesticides, 97–105, 218n.
        18, 219nn. 24, 25
    against Sierra Club, 188–89
    UFWOC, 90–97, 218n. 20
League of United Latin American
    Citizens (LULAC), 49
legislation, 65–66, 84, 85–86
Little Chama Valley Ranch, 160,
    224n. 25
Livestock Growers of the Valley. *See*
    Ganados del Valle
lobbying, 21–22

Lodi, 117
Lopez Tijerina, Reies, 50, 133
Los Angeles, 36, 49
Los Angeles County, 81
Los Ojos, 131(fig.), 144, 164, 188, 189
LULAC, 49

McFarland, 70, 122
McWilliams, Carey, 63
Maestas, Gerald, 170, 171, 175, 177, 183
Malcriado, El (newspaper), 92(fig.), 97, 108, 110(fig.), 201, 219n. 26
Manzanares, Antonio, 164, 168–69, 178(fig.), 183
marginalization, xvii–xviii, 48, 64, 125
  and environmentalism, 3–4, 16–17
  and identity, 32–33, 34
Marquez Wildlife Management Area, 180
Marxism, 11, 208
Mazocchi, Tony, 105
Medina, Anastacio, 85
Mengle, Donald, 76
mestizos, 43
Mexican Americans, 49–56, 64, 72
Mexican-American War, 42
Mexican Era, 62
Mexicanos, 36, 37, 42–43, 198, 213n. 1
Mexicans, 43, 49, 63–64, 68, 216n. 4
Mexico, 19–20, 101, 122, 194
middle class, 26, 37, 51, 72, 127, 216n. 4
Milagro Fund, 165
Milby, Thomas, 76

minorities, 16–17, 42. *See also* ethnicity; race
mobilization, 8–9, 12, 105, 213–14n. 3
Mondale, Walter, 114
Montoya, Bill, 158
Morley, Thomas, 76, 77, 91, 93
Morrill Act, 62
Moses, Marion, 85, 105
Mouffe, Chantal, 161
Movimiento, el. See Chicano movement
Muir, John, 22, 227n. 1
multiculturalism, 52
Munoz, Carlos, 49
Murphy, George, 100, 112

Nader, Ralph, 105
Nash, June, 10
National Farm Worker Association (NFWA), 70–71
National Parks Association, 23
National Park Service, 88, 156
National Rifle Association, 154
National Wildlife Federation, 23, 150, 151–52, 154, 221n. 21
Natural Resources Defense Council, 23, 57
Nature Conservancy, 150, 152, 168, 173, 181, 221n. 21, 224–26n. 27
Neblett, Judge, 96
Neo-Marxism, 14
New Mexico, xiv, 35, 49, 50, 126(fig.), 129–30, 150
  community development in, 125, 127
  economy of, 133–35, 223nn. 12, 13, 15
  hunting in, 153–56
  land in, 132–33

New Mexico (*cont.*)
    ranching in, 146–53, 224nn. 18,
      22
    resource agencies in, 156–63
    tourism in, 141–43, 151, 205–6
New Mexico Community Founda-
    tion (NMCF), 164
New Mexico Department of Game
    and Fish (NMDGF), 127, 149, 152,
    184
    on grazing, 167–68, 169–70,
      173–74, 175, 177, 179, 182,
      224–25n. 27
    on hunting, 154, 156
    operations of, 157–63
New Mexico State University
    (NMSU), 179, 183
New Mexico Wildlife (magazine),
    156
new social movements (NSMs), xv, xx,
    25, 30, 208
    discourse of, 10–12
    environmentalism in, 28–29
    goals of, 7–9
    identity and, 46, 47
NFWA, 70–71
NMCF, 164
NMDGF. *See* New Mexico Depart-
    ment of Game and Fish
NMSU, 179, 183
NSMs. *See* new social movements

O'Brien, Charles, 96
Oil, Chemical, and Atomic Workers
    Union, 105
organophosphates, 103–4, 120

panethnicity, 52
parathion, 120

Parteros, 132
Partido, El, 200
pastoralism, 53, 137, 174–75, 204,
    205
Pastores Feed and General Store,
    165, 166(fig.)
Pastores Lamb, 165
Perelli-Minetti and Sons contract,
    115, 116–17
pest control, 89. *See also* pesticides
pesticides, xiv, xviii, 107
    controlling use of, 39, 115, 118–
      20, 121
    development and use of, 72–76
    as environmental issue, 25–26,
      57–59, 86–90
    injuries from, 77–81, 217–18n.
      15
    lawsuits regarding, 90–105,
      218nn. 18, 20, 219nn. 24, 25
    regulation of, 81–83, 217nn. 13,
      14, 219–20nn. 28, 32
    UFWOC on, 83–86, 109–14,
      123–24, 191
Pinchot, Gifford, 22
Pittman-Robertson Act (PR), 155,
    160, 180, 224nn. 23, 25, 226n. 27
PLAN, 151
Plotke, David, 11
politics, xvii–xviii, 16, 27, 191, 209
    identity, xvii, 7, 9, 195, 197–98
    UFW and, 121–22
pollution, xiv, 24, 45, 102
Ponce, Vicente, 101
postmodernism, xvi–xvii, 9–10, 207
poverty, xiii, xiv, xvi, xix, 31, 64,
    187, 222n. 9
    and economic growth, 14–15
    environmentalism and, 5–6

factors of, 34–40
in northern New Mexico, 127,
129, 130, 133–34, 163–64
power, xvii–xviii, xix, 68, 71–72,
128, 218n. 17
praxis, 54–55, 198–99
Proposal to Improve Wildlife Habitat on the Rio Chama, Humphries, and Sargent Wildlife Areas
(Ganados del Valle), 171–72
publicity, 114, 171, 178(fig.), 218n.
22, 219n. 28
Public Lands Action Network
(PLAN), 151
Pure Food and Drug Act, 75

quality-of-life issues, 8, 29, 30, 147,
194, 196
Questa, 150

race, 31, 60, 62–63, 67, 145,
215n. 1
racial project, 44, 46
racism, 4, 6, 13, 16, 36, 215n. 3
economics and, 194–95
environmental, xiii, 17–20, 26
factors of, 40–46
and identity, 31–32
and Mexicans, 63–64
and power, 125, 129
resource management and, 170–
71
ranching, 224nn. 18, 19
and environmentalism, 146–53
sheep, 137, 139
Raza, La (newspaper), 200
Raza Magazine, La, 200
Raza Unida, La, 50, 200
Reagan, Ronald, 100, 112

regulations, on pesticide use, 75–76,
77, 81–83, 93–94, 115–16
religion. *See* Catholicism
"Reports of Occupational Disease
Attributed to Pesticides and Agricultural Chemicals" (DPH), 77
research, on grazing, 178–87, 226n.
28
resistance, 33
resource management, 125, 145, 184
and Ganados del Valle, 164–79,
188–90
by NMDGF, 156–63
as social construct, 185–87
resources, xiv, 16, 68, 133, 143, 213–
14n. 3
revenues, 157
Ganados del Valle, 165, 167
tourism, 140–41
right-to-know laws, 97
Rio Arriba County, 126(fig.), 130,
134, 138(table), 222–23n. 10
development in, 143–44
tourism in, 141, 142–43
WMAS in, 159–60
Rio Arriba Wool Washing plant, 165
Rio Chama Wildlife and Fishing
Area, 159, 160, 171, 172, 180,
183
Riverside County, 95–96, 101, 219n.
25
Road Runner, The (newsletter), 88
Rodriguez, Arturo, 122
romanticism, 22, 214n. 7
rural communities, xviii, 14, 66
economies of, 133–34, 161, 162
in New Mexico, 129–32, 136–
37
Rutherford, John, 32

safety
    UFWOC demands, 115, 117–19,
        220n. 36
    worker, 82, 84, 94–96, 109, 111,
        116, 119–20
Safeway, 107
Salazar, Gumercindo, 164, 174
San Francisco Bay area, 88
San Joaquin Valley, 60–62, 84, 216n.
    3, 217n. 6, 227n. 4
Sargent Wildlife Management Area,
    224n. 26
    ecology of, 171
    grazing on, 167–69, 173–74,
        183, 224–26n. 27
    purchase of, 159–60, 180
Savory, Allan, 171
Schryer, Frans, 194
Scientific Institute for Public Infor-
    mation (SIPI), 105
Scott, Alan, 7, 10–11
Sheep industry, 127, 137–38, 165,
    167, 223n. 12
SHRIC. See Southwest Research and
    Information Center
Sierra Club, 23, 57, 87–88, 150, 151,
    153, 181, 188–89, 224n. 21
Sierra Club Foundation, 153
Silent Spring (Carson), 99
SIPI, 105
ski resorts, 142–43
Smithsonian, 205
social movements, 4, 7, 12–13, 206–
    7, 213–14n. 3. See also new social
    movements
Soil Conservation Service, 158
Solis, Robert, 203
South Central Farmers Committee,
    66
Southern Pacific Railroad, 66

Southwest Research and Information
    Center (SHRIC), 153, 187, 224n. 20
Spanish language, 44–45, 48
sprayers, 93–94, 219n. 24
State Water Project (SWP), 68
status, 38–39
Steinberg, Lionel, 116–17
strategy, 197
strikes, 64–65, 71, 217n. 10
subalterns, subalternity, xiv, 4–5, 12–
    13, 127–28, 192, 227nn. 1, 2
    community goals of, 193–94
    culture of, 52–54
    environmentalism and, 3–4, 5–
        6, 14–16, 28–30, 192–93,
        210, 211
    public land use and, 145–46
    racism and, 19–20, 41
Suffolk County Mosquito Control
    Commission, 86–87
SWP, 68
symbolism, cultural, 199–200

Taylor Grazing Act, 147–48, 224n.
    18
teamsters, 121, 220nn. 33, 36
Tehipite chapter (Sierra Club), 87
Tenneco, 66
TEPP, 120
Texas, 73
Third Wave, 27
Third World, 14, 15, 213nn. 1, 2
Tierra Amarilla, 177
Tierra Amarilla Land Grant, 130,
    159, 173, 222n. 5, 227n. 6
Tierra Wools, 165, 199
Torres, Lazaro, 203
tourism, 130, 151, 223n. 13
    culture and, 205–6

planning and, 142–43
revenues from, 140–42, 157
toxic hazards, 23–24
transcendentalism, 22
Treaty of Guadalupe Hidalgo, 132
Trevor-Roper, Hugh, 52
Tulare County, 60, 76, 81, 117, 217–18n. 15
2,4-D, 120
2,4,5-T, 120

UC. *See* University of California
UFW. *See* United Farm Workers
UFWOC. *See* United Farm Workers
    Organizing Committee
underemployment, 135–36
unemployment, 134, 136
unionization, 64–65, 67, 71–72,
    122–23
unions, 59–60, 69–70, 84
United Farm Workers (UFW), 34,
    121–22, 123, 216n. 2
United Farm Workers Organizing
    Committee (UFWOC), 216nn. 2, 3,
    217n. 10
    boycott by, 55, 105–9
    and the Chicano movement, 32,
        49, 200–201, 206, 227n. 4
    collective identity of, 195–96,
        197–98
    contracts, 114–20, 220n. 36
    cultural symbolism of, 199–200,
        201–2, 203
    gender and, 34
    goals of, 39, 40
    and growers, 109–14
    lawsuits of, 90–105, 218nn. 18,
        20
    organization by, 59–60
    origins of, 70, 71, 216n. 2

pesticides campaign of, xviii, 58–
    59, 82, 83–86, 89–90, 102–5,
    123–24
as a subaltern social movement,
    xiv, 28, 29, 37, 191, 192–93,
    208–9
United Mexican American Students,
    200
United States Court of Appeals, 100
United States Department of Agricul-
    ture (USDA), 74–75
United States Environmental Protec-
    tion Agency (EPA), 100, 217n. 13
United States Fish and Wildlife Ser-
    vice (USFWS), 156, 160, 168
United States Forest Service (USFS),
    133, 139
United States House Interior Over-
    sight Subcommittee, 174
University of California (UC), 68–69,
    102, 217n. 9
Uribe, Amalia, 95–96
USDA, 74–75
USFS, 133, 139
USFWS, 156, 160, 168

Varela, Maria, 164, 170, 183
Virgen de Guadalupe, La, 54, 201–2,
    227n. 5
Virgin Mary, 54
Voss, Henry, 83

wages, xviii, 59–60, 63, 69, 71, 114,
    117, 122. *See also* income
Wagner Act, 70
Walker, Richard, 39
Wall, Stephen, 91–92, 94
War on Poverty, 51, 108, 133
water projects, 68, 223n. 16

weaving, 54, 127, 137, 139, 164–65,
    198–99
Webster, Yehudi, 44
West, Irma, 76
Whitaker and Baxter, 114, 219n. 29
wilderness industry, 155–56
Wilderness Society, 23, 150
wildlife, 146–63, 181, 186–87, 188–
    90, 224n. 24
wildlife management areas (WMAS),
    127, 130, 222n. 5
    grazing on, 167–79
    management of, 158–60, 188,
        189
    research on, 179–87
Wilkinson, Charles, 146
Winant, Howard, 44

WMAS. *See* wildlife management areas
Wonder Palms Ranch contract, 117,
    118–19
wool industry, 54, 127, 137, 139,
    198–99
Wrath of Grapes, The (video), 122
Wurster, Charles, 105

Yannacone, Victor, 86–87
Yellowstone National Park, 186
Yosemite National Park, 88
Young, Iris, 46, 184

Zaninovich, Jack, 88
Zapata, Emiliano, 109, 111(fig.)
Zwank, Phil, 179, 183

About the Author

Laura Pulido is an assistant professor of geography at the University of Southern California, where she teaches courses on environmental issues, the Southwest, and inequality. She received her doctorate in urban planning from UCLA. A native of Los Angeles, she has been a member of the Labor/Community Strategy Center since 1990. She has served as a commissioner for the Environmental Affairs Department of the City of Los Angeles and has been involved in a number of environmental and social justice struggles.